Children of the Second Spring

Father James Nugent

and the Work of Child Care

in Liverpool

Very Rev Mgr. John Furnival STL VG

GRACEWING

First published in 2005
By
Gracewing
2 Southern Avenue
Leominster
Herefordshire HR6 0QF

ISBN 0 85244 653 5

Typeset by Print Origination
Ince Blundell Merseyside L38 6JF

Printed in England by Antony Rowe Ltd,
Chippenham, Wiltshire SN14 6LH

Contents

Foreword   1
Acknowledgements   3
Dedications   9
A Chronology (1822 – 1924)   11
Prologue   17
Introduction   35

Part One (1822-1863)

1   His First Home   51
2   The Gift Of An Education   67
3   Rome, Lancashire and Plague   81
4   Children of the Second Spring   105
5   The Catholic Institute   123
6   Catholic Times and Turbulent Times   141

Part Two (1863-1905)

7   A Time To Serve   149
8   Reform and Training on Land and at Sea   167
9   The Old Country and The New world   193
10 Temperance, A Virtue   201
11 In The House of Providence   223
12 Father Berry's Homes   233
13 Golden Days and Last Days   249
14 The Children's Bishop   259

Part Three (1924-2005)

15 The Nugent Care Society Yesterday and Today   277
16 Father Nugent's Legacy, and a Final Portrait   295

Bibliography   335
Appendices   340
Incorrigible Women   341

Monsignor J. Nugent

A portrait by J. J. Shannon Walker Art Gallery Liverpool

Foreword

2004 in Liverpool was the Year of Faith. Recognition was given to the many ways in which women and men inspired by their fidelity to God have served their sisters and brothers to bring them life in abundance in body, mind and spirit.

2005 is the Year of the Sea. Liverpool's past and present cannot be understood without its experience of all it has meant and still means to be a major port. In the nineteenth century tens of thousands arrived at the port in desperation from famine and injustices they had experienced in Ireland. In Liverpool Father Nugent, assisted by so many others, and not by Catholics only, welcomed and cared for them in their desperate need. Recognition of this is wonderfully expressed in the statue built in his honour in St John's Gardens.

In 2008 Liverpool will be the European Capital of Culture. Father Nugent understood that we do not live by bread alone. Life in abundance is about so much more, education, sport, drama, music, in a world culture. It is good that the centenary of this very great man is gratefully celebrated in this book by Monsignor John Furnival.

And we rightly rejoice that what inspired Father Nugent inspires many today, what concerned him, concerns many today, and his breadth of vision of care guides many today, not least in Nugent Care, the society named for him and faithful to him still.

+ Patrick Kelly

Hunter Street
The birthplace of Father Nugent
A typical dwelling (circa 1927) *much the same as in Fr. Nugents time*

Acknowledgements

The opportunities given to me to study and research for this book were as important as the materials and resources themselves, and so I owe a big thank you first to John Kennedy and Kathleen Pitt, the former Director and present Chief Executive of The Nugent Care Society. They provided me with the information and encouragement I needed. The intention of the Society to mark the Centenary Year of their Founder's death changed this project from one of private interest for me into one of a wider celebration of the Society's continuing work.

I found a willing publisher in Tom Longford at Gracewing Publishing based in Leominster, and enthusiasm and experience in Tom Morley of the Merseyside-based Charity Survive-Miva who saw the importance of Nugent's story for Catholic history. I am grateful to them both for helping to turn my efforts into a published biography.

There has also been willing and invaluable support from Pat McEvoy whose interest in Father Nugent ensured that records at Clarence House School, Freshfield, were preserved and made available to me. I am indebted to her also for keeping my attention fixed on the project over a period of nearly three years. I also owe a debt of gratitude to Christine Dunbobbin, widow of the late Ray Dunbobbin whose play "Black Spot on the Mersey" created renewed interest in Father Nugent and the Irish Famine when it was broadcast as a play for radio and staged at The Liverpool Play House in 1970. To everyone who made papers, letters, notebooks and written records available to me, my sincere thanks.

Certain books stand the test of time, and indispensable in my research have been Thomas Burke's inimitable "Catholic History of Liverpool" (1910) and John Osmond

Bennett's standard text "Father Nugent of Liverpool" (1949). These give us a chronicle of Father Nugent's place in the pioneering days of Liverpool's resurgent Catholic Community. Although both were written a long time ago, and from very different perspectives, they have been the key texts for a study of Nugent's life and ministry. They are almost entirely sympathetic approaches to what must have been a much more fiery and controversial life than they convey, and more recently others have given us the benefit of further research. John Belchem has been one of several authors who have tried to place Nugent in perspective and give him his rightful place in Liverpool's social history. His book 'Merseypride – Essays in Liverpool Exceptionalism (2000)' helps to redress the imbalance, since only in more recent times has social development been recognised as an important aspect of historical analysis.

In the same way, Patricia Runaghan's "Father Nugent's Liverpool" (2001) is a welcome and helpful publication which emphasises Nugent's relationship with the Irish in his home town and his concern with Irish issues generally. Richard Whittington-Egan's article in "Liverpool Shadows" (2002) is also very interesting and inspired me to look deeper into a life of intrigue and complexity. From another perspective I have been greatly helped by papers received from Paul Shaw at the archives of St. Mary's Convent, Brentford, Middlesex, which contain a record of the work of the Congregation of The Poor Servants of The Mother of God and their connection with Nugent in Liverpool. Information has also been supplied by Michael Sharratt at Ushaw College Library and by James McAuley at the archives of the English College, Rome, in regard to Father Nugent's seminary days. Mgr. Peter Fleetwood, at the Pontifical Council for Culture in Rome, also kindly provided me with some notes on Catholic Culture. My sincere thanks go to them.

A more extensive bibliography is given at the end of

this book. The problem with extensive bibliographies is they can give the impression that all the books and papers have been read from cover to cover– they have not, but they have all been used in some way towards this project. The sheer quantity of material serves to emphasise the impossible scale of the task, and the limited nature of my own efforts, but the published material is there for those who want it and it is offered as 'Further Reading'.

The fruit of unpublished research has also been of value. I would like to thank those who made available their own MA research, such as Father John Seddon, whose work on Father Wilfred Carr highlights part of Nugent's influence in the Church's Social Teaching, as background to the promulgation of Pope Leo XIII's Encyclical 'Rerum Novarum'. I also want to acknowledge Father Peter Morgan's work on the Gillow Family which touches on the life of Father Nugent's priest companions in Liverpool in caring for refugees of the Famine in Ireland and gives an account of the Martyr Priests who died as a result of caring for the fever victims amongst the Immigrant Community.

Thanks are due to Peter Doyle for several references and background materials on the history of the Diocese of Liverpool and the book entitled 'The Edwardian Story'(2003) – the history of St. Edward's College, Liverpool, which had its origin in Nugent's foundation of The Catholic Institute. Likewise, my thanks to John Davies, Lecturer in History at Liverpool Hope College, for his helpful article on Father Nugent as Prison Minister, printed in the periodical 'North West Catholic History' (1995). Cannon Brendan Alger of St Mary's Douglas, Isle of Man, pointed me in the right direction for certain library resources and articles which have been very helpful. My thanks also go to Professor Simon Lee and other members of staff, past and present, at Liverpool Hope University College for giving me access to the College library, in particular to copies of 'The Tablet' of the period. In the same way, those in charge of the resources of the Liverpool Central Library, and the Metropolitan Cathedral Archives, especially Meg Whittle and Mgr. Peter Cookson, have made important material accessible to me, for which many thanks.

The Cistercian Community of Mount St. Bernard has been welcoming and provided a quiet place to write. The part played by the Cistercians in this story is not insignificant, as the role of the Agricultural Colony, in the grounds of the monastery many years ago, had its connection with the Catholic Reformatory Association in Liverpool and Father Nugent's work of Child Rescue and Reform. My thanks go to The Abbot and Community, in particular Father John Paul Sanderson. I would also like to acknowledge the help given by Maureen Havers who shared with me her findings in regard to the fascinating story of The Colony at Mount St. Bernard.

It is well known that Father Nugent visited America often. I have not had the advantage of tracing his footsteps there but I owe special thanks to Idelle Schwartz in Harrisburg, P.A., and those who helped her in obtaining information and sending archive material relating to the Nugent family in Minnesota. In particular I would like to acknowledge with thanks the papers entitled 'Irish America' (Coming into Clover) by Maureen Dezell which traces part of the story of Irish Emigration to America. It is an important part of James Nugent's life story.

Technical help from those who have typed texts, advised on the text or helped to proof read texts with great patience, has been crucial. In this regard may I thank Tom Morley, Mrs. Ann Foran, Reverend Tony Johnson, Reverend Ernest Diggory and Father John Seddon. They have provided much needed help on occasion to get the computer technology back on track (since it is still holds many mysteries for me).

I am very pleased and grateful that Archbishop Patrick Kelly, my Archbishop, Chairman of The Nugent Care

Society, has continued the fine tradition of episcopal support for Catholic Social Welfare in Liverpool and kindly agreed to write the Foreword to 'Children of The Second Spring'

Scriptural quotes are taken from the New Jerusalem Bible as published by Darton Longman and Todd, with permission. All direct quotes requiring copyright permission have been sought and obtained as far as possible. The cover photograph, from the archives of The Nugent Care Society has been used with the agreement of Kathleen Pitt, whilst other photographs in the book have been supplied by Tom Murphy of the 'Catholic Pictorial', Carmel Brinkley from Nazareth House, Crosby, and the (flattering) photograph of the author was taken by John Callaghan; many thanks to all of them.

It has taken me nearly three years to research and write this book. After that time my ticket for the Archive Room in Picton Library expired – and I almost did too! The helpful members of staff there were probably glad to see the back of me. A general word of thanks to them will have to suffice. Besides material on Father Nugent there were helpful references to Father Berry. In that connection I would say a word of thanks to Paul and Mary Weston for their help; they are distant relatives of the Berry Family. Paul Weston has also kindly provided photographs.

Finally, I apologise to anyone who may feel I have not adequately acknowledged their help or to anyone whose permission was inadvertently not obtained. There was no deliberate intention in this. They know who they are and they know I am grateful to them all. There may well be errors in the information contained in this book but every effort has been made to produce an accurate record.

The statue of Father Nugent erected in St. John's Gardens
with St George's Hall in the background

Dedication

This book is dedicated to my parents, Joe and Monica, Furnival, fifty-five years married this year, and to my sister Marie and my brother Bernard and their families who helped to nurture my own vocation as a priest. Also, to all the hard working souls, striving, often without visible reward, for greater social justice, education, and the pastoral care of young people today, this book is prayerfully dedicated.

A Chronology
of Father Nugent's Life
& A Hundred years
Of Catholic Child Care in Liverpool
(1822- 1924)

1822   3rd. March, James Nugent born in Hunter Street,
Liverpool
17th. March baptised at St. Nicholas Church,
Copperas Hill

1824   Opening of new Workhouse, Liverpool

1829   Act of Catholic Emancipation

1830   Nugent attends The Academy School, Queen's Square

1838   A student at St. Cuthbert's College, Ushaw

1841   Foundation of Catholic Blind Asylum, Liverpool, by Dr.
Youens

1843   Nugent a student at The English College, Rome

1845   Ordained to the Diaconate in Rome

1846   30th August ordained to Priesthood at St. Nicholas's,
Liverpool. Appointed to St. Alban's parish Blackburn

1847   Recalled to Liverpool to help at St. Nicholas's

1847   Appointed to St. Mary's, Wigan and to found St.
Patrick's, Wigan

1848   4th December, St. Francis Xavier's opens in Liverpool

1849   1st January Nugent appointed to St. Nicholas's,
Liverpool. Starts a Ragged School in Spitalfields

1850   Year of The Restoration of the Catholic Hierarchy and
appointment of Bishop George Brown, first Catholic
Bishop of Liverpool.
7th January, opening of Middle School for Boys
in Rodney Street, by Fr. Nugent with Fr. Worthy

1851   Arrival of Notre Dame Sisters in Liverpool
for School and Orphanage work
St. George's Industrial Schools opened at Everton
Crescent

1852   Sermon by Nugent at Fontenoy Street Schools on
        Education

1853   31st October , opening of Catholic Institute in Hope St.
        Easter Monday, Holy Cross School Sermon by Nugent
        on Temperance

1854   'Save the Child' Inaugural Meeting at Town Hall

1856   Catholic Reformatory Association established
        (Nugent as secretary)

1858   St. Vincent's School for Boys and Boys' Orphanage,
        Everton (transferred to Beacon Lane 1862, Sisters of
        Charity)

1859   Nugent named as owner and editor of 'The Northern
        Press'

1860   Founded 'The Catholic Times' and other publications

1863   1st January, appointed first Catholic chaplain to Walton
        Gaol
        St. George's Schools transferred to West Derby Road

1864   Night Shelter and Boys' Refuge opened in Soho Street,
        Liverpool
        "Save the Child" meetings in Liverpool
        15th August 'The Clarence' Reformatory Ship
        commissioned on the river at New Ferry
        St. Elizabeth's School for Catholic Girls in Soho Street
        (later transferred to Breckfield Road, Sisters of Mercy)

1866   Nugent appointed to board of St. George's Industrial
        Schools and acting Headmaster

1867   Opening of St. Anne's School for Girls, Mason Street
        (Sisters of Charity) (later transferred to Freshfield)

1869   Opening of Boy's Refuge in St. Anne's Street, Liverpool
        Closure of Night Shelter and Refuge in Soho Street

1870   Nugent sails for Canada with first group of child
        emigrants

1872   'League of the Cross for Total Abstinence' is launched.
        9th March Birkdale Farm School opened

1875   Opening of the 'League of the Cross Hall, in Rose Place.
        Monday Night Concerts inaugurated

1876   Girls' Reformatory opened at May Place run by Sisters of
        Charity

1880 'The Clarence' Ship damaged by fire
Nugent in Ireland for Emigration Society
1881 16th April 'The Liverpool Catholic Children's Protection
Society' founded jointly by Bishop O'Reilly and Father
Nugent. Began systematic emigration of children.
First group sailed to Quebec, Canada and on to Lindsay,
Ontario (1100 children would emigrate over next 8 yrs)
Appointment of Richard Yates as Society President
Party of 16 children to Quebec with Mrs Wain
Grey Nuns in Ottowa offer help
Mrs Lacy takes two parties of children to Canada
1884 Fire again on 'The Clarence' which is destroyed
1885 31st December Nugent resigns from Prison Chaplaincy
1886 Mutiny on 'The Clarence' and crisis in Reformatory
Association
Father Nugent appointed to Blundellsands to start
mission at St. Joseph's (Church opened November1886)
1887 Resigns parish work at St. Joseph's
1889 Nugent speaker at First Catholic Laity Congress,
Baltimore
1891 Opened Refuge for Fallen Women (St. Saviour's Refuge,
Paul Street, in care of The Poor Servants of the Mother of
God)
St. Vincent de Paul Society leased 105 Shaw Street,
Liverpool, for establishment of St. Vincent's Working
Boys' Home and Night Shelter for Homeless Boys
1892 12th June, in Rome, Father Nugent made Domestic
Prelate with title of Monsignor by Pope Leo XIII
Father Berry leased 1 Marble Street, Williamson Square,
as St. Philip's House for Street Trading Boys (calculated
1100 boys roaming the streets in Liverpool)
1893 17th. February, Bishop Bernard O'Reilly assumes control
of St. Vincent's Boys' Home from S.V.P. Fr. John Berry
in charge and arranged opening of St. James's House
Night Shelter on same site. (Later moved to Everton
Crescent)
1894 Bishop O'Reilly dies. Bishop Thomas Whiteside
succeeds him

Poor Law Schools and a Committee set up by Bishop
Whiteseide under supervision of Father Pinnington
Death of Mrs Lacy (supervisor of Shaw Street Home for
(Child emigration) and her replacement by Miss Yates

1895   St. Bernard's Training House in Bute Street opened as
preparatory School for admission to St. Vincent's Home
(named after late Bishop)
Monsignor Nugent in Florida for Annual Convention of
The National Editorial Association of America

1896   30th August, Golden Jubilee of Priesthood. Lord Derby
(Lord Mayor of Liverpool sets up Testimonial
Committee)
Appointment of Mr Doughan as Society President

1897   Nazareth House Children's Home established at Great
Crosby.
Girls from Shaw Street Home move to Crosby
20th May, closure of St. Philip's and St. James's Homes
due to financial problems. 30th October closure of St.
Bernard's Home (3000 boys had been assisted in 5
years) Retirement of Fr. Berry.
New Committee set up by Bishops with help of
Reynolds and Shute Families
Arthur Chilton Thomas Manager of Father Berry's
Homes
'House of Providence' Opened by Monsignor Nugent

1898   Re-opening of St. Bernard's and St. Philip's. Death of
Francis Reynolds, benefactor.
Liverpool Catholic Childrens' Protection Society moved
from Shaw Street Hostel to 53 Everton Road

1899   Father James Hughes offers help for emigration work in
Canada and America. Catholic Children's Aid
Committee established by Bishop Whiteside at Trueman
Street, Father Pinnington as Secretary,
A 'Receiving Home' established by Sisters of Charity at
Everton Crescent and later Residential Homes
Canadian Authorities complained of children being sent
out medically unfit for emigration.

1900   Arthur Chilton Thomas rented property for Boys'

Homes in name of Father Berry's Homes

Publication of St. Vincent's Record Magazine of news for former residents of Boys' Homes

1901   Talks on the Amalgamation of Catholic Emigration Societies

Canon St. John helped found New Orpington lodge, Ottowa, to receive emigrant orphans

1902   Resumption of title 'Father Berry's Homes'. This took over use of Hostel at 55 Everton Road as Remand Home

The Lenten 'Good Shepherd Collection' started by Bishop Whiteside. Voluntary payment scheme started for Children in Father Berry's Homes through Catholic Children's Aid Committee in Liverpool.

Catholic emigration of children ceases.

Publication of Bans Report on Emigration policy

1903   Opening of St. Edward's Orphanage for Boys

Bishop Whiteside and Lord Mayor host Dinner in Adelphi Hotel Liverpool on Nugent's return from triumphant tour of America.

Idea of Memorial Statue is put forward

Catholic Truth Society Conference in Liverpool

Catholic Emigration Association formed to include: Crusade of Rescue, Birmingham Rescue Society and also Father Berry's Homes

Babys' Home (Our Lady's) started at 93 Shaw Street

1904   Nugent opens Maternity Home 'House of Good Counsel' in West Dingle, Liverpool

Embarks on (final) journey to America and Canada with Abbot Casquet for Lecture Tour. Visits family in Minnesota where he falls ill

1905   16th May Nugent sails home on S.S. Oceanic. Bad fall on deck, sustains head injury and impairment of eye-sight (aged 83)

27th June, death of Monsignor Nugent at Harewood House, Formby after contracting pneumonia. Requiem Mass St. Nicholas's Pro-Cathedral 30th June. Burial at Ford Cemetery.

1906   James O'Connell appointed as Assistant to Father

Pinnington.

21st July, death of Arthur Chilton Thomas

8th. December - memorial Statue of Nugent in St. John's Gardens

1908   More children emigrate to Canada

1909   Resignation of Canon Pinnington as Administrator of the Society

1910   Visit of Fr. Bernard Vaughan (later Cardinal) to the Philharmonic Hall Liverpool for fund-raising Concert

1911   Appointment of Father Thomas George as Director of Children's Homes in Liverpool, extended the facilities, laundries and workshops. Thomas Whiteside named as First Archbishop of Liverpool & Metropolitan

1914-18 Cessation of activities during the First World War and subsequent closure of several Industrial Schools and Homes

Staff and 200 Old Boys of Homes on active service

1920   Recuperation of activities and fund-raising by The Society

Seabank House, Formby bought as children's Holiday Home

1921   Death of Archbishop Whiteside.

1923   Re-opening of St. George's Industrial School. Archbishop Keating leads discussions on merger - 15th November Proposed amalgamation of The Liverpool Catholic Children's Protection Society, Father Berry's Homes and The Catholic Children's Aid Committee.

1924   Decision to amalgamate effective from 1st March under title of Liverpool Catholic Children's Society and official end of Father Berry's Homes Monsignor Pinnington Administrator and Father John Bennett as Secretary.

Prologue

(An autobiographical sketch)

"Nobody's Children"

(Taken from Notes used by Father Nugent for a speech about the plight of the street children he met in Liverpool)

Part I

You may think it a strange proposition for me to make when I say, that there is no more practical school to study mankind than within the walls of a prison. There you find every variety of character and disposition, as you have every form of human weakness. Constant intercourse with a class who are naturally quick and clever, who are keen observers and have to live by their sharpness, who too are thoroughly experienced in the 'ups and downs' of the world, must give not only an insight into the mysteries of criminal life, but a practical knowledge of the causes which lead so many to adopt it. My daily duties for three & twenty years lay within the walls of one of the largest prisons in England and afforded me ample opportunity to study mankind. Each year from ten to fourteen thousand prisoners fell to my charge.

Fully alive to the responsibilities of such a position, both to the individuals and to the country at large, my earnest efforts were directed to reform those who came under my care and restore them with improved principles and habits to society. The work of reformation among the adult criminal class is a hard if not an impossible task. It is a duty which one must not shrink from or grow faint-hearted over, though it is always disappointing. The experience of years has convinced me that the most effectual means to check crime is to strike at its root or foundation. There is no truer axiom than the old one *'Prevention is better than cure';* once stop the source of any evil, and society is no longer corrupted by its influence. Many years ago, I was on my daily rounds through the wards of the prison and turned into the cell of a prisoner not more than twenty years of age. He was a bright, intelligent, Irish lad, with a sparkling humorous eye and a face which did not bespeak a bad heart. He came to Liverpool when nine years of age and having no friends (here in that city) was cast upon the streets and soon afterwards became a frequent visitor to the Borough Gaol. Before he was fifteen he was transported for five years, and now again he is condemned to seven years penal servitude. Turning to me he said "Well yer Reverence, I know what you say is all true but its no use you wasting your money and time upon us old 'guns', just try your hand upon the lads. If you can keep them from being thieves up to sixteen you'll find very few of them take to it after that. We never forgets the bad".

You may consider it a strange proposition for me to make, that talent runs to waste in the gutters of England. This is not an opinion which I utter for the first time, but one which I have held for years and my daily duty in the prison convinces me more and more of its truth. Criminals, as a class, are not dull and stupid, but on the contrary are quick and clever and most of them display more than an average amount of natural talent. But this, through neglect or the circumstances of their early life, has been perverted.

At the present time the public mind is occupied with the various economic plans; one is a labour saving system, another is for a saving in the consumption of fuel, another of steam, water etc. But the terrible loss of the immortal soul of innumerable men and women, the loss of human energy, ability and enterprise, which is daily taking place under our very eyes, poorly attracts attention. The wasted power of human life and therefore of national capital and greatness, is something to startle political and social economists. The boy I mentioned before said: "a lad who has been a knocking about the streets is ` fly' to too many things and knows too many 'pals'; that if he wants to lead a square life they'll not let him". This was a true and a practical lesson. He felt that habit had become a second nature - that it was next to impossible for him to change his life, but he was anxious that others should not fall into his footsteps, for in all earnestness he said – "believe me, Father, dishonesty is a hard crust to eat." You will see at a glance that this poor fellow, abandoned as he had been, was intelligent and a keen observer. I tell you upon the authority of one of the best informed men on the condition of the London Poor that there are One Hundred Thousand children knocking about the streets of that city daily. He wrote: "Winter and summer within the limits of the vast metropolis of England, the city of London, there wander destitute of proper guardianship, food, clothing or employment, a hundred thousand boys and girls in fair training for prison life and finally for penal servitude."

According to an official report made by the Police in 1868, we had 48,782 children between the age of 5 and 14 who attended no school and of these 25,000 at large upon the streets (exposed to every vice). Wherever you turned, at that time, you saw crowds of dirty, naked, shoeless children. It would seem as if they were 'Nobody's Children,' for they roamed unheeded through those busy thoroughfares and along our seven miles of docks, desolate and homeless wanderers, without a heart to love them or a hand to guide them. They prowled about that busy city, the keen and cunning succeeding by various devices to live, whilst others suffered all the hardship of hunger and absolute want. In the long cold winter nights, when the snow lies thick upon the ground and the stormy blast makes comfortable luxury draw close to the fireside; the birds of the air have their resting places and the very dogs their warm kennels, but these poor little ones huddle together under railway arches, in empty boxes, under theatre show boards, over bakers' ovens - in fact anywhere to get a little heat and protection from the frosty and nipping night air.

How many died of actual starvation and were buried in the paupers' heap without a mourner to follow their coffin or a single tear shed over their grave? Poor children of the streets! They grow up in the lap of misery, as the flower grows amid the mire. Already evil in its two-fold form of vice and sorrow blocks their pathway in life, to corrupt and afflict them. What an existence, what an education, what a future! The streets are the schools of crime, where the girl, scarce in her teens, is degraded into a fallen outcast; the boy into a rowdy duffer, thief and convict. These neglected ones are the seeds of a future generation, the men and women who have to build up or to destroy the social fabric. These are immortal beings created by God, with a destiny far more glorious than the mind of man can understand or human language picture.

They are endowed with powers and faculties to gain, by honest, industrious labour in the struggle of life, their own bread, and to prove useful members of society. Here is a population which if only cared for and taught their duty to God, to their neighbour and to themselves, might grow up to adorn any position and shed an honour, by their energy, talent and virtues, upon any country. True they are neglected and homeless; many of them may be the offspring of drunkards or thieves or they are orphans - in fact 'Nobody's Children'. Believe me, their condition is their misfortune rather than their fault. They are no more vicious or inclined to evil by nature than we are. They are God's creatures formed by His Hand, endowed with a soul and mind, stamped with His own image and likeness. Therefore, it is unchristian to admit that opinion which is so current nowadays that vice and virtue are inherited from the parent stock, just as their bodily form. Vice is not hereditary, no more than genius or talent; these belong to the mind and will of man and are not generated, and only in what is generated is there a natural inheritance.

You will not, ladies and gentlemen, charge me with exaggeration if I say, genius and talent runs to waste in the gutters of our large towns and that the poor little street wanderers, when they have once the chance of knowing better and doing right, would put to the blush the children of the upper ten thousand. I could find a match in every good quality, either bodily, mental or moral, for the pick of the young aristocrat or 'nobs' of Harrow, Rugby and Eton, among the newsboys, shoeblacks, fuzee-sellers and ballad singers, that run with sore and shoeless feet, with naked limbs and unkempt hair, from mid-day to mid-night and from midnight to mid-day again.

Would there be any difficulty in finding matches for the dregs of these same urchins among the refuse of the 'nobs'? I think not. I fancy it would be an easy matter to pair the moral, mental and bodily defects of these and those, in spite of the blue blood of the one and the base breed of the other. This talent which runs to waste in the streets is a fountain of wealth were it only utilized and directed into a proper course. The fresh energy and invention which are called into action by the street children, in their various avocations as traders and artistes, prove this beyond a doubt. Here is a troupe of these boys and girls by nature clever, quick and energetic; each of them striving to pick up a few coppers, and though many of them are mere infants, yet we find them as anxious to secure public patronage as the adventurous tradesman who turns over hundreds, yea thousands of pounds for their copper. (Father Nugent then describes one group of young street traders):

"Buy any oranges, Sir? Nice sweet oranges, Sir, two a'penny oranges, two a'penny. Real St. Michael Oranges, two a'pen."

"Feuzees Sir! Buy a box of Feuzees Sir! Honly a halfpenny a box. Regular stunners, go off of 'emselves. Buy a box?"

"Jist put yer feet on my block and I'll do von on `em for nuffin, Sir."

"Morning Papers, Morning papers. Times; Daily Telegraph; Standard, Daily News, Punch, ... Morning Papers".

"Shine 'em, Sir: Shine yer boots Captain". "For a copper. Jist let me giv 'em the flash o' lighten touch, so as yer honer can see yer face in 'em without a looking in a looking glass!"

"Here your..... Don't you go a believing on him, Sir. He can't shine yer boots. He can black yer boots and he can crack yer boots; but he can't shine 'em, no .... Cos he 'aint got no

blackin; he's got nuffin but soot and vitriol. His father's a chimney sweep and he collars the soot. I'll do von on 'em for nuffin, Sir". The gentleman submits to the operation.

"Now stupid, black the other".

"Not if I knows it, until you forks out sixpence. You don't catch a weasel asleep".

"Why that other boy would have done them for a penny".

"Yes, he'd have blacked yer boots and cracked yer boots, but he couldn't shine yer boots."

There is no alternative unless he wishes to make an exhibition of himself. He pays his 6d and confesses that he has been outwitted by this street urchin.

Part II

Tiny Bill

"Please Sir! Will you spare a poor boy a copper to get a bit of bread with? Do Sir, I'm starving! I haven't tasted anything today. Father's dead and mother's sick and can't get work and we aint got anything to buy nutting with. Do kind gentleman, just one penny".

Stop and question this poor little fellow and he will astonish you with his clever answers, his ready wit and natural talent. "Well, my boy, where do you live?"

"I don't live no where".

Don't be annoyed at any little lack of truth his answers may evince. It seems misery, aware of something shameful in its real position, considers any false one, good or bad, must needs be preferable. So, if you happen in your cross examination to elicit that his father, whom he said was dead has only gone to sea and never come home again; or that his mother instead of being laid up with the ague, is only laying down drunk, don't turn your back upon him disgusted with his lies or looks. True he has a very dirty face, is very sparing of his pocket handkerchief, but if you look fairly at his true position, you may find it quite as worthy of commiseration, if not more so, than his assumed one would have been had all he said been true.

"Well, my boy where do you live? Wouldn't you like to get a place?". *"Yes, Sir!"* What sort of a job? What can you do?

His little eyes begin to sparkle, the little blood he has mounts to his cheeks, as pulling at his little flaxen curls he says: *"I'd like to be a Conj'rer"*. "A what?" *"Why a Conj'rer, Sir. Like they been at the Cirkis. I does lots of thins. See, Sir. This is the Splits"*: Down he goes upon his hamstrings, sending his two big toes as far from each other, as if his two legs, cut off at the trunk, were placed straight along the pavement - thigh to thigh: thus he remains some seconds, doubling his body over first on one side and then upon another, so as to bring the crown of his head and instep close together; up like a spring upon his feet and throwing back his head and arms until the back of his head touches his heels, he picks a button off the pavement with his mouth and rises with it, without breaking down.

"Benback, Sir", and now reversing his position and operation, with head on ground and feet in air, he stretches out his arms, gently brings his feet down behind his head, picks a stone up with his toes, with which he also hurls it many yards, then without coming on his feet he raises himself upon his hands and walks after it, picks it up this time between his two big toes and passing it up this way over his body, puts it into his mouth. Neat round and round he goes, from feet to hands from hands to feet, sideways on one hand, straightforward or backward on two, until his 'lot o thins' that he can do, seeming exhausted, he tries his hand or rather his feet at what he cannot do.

The simple question of what he would like to be and what he could do have raised such pictures in his young imaginative mind, of boys in thickly spangled skins, dangling high up in space from the trapeze by head, hands, feet, back, neck and teeth, that he forgets his bleeding feet, forgets his hovel of a home, his neglectful drunken mother – No! She alone, cruel, drunken, as she is, he never will forget. She forms the principal object in his tableau of glory; of all the kindly cheering faces around, he sees but hers; of all the clapping hands, applauding voices, he can hear but her "Brave boy"!! This is the embryo of a Blondin, a Leotard, An Olmar Eurardo, a Leon, a Steikchel, or a Delavanti, and more than one of these with many scores of scores of inferior note have risen by their daring from his level.

Circumstances have a great influence in moulding and forming character and of developing and maturing genius and talent. Imagine a boy or girl cast on the streets at the age of nine or ten years with no natural protector - with no one to love them, no one to guide them. What must be their career in life? Who has to impress upon them principle; who form and cultivate their character? Is it not to be wondered at that they grow up without principle, without any moral sense between right and wrong? Can you be surprised if they gradually fall into the ways of vice, and as their natural powers develop, that they become experts in that line of wickedness which they adopt and for which they have a special aptitude. The criminal class spring chiefly from the neglected class or they owe their downfall to the influence of companions. You have seen men sometimes in your streets or at race meetings, or on the shore at Blackpool, Douglas or Scarborough, doing the three card trick - the purse trick or giving away broaches or .... Pins. These men if you listen to their wonderful, glib and clever speeches, profess to be benefactors to their fellow men: the one object of their lives is to make people happy. They wish to scatter broadcast the wealth which has been entrusted to them by some foolish but well meaning young nobleman whom, they say, has more money than sense.

You can judge for yourself the talent which a youth, springing from the gutter, is gifted with and how it has been employed, when I tell you that he is one of the cleverest card sharpers out. Another of them is an expert in precious stones and has often with effect carried off a real diamond and left a counterfeit in its place and that he has more than once been concerned in some of the largest and most cleverly planned jewellery robberies in Paris and London. He has graduated into the highest rank of criminal life and now scorns the purse trick, the three card trick or any of the lower arts of the profession.

On your streets this evening close by the railway station you will see three or four pavement sketches by one of these lighting artistes.

Pilate's Hall. The crowned head, the trickling drops of blood, streaming down that suffering but adorable face, the purple garment of mockery and the reed for a sceptre were so true and so speaking in their execution, that one might imagine a young Carle Dolce was throwing off the infantile efforts of genius. Here was talent, running to waste in the streets and the well finished pictures of the French Napoleon, delicately tinted mackerel, moon-light scenes, cats' heads purring with life and full length children which seemed almost to move and speak, excite no further sympathy or interest towards the young artist than an odd copper from the passers-bye.

We have heard of infant prodigies on the stage, but never expect to meet them in the gutters. What is this two feet six of insolent assurance in an urchin's garb, with deep black painted eye-brows, moustache, imperial face besmeared with rouge and chalk?

The streets are still full of life and our illustrations drawn from the realities are far from being exhausted. Here is a group of three lads, their respective ages being, if we may trust our eyes, 6, 8 and 10. They are a troupe of artists, a travelling company of 'motley players'.

This is no exaggerated picture, but a troupe of artists, a travelling company of 'strolling players', who have in their professional capacity toured most of the large towns in England. This little band, who were well known to me some years ago, actually tramped from Liverpool to London, giving their dramatic performances al fresco in every town and village they passed through. Their theatrical wardrobe was not the least encumbrance upon their journey, for their only change of costume consisted in the amount of burnt cork that was necessary to give fierceness and determination to their tiny faces for the deeds of darkness they were bent upon.

Often have you and I seen their tragic company, around the door of an omnibus or in the vicinity of the Liverpool Exchange Flags, act Shakespeare's tragedy of Richard the Third in something over five minutes. Tragedy is their legitimate line, unless they vary it with some scene from a Metro Drama which is full of terrible situations either by land or sea, hair-breadth escapes, a terrific combat with imaginary broadswords, ending in a back-fall to show the skill of these artistes in dying. Sometimes these dramatic efforts represent the worse side of human life, robbery, murder, seduction, which are the first lessons these children learn by heart in the gallery of some low theatre or 'penny gaff'.

In August 1865 one of this group came under my charge in the gaol when he was just nine years old. He and a girl a little older than himself stopped an old lady one night in the vicinity of the Adetphi Hotel and attempted to take her purse from her. She cried out for assistance and these two highway robbers were instantly taken prisoners and eventually sent to a reformatory school. This boy did not know a letter in the alphabet; he could not say the "Our Father", in fact he scarce knew the existence of a God, yet he repeated for me, on the floor of his prison cell, as he had seen them acted, Richard the Third, Jack Sheppard, the Dukes Motto, Dr. Faustus and scraps of other plays. Poor child, what did he know, he was "Nobody's Child"; and who cared for him? The gallery of the theatre was his only school and the heroic deeds of high-way men were the noblest aspirations that had ever been set before his mind. He was withal a genuine, straightforward lad, and I felt at the time that he had a heart and talent to make a position for himself if he only had the chance. Strange to say, I met that boy on board of the steamship Austrian in which I crossed the Atlantic in 1870, when I took out a number of destitute and orphan children to Canada; a fine strong well-built and now a fairly educated youth. I did not recognise in him the former half-clad and neglected urchin tragedian. When I asked his name, he replied "Why Father, have you forgot me?" Looking into his face more closely, I said "what, is it little Don?" "Yes, Father". Suffice it to say that my heart had long before that warmed to that boy and my early hopes, that if he were only taught better and had a chance, he would one day be a respectable man, are now more than realized. He is doing well, and long ago become a large farmer in Canada. I have no fear of poor Don ever turning back to street life again or putting into practice those lessons of his neglected childhood.

Part III

To "Save the Boy" from the fatal influences of pauperism, ignorance and crime and the temptations of the "Streets" has been the chief aim of my life. "Save the Boy" is my motto - inscribed on the flag which I unfurled nearly thirty years ago and time, with its experience, only binds me more faithfully to its call.

I ask then to "Save the Boy" from what? Not from labour, which is his birthright, for which he may be thankful to Heaven yet, before he dies, but from Temptation. To the child nurtured by affectionate parents, supplied with daily food and daily kindness, educated in religion and morality and helped by wise and able friends, anxious for his welfare, to the means of living by honest and intelligent labour, even to such a child, Temptation is more than a name. To the child whose fate is to hunger and wander about the streets, where limbs are familiar with cold and fatigue, whose stomach is familiar with starvation and whose eyes are familiar with misery and vice - Temptation is a Power - a Demon whose influence not one of a thousand such boys can long resist. To him Theft is the stepping stone to Wealth. Honesty is represented by the people who seem to have all they need and to find life easy and comfortable, and Justice is personified in the Policeman who drives him from one street corner to another in the day and from one stone bed to another in the night. Fame and distinction, as he learns to think of them, are to be gained by daring acts of crime, and heroism is to be displayed in the prisoner's van, in the dock or at the hulks and, when Fortune favours him, by "dying game" upon the gallows. The streets are seldom the schools of honesty, morality or virtue to those who study and live in them; and year by year the lad who today would be honest for his food and lodging, tomorrow steals the loaf of bread he cannot buy but must eat, and thus turns into the road which leads through all human misery and shame, which no right-minded man can contemplate without sadness and regret. Impressed with this conscious knowledge, gained from my daily experience in the prisons, I opened the Refuge and Night Asylum in Liverpool in 1865 with the object of giving a shelter to boys who had no place to sleep but on the streets. They were there provided with a wash, a basin of coffee and half-a-pound of bread, with a dash of treacle upon it, when the funds would admit of such a luxury. You can judge of the extent of the work when I tell you that in a period of five years we had given 97,831 suppers and 7,743 nights lodgings, whilst 1,728 boys had been permanently dealt with. No boy was ever turned from the door of the Refuge on account of his creed. It offers a shelter and food to Protestants as well as Catholics and those who know me, know that I am incapable of taking advantage of the orphanage and destitution of a child to tamper with his faith.

I appeal, with confidence, to all classes to co-operate in this movement. Why should not willing hearts and firm hands be bound and clasped together, seeking to save and elevate our common race? Protestants and Catholics: men of all shades of opinion can have work: the numbers are large enough, the field is wide enough for the well-directed energies and zeal of all. Whatever may be our religious or political principles, here is a great social question where large-hearted men can work together and prove by our actions that the true foundation of religion and politics is to do good to our fellow creatures. In the interests of humanity, in future progress and stability of this country, in the work of saving those souls that have been Redeemed by the Blood of the One Saviour of mankind, let us bury before the Altar of Charity every sentiment of religious jealousy and intolerance, and let us seek to do for these poor children what we would desire to be done for our own were they placed in similar circumstances.

To feed the hungry, to clothe the naked, to shelter the homeless and to suffer little children to come unto Jesus, are precepts binding upon all men. God, who one day will judge us all, has said that what we do for the least one of these little ones for His sake is done unto Him.

If you saw a child fall into the river, would you not make some effort to save him? This is the common instinct of our humanity. Some years ago, the brother of one of these boys fell overboard from the Reformatory Ship Clarence into the River Mersey. Instantly a cry was raised "A Boy overboard". "Save the Boy"; "Save the Boy"!! rang across the waters, from ship to shore, and was re-echoed from the deck of every vessel that lay at anchor. As quick as lightning one of his companions leaped from a porthole into the dark and angry flood. With dauntless courage he breasts the surging waves, gaining ground at every stroke. Now his companion, exhausted, sinks: - again he rises to the surface. Already he is borne by the swift flowing tide half a mile down the river. "See"! "See"!! his strength has gone; his hands are motionless, he reels, he sinks. His little companions look on with wild anxiety; it would seem as if their voices and hearts were lifted up to the common Father of all "Oh God, Save the Boy!!_

As he sinks for the third time, that brave heroic boy seizes his sinking companion and our joyous shout rends the air: "He's saved!" "He's saved". If such be the noble instincts, even of these poor outcast and criminal boys, surely Men and Christians will not turn a deaf ear to my cry when in the Sacred Name of the One Father and Redeemer of all, I ask you to "Save the orphan and destitute Children", who are perishing on your streets, borne along to destruction by the torrent of pauperism, ignorance and crime.

Street Trading

During Father Nugents time *(circa 1900)*

Introduction

The Man behind the Mission

"I freed the poor in distress

and the orphan who had no helper.

The dying man's blessing rested on me

and I gave the widow's heart cause to rejoice.

I was eyes for the blind

and feet for the lame.

Who but me was father of the poor?

(Book of Job. 29;15. The New Jerusalem Bible)

Imagine a time before the days of Queen Victoria, before the motor car, when the streets were full of horse-drawn carriages, when many roads were dirt tracks, a time before the train, electric light, television, radio, cameras and computers. Imagine a time when coal and cotton were Britain's mainstay in trade and commerce, a time when plague and great poverty stalked the streets, when there was no welfare state and the workplace was a place of slave labour, when children were abandoned and half-starved in the streets and the local church was the provider, with thousands of people "living off the parish". Imagine a time when Catholics had no vote and few could go to school, when the Catholic priest was the father of the community and churches were full. Imagine a small town next to the sea, bordered by green fields where the traces of Dutch and Viking settlers could still be seen on the landscape and dockland was only in its infancy. Then you are beginning to imagine the world that James Nugent knew as a child in Liverpool.

James Nugent belongs to two distinct but related traditions in modern history. He takes his place in the long line of philanthropists, benefactors and community leaders who, in Liverpool, rose like giants to tower above the destitution and misery that lay all around them and helped to shape the life and the heritage of the city we now know. He compares favourably with the greatest of them: William Roscoe, William Rathbone, Josephine Butler, and many more. If James Nugent has not gone down in history with quite the same acclaim as other fellow - reformers this does not imply that his contribution was any less significant or that his influence was any less profound.

The other tradition to which he belongs is that of a special band of people whose prime concern was the protection and formation of the young. He is part of the story about the spiritual care of children epitomised in the life of St. Joseph of Nazareth, St. Vincent de Paul, Blessed Edmund Rice and St. John Bosco, to name but a few. Their work is reflected in memorial statues that show them with a young child at their side. The bronze statue of Monsignor Nugent, in the ceremonial robes of his office, and the ragged boy next to him, proclaims the salient characteristic of his mission to care for the underprivileged child, whilst the contrast of his rich apparel with the wretched state of his protégé reflects how he used position and privilege to serve the poor.

The broad historical context of James Nugent's life was the hundred years period between two great conflicts. The Battle of Waterloo in 1815 and the outbreak of The First World War in 1914 provide the parameters of a comparative time of peace in Britain which gave scope for consolidation, empire building and progress, although hostilities were never far away. Nugent knew the days of the Crimean War, the American Civil War and the Boer War. As an Army Chaplain of long-standing he had some insight into the mentality of War but his call to arms was a battle waged against poverty and ignorance, prejudice, inequality and crime, on the streets of Liverpool rather than in the theatre of war. That remarkable century in Britain was the setting of Nugent's life-span.

James Nugent's place in history is assured and immortalised in Frederick Pomeroy's statue of him, placed for all to see in St. John's Memorial Gardens, sometimes called The Peace Gardens, in the heart of Liverpool. It has stood there since its unveiling on 8th. December 1906, in all weathers and seasons, a reminder of Father Nugent's steadfast and determined ministry throughout arduous times. The pose is one of protection and blessing, portraying Father Nugent's double mission of bringing to the needy the practical arm of charity and the providential hand of God. The inclusion of Nugent's statue in that place is a recognition that spiritual warfare is something noble and honourable. He finds his place among Liverpool's heroes of war and peacetime.

In Father Nugent's estimation, charity definitely began at home. "To do the work that lay at his own doorstep was the cardinal feature of his work", the historian Thomas Burke wrote of him in his book 'Catholic History of Liverpool'. Archbishop Whiteside, speaking after Nugent's death in 1905, expressed what everyone felt about Nugent; that the story of his work was written in the history of the streets. Thomas Whiteside, fourth Catholic Bishop of Liverpool and first Archbishop of Liverpool, continued the work of his predecessors and Nugent's pioneering efforts for child welfare, and is a bridge between two important phases in the history of the Liverpool Catholic Children's Protection Society. This is why a chapter has been devoted to him in this book. He noted the important aspect of Father Nugent's ministry - that it was rooted in the immediate and the practical and that he had spent his adult life caring for the poor in the streets where he had spent his childhood.

Whilst it is true that James Nugent's charitable work

would take him half-way around the world, making him an ambassador for Liverpool and its people, in his own words he professed that he "belonged to Liverpool". He was born there, grew up there and expressed the hope that he would end his days there. Liverpool gave him the motivation and the drive, as it has done for so many of its citizens, to accomplish great things from small beginnings and, in the face of enormous social problems, to make a difference by being resolved to make a start.

During his Pastoral Visit to Britain in 1982, Pope John Paul II, speaking in Liverpool, referred to Father Nugent as "your own pioneer of charity". The phrase implies that Nugent is in the ownership of Liverpool's community and a present reality not a past shadow. He is part of what is 'ours' and what makes 'us' today in Liverpool, in society and in the Church. But as we can only understand ourselves fully in the light of the history that has shaped us, James Nugent needs to be seen within the social and religious development that has moulded and influenced our society to the present day. This is what I have tried to do in this book, to see Nugent's place in the cultural heritage we are now part of, bearing in mind the Pope's words on that same occasion in Liverpool: "perhaps the greatest heritage was to be found in all those who have struggled here to overcome the ills of society and to build up a common brotherhood".

In his own day too Father Nugent was praised at the highest level by the Catholic Church. Pope Leo XIII, in 1892, in private audience, made him a Domestic Prelate in recognition of his services to the Church, to the Catholic Press and to the poor. From that time on he was known as 'Monsignor Nugent'. A great friend and ally of Nugent, Archbishop Ireland of St. Paul's Minnesota, USA, whose enterprising work helped Nugent find homes for immigrant families from Ireland, paid tribute to him saying: "someone in England with mind to understand him, with heart to value him, with pen to picture him, will no doubt before long give us his biography", and he thought it would be "a blessed book". It presents a daunting challenge which I am not sure will be met! A challenge also came from the pages of the 'Ushaw Magazine' at the time of Father Nugent's death warning that "his life was too big, his interests too manifold to be dealt with in short pages". I hope I have heeded this warning.

Even Father Nugent's harshest critics (and there were a few as we shall see) would have had to agree that the words quoted above from the Book of Job present an accurate summary of his mission. They are the inspiration for what must be one of the most impressive epitaphs ever written. Pomeroy's bronze of Nugent, like Sir John Shannon's portrait in oils, and the marble bust of him by Aniza McGeehan, might convey something of the strength and compassion of their subject; a towering presence who "for over fifty years strode like a colossus over the life of Liverpool". Yet for all their artistry, these memorials in bronze, oil or marble cannot convey the flesh and blood man behind the mission, the real life behind the legend.

I have looked in vain in all the recent extant commentaries on Nugent for a hint of that humour and sparkle he must surely have had - being from Liverpool and working with children - even in the dour and irascible times of his declining years when the sad wistfulness of long experience overtook him. This book is an attempt to provide what we cannot see in the accolades and memorials. Canon John Bennett, Nugent's biographer in 1949 pointed out that few passers-by notice the statue and even fewer bother to stop and read the inscription on it. Perhaps this book will bring a few more people closer in order to know and appreciate Father Nugent better.

More important than external monuments is the internal disposition of those whose continuing work of practical charity, started by James Nugent, is carried out generously and well. The Society he founded nearly 125 years ago continues the work in his memory and in the name of the Gospel, in a way that has widened and spread beyond even that which Nugent's great vision could have foreseen. We see Father Nugent acclaimed as an 'Apostle of Temperance', 'Protector of the Orphan', 'Consoler of the Prisoner', 'Reformer of the Criminal', 'Saviour of Fallen Woman-hood' and 'Friend of all in Poverty and Affliction', but this stirring litany has to be evaluated in the cold light of the circumstances of his day. These titles are only clarion calls to an urgent mission which was relevant then and continues to be relevant now.

What is missing from the litany, surprisingly, is a description of him as an 'Apostle of Emigration' since he pioneered the process of sending Catholic children to new homes in the New World. This is a more ambivalent issue and his role in this regard has perhaps been less well understood. As his statue faces the River, the Irish Sea and the Atlantic Ocean, which carried so many hopeful migrants to and from Liverpool's shores, it is left to our imagination perhaps as to how significant a part this played in his work. He would make the crossing many times in the quest for a suitable home for orphaned children.

Few Catholic priests in Britain have been so publicly honoured and acclaimed as Father James Nugent, but I sense that he would rather we applied to him the words written on Sir Christopher Wren's memorial in London: "If you wish to see his monument look around you". The words refer, of course, to the great building of St. Paul's Cathedral which Wren inspired, but their wider meaning is clear. The living memorial of Father Nugent's work is in the people of yesterday and the people of today, in the charitable institutions around us and in the continuing service of the poor.

Before I read anything about Father Nugent I re-read the 'Letter of St. James' in The New Testament. What Martin Luther once called a 'gospel of straw' has become an accepted charter for Christian belief and action, a living gospel which precedes the historic division of the churches, and which forms the basis for much of the

Christian mission. The 'gospel of straw' tag would hold good only if the gospel remained idle words and promises. When I read St. James I sensed that it had been the charter for Nugent's own mission too, and that it had been the driving force behind so much of his apostolic work with the underprivileged. He always insisted that he had adopted a practical approach and that his concern was not only to give physical shelter to the needy but also spiritual guidance to the soul. His particular brand of 'unspoilt religion' was exactly how St. James expressed it: "to come to the aid of widows and orphans in their need". Nugent himself once wrote: "The true foundation of our religion is to do good to our fellow-creatures".

Not all recent commentaries on Father Nugent have been without criticism. John Belcher for example, though praising Nugent's part in the development of social welfare, sees him motivated by a sort of religious competitiveness which, from within his Irish-Catholicism, made him want to 'outdo' the Protestants in Charity. This has to be set against Thomas Burke's more partisan approach of regarding Nugent's greatest service to Liverpool, and perhaps to the whole of England, as being able "to enlist the aid of enlightened Protestantism in Liverpool for the salvation of the child". A strong claim, but one that seems to be justified when we consider that Nugent secured the presence of Orangeman, Jew, Unitarian, Non-Conformist, Catholic and representatives of many other religions on the same platform as long ago as 1865 in his campaign to 'Save The Boy'. Whichever view we take, there is no doubt that Nugent helped to redefine the nature of the Catholic mission in light of the sea change in social needs which mass immigration from Ireland brought about. He pearheaded Catholic Social Welfare in England.

I am sure there was much more to Father Nugent's work than a kind of religious 'one-upmanship'. In his work for the Boys' Refuge and in his Prison Ministry, for example, he demonstrated his belief in what St. James describes as "the law that sets us free"; the perfect law of love. He wanted to show to the vulnerable and the hurt that a law of kindness existed as well as rule of law and punishment. His reform work was often a matter of the steel fist in a velvet glove, but underpinning this was what St. James' Letter presents as a belief in the redemptive power of good works - Nugent thought of work as 'the elevating power'. In St. James, even the harlot, Rahab, is exonerated by her kindness, and in the conclusion of this Letter of James we are offered these encouraging words: "If one of you strays away from the truth, and another brings him (or her) back to it, he may be sure than anyone who can bring back a sinner from the wrong way that he has taken will be saving a soul from death and covering up a great number of sins". Here is the essential image of the 'Good Shepherd' which, among all the titles ascribed to Father Nugent, remains his greatest sobriquet.

A hundred years have gone by since Father Nugent's death on 27th. June, 1905 - a span of time long enough to forget, but also long enough to justify another look at the details of his life and work. Some may say that Father Nugent is a figure belonging to an unreachable past. He lived in a time so different from our own that practically all the landmarks of the society and the Church he knew have disappeared, and the layers of change, that a century of progress and conflict has left, form an impenetrable curtain.

There is another view, which I share, and that is that a Centenary Year is an important juncture at which to recall the contribution of someone whose impact on Church and Society is still strong and who, although separated from us by a century, somehow remains tangible and real. I feel it is important to dispel the collective amnesia that settles in time over the details of a person's life and to lift the veil to take another look, to rediscover and re-evaluate the real Father Nugent. A major aspect of this book is also to celebrate the work of the Society he and Bishop O'Reilly founded over 120 years ago. The centenary of Father

Nugent's death is an important moment of reflection and commemoration for the Nugent Care Society. It is also a good time to revisit the personal attributes and many-sided achievements of Father Nugent in his own right, as he may be in danger of being consigned to the footnotes of the local history books.

This biography is an attempt to rescue James Nugent from this potential obscurity and to examine the deeper aspects of his contribution to Liverpool as the city approaches the celebrations for the 800th Anniversary of its Charter in 2007 and 'European Capital of Culture 2008'. Liverpool has advertised itself as a City of Faith, which some may regard with a touch of cynicism. The title 'Capital of Culture' may call forth some of the humorous reaction for which Liverpool is famous, but however it is viewed it should be clear that such a claim owes much to those who have gone before us. It is time for a new appraisal of Father James Nugent's contribution to the faith story of our country. He should be seen as one of the greats of Liverpool, part of it's precious heritage which makes it, for most of the time at least, a 'wondrous place' in which to live.

What if James Nugent was to come down from his pedestal in St. John's Gardens and stand once again where he would want to be, with those he loved and served so well; the people of Liverpool? They were people like those of any great community, of different creeds and nationalities, needy, vulnerable, prisoners, young and old, homeless, single parents, children. They included the helpless drunkard and the asylum seeker. What sort of person would we see, and what sort of things would he reveal to be the influences that shaped and drove him in his ministry in those by-gone days?

Father Nugent cannot be appreciated fully in isolation from the town of his birth. Throughout its long and eventful past, Liverpool has known some dark days and when the visitations of evil came in a variety of guises - fever, famine, pauperism, squalor, economic depression and sectarian strife (sometimes all at once), adversity and hardship were often overcome by means of the positive spirit in the community and a firm belief that things could change.

Not only self-belief but also resourcefulness and ingenuity have made things happen in Liverpool. The inherited stigma of the Slave Trade and the shifting sands of fortune in industry and commerce, the arrival of immigrants in huge number and the problems of infrastructure this revealed, have largely been overcome by an indomitable spirit within the ranks of the community itself. With good reason the political and religious leadership of Liverpool over the years is something of which the city can be very proud. An unimaginable rise to riches also brought an unimaginable slough of poverty - twins born of the same mother called progress, and it was in the painful inter-action of these that Father James Nugent spent his life ministering to the poor in the town where he grew up.

As Father Nugent took up his position as a priest in Liverpool in 1849, the Catholic Diocese there was in its infancy and the times, like no other times since The Reformation, were ones of crisis management. There was no clear strategy or direction from Central Government and as yet no proper understanding or analysis of the root causes of social and moral evils, or of the psychological factors in crime. Charitable Societies abounded everywhere, like 'The Benevolent Society of Saint Patrick', 'The Irish Sons of Freedom', 'The Total Abstinence Benevolent Society' and 'The Catholic Benefit Society': the names themselves reflect the peculiar needs and ethos of the time. A culture grew up around these Institutions whilst various Guilds and Associations, which were often nurtured and inspired by the local parishes, jostled for position in a general charitable effort.

Behind these Organisations there was also an attempt to address a deep-seated religious divide that had been inherited from Reformation times and manifested itself in social and political life. In 1883 and 1884 a Catholic bishop, Bishop Bagshaw of the Diocese of Nottingham, wrote a series of Pastoral Letters in which he attributed the blame for pauperism in England to the Reformation's systematic dismantling of the agencies for Poor Relief. The monasteries had provided a safe haven for many social refugees. The political will to replace this provision was lacking, and Bagshaw argued that the community had been left to provide for people, without the necessary resources to do so. He believed that when religious principles were compromised the rule of economics took over. The Letters were given publicity in Father Nugent's newspaper 'The Catholic Times'. They fitted well with Nugent's own ideas and exemplified how he was able to harness the power of the Press in his own agenda for reform.

Perhaps it was because of the stormy and uncertain nature of those times that it is hard to see a logical pattern in Father Nugent's work. He sometimes comes across as a rather lonely figure moving from one charitable project to another in an unconnected series of schemes dictated by changing needs. This partly reflects the nature of those times and partly reflects his own restless nature. 'A soul too big for his body' was how Bishop Brown described it, whilst Bishop Goss worried that there was too much ambition in him.

Father Nugent's work cannot be easily chronicled or divided up, as some biographers try to do with their subjects, because he was compelled to move quickly and, like a latter day Saint Paul, wanted to "forget what lies behind and strain forward to what lies ahead". This is the real reason why James Nugent defies attempts to put his life story into neat compartments, as I have found to my cost! In all the complexity of his work there was a simple underlying motivation - the mandate of the Christian gospel to help the underprivileged by the practical and generous sharing of resources.

For the sake of clarity, I have divided Father Nugent's career into two phases, even though this is somewhat artificial as there is an overlap between the two. The first part is from the time of his birth in 1822 until his appointment as Prison Chaplain in 1863, and the second part is from 1863 to the time of his death in 1905. The third section of the book is an outline of the history of Catholic child care since his death and an evaluation of the legacy he left us through his life's work. Despite this three-fold division I know it will be understood that Nugent stands within a much longer tradition of charitable endeavour that went before him and continues today beyond the confines of the Diocese of Liverpool, but it is not possible to do justice to that in this book.

It is not possible to know or understand every detail of a person's life and no life can be expressed completely in a book. I don't presume to have attempted that, but I felt it was important to try to piece together as many of the strands as possible of a life that was as complex as it was long. Emphasis only on Father Nugent's successes and strengths and not on the failures too would serve only to present a false picture, but at the same time we should give praise where praise is due. His early years are not recorded in any contemporary account and in the absence of written records what happened at that stage of his life can only be conveyed by reference to his future activities and reflections, his parental and environmental influences and a measure of conjecture.

I have tried to make some evaluation of the significance of Father Nugent's work for our own day by looking into the community to which he dedicated all his energies. I have looked for any indication in accounts of his life for an insight into how he was feeling; what were his thoughts and emotions as he encountered and addressed sad and emotional scenes? I have wondered how he coped with the wretched sights of human misery that met his eyes, and from where he derived solace and support.

For all the praise given from the higher dignitaries of the Church, it was the widespread love of everyday people which set Nugent apart in the folk-lore of Liverpool. He was a human sign-post in the dark streets of his day, a shepherd and a comforter to those who lay dying in the fetid cellars full of plague victims. At a time when morale was at an extremely low ebb, when people badly needed providence to take a hand, Nugent was there, and like a modern John the Baptist, people were content to enjoy for a while the light that he gave. The 'Liverpool Daily Post and Courier in its fulsome obituary of him in 1905 said: "No one thought of differences under Nugent's gracious glamour, except the differences between good and evil, light and darkness, hope and despair".

Paradoxically, it was his decision to stay with the poor that prevented Nugent from attaining a more prominent place on the ecclesiastical ladder or in the pages of history. Cardinal Manning tried more than once to coax Father Nugent to Westminster when he recognised the work he was doing and how it accorded with his own ideals. Nugent resisted the blandishments of life in the capital and decided that he had a more important task to do in Liverpool. He frequently and proudly stated; "I belong to Liverpool". His conscious decision to identify with the needy people on the streets of his home town, to see the importance of the local mission, is key to understanding him - more so than any list of his accomplishments. The belief among Londoners that nothing of significance happens elsewhere, clearly prevailed in those days too. By staying and working with Bishop O'Reilly in Liverpool, Nugent went on to found a Society for child care that continues to the present day as a legacy to the city.

Several factors have prevented Nugent from enjoying a higher profile in the general record of recent history. He and Cardinal Newman were two giant figures in Catholic resurgence and renewal in England but Nugent grew up in the shadow of his more famous contemporary. That Cardinal Newman's ideas, writings and life-style influenced Nugent deeply cannot be in doubt and although Church History has not given the same degree of eminence to James Nugent as to John Henry Newman, yet

the resurgence of Catholic life and culture in 19ᵗʰ· Century
Britain - the so called 'Second Spring' - was in no small
way due to Nugent's early attempts to implement the
teachings of the future Cardinal at a local level. There is a
real sense in which the children Father Nugent helped to
rescue and rehabilitate into citizens for this world and the
next, were children of a new season of hope in the Catholic
Church. They were the children of the Second Spring.

As well as doing a lot of good in the field of Catholic
devotion and learning, through the Catholic Institute
which he founded in Liverpool in 1853, James Nugent,
under Newman's influence, and inspired by the example
of Cardinal Wiseman's national 'Crusade of Prayer',
helped to create a new confidence in the Catholic people,
distinct from, but built upon, the Catholic-Irish tradition.
Nugent admired the work of Cardinal Manning and
Archbishop Temple and the united witness they gave in
the work for Social Welfare and Workers' Rights in
London. There was also a clear link between Manning's
activities and Nugent's brave call to the Poor Law
Guardians to promote the Rights of Catholic paupers in
the Workhouse, whilst his defence of Prisoners' Rights was
something he spoke out about boldly before Parliamentary
Select Committees.

In many instances Nugent was following the lead of
others, but he was probably one step ahead of Cardinal
Manning of Westminster in starting "The League of the
Cross for Total Abstinence" in the North of England,
which The Cardinal spearheaded so effectively in London.
James Nugent was well placed to do all this as someone
with Irish and Lancashire blood. As Bennett describes him
in his book, he was, through to the end of his life,
"characteristically Irish, characteristically Lancashire, and
above all characteristically Nugentesque" in style and
manner. Without exaggeration we can say that he was one
of the principal architects of a new Catholic identity which
emerged from a very mixed community, comprising
people of many different backgrounds - from the north

and south of Ireland, from the Continent of Europe and from among English Recusants families. The success in building up the Faith Community from these was no small achievement.

Another reason for his comparative obscurity is that he was part of a second raft of reformers and community leaders in 19th Century Britain. Local histories will attest to the crucial part played by legends of social reform in Liverpool, men of the stature of the three Williams - Rathbone, Duncan and Roscoe, and women of the calibre of Kitty Wilkinson and Josephine Butler and Agnes Jones. Again, James Nugent was in the shadow of his famous forebears in Liverpool's civic and political life, who steered the ship of Liverpool's progress to its present course. As such he is not always given due credit for the specific steer he gave or the light his particular star shed on society amidst so many bright suns.

Nugent's poor ratings in local history books may well be due to the fact he struggled to assert Catholic life in a Protestant town, in an atmosphere still characterised by fear and scepticism that arose from a long history of internicene warfare. He was compelled to work in a robust and overt way for a statement of the Catholic view-point without incurring the wrath of too many opponents. It was a time of tension among the Churches, but a measure of Nugent's calibre, as already quoted, was that he was able "to enlist the aid of enlightened Protestantism" and much more than that. His rallying call to friends and enemies alike to get behind the all-important needs of the child, uniting almost everyone in a common cause, may have been his greatest legacy, of which we shall say more later, but it also resonates strongly with our own times. Suffice it to say here that it helped to break down barriers and create a more tolerant climate in the community at that time and blazed a trail for future ecumenical partnership. In a special way, his friendship with the Anglican priest, Canon Thomas (Major) Lester blazed a trail to Christian Unity at a very difficult time in inter-Church relations.

His life shows us, for all its shortcomings, that the tender and timeless quality of a holy life spent in service to others, transcends the barriers of class and creed and the failings that come with the passage of years. Father Nugent's example remains valid always because it was born of a personal and sincere sense of God's presence in the people he met, a sense of the presence of God's hand in events, a strong awareness of his own particular vocation.

It is not possible to make an exact assessment of all aspects of Father Nugent's life with the incomplete information we have about him. The modern tendency to judge past events and attitudes by the very different standards and requirements of our day, obstructs a proper evaluation. Nugent would have been as horrified by the red tape surrounding child care and social welfare today as we might be by some of the methods he employed. By our criteria he would probably be accused of naivety and impropriety, and by his criteria we would be accused of being squeamish and pusillanimous. Such is the problem of making comparisons between one era of history and another. There is no doubt he would have shared the sadness that all right-minded people feel in the face of current incidents of child abuse.

Nugent was not immune to criticism. His active and outspoken style could not fail to attract opposition from groups such as the Irish Nationalists, who accused him of being interested only in the symptoms and not in the root causes of the plight of the Irish People. The fact remains that political expediency did not stand in the way of practical charity and compassion. Perhaps, looking at the global scene today we are not so far removed from the reality of Nugent's day and hopefully we, like him, will still be allowed to act according to our hearts as well as our heads.

Part One (1822 – 1863)

Chapter 1

His First Home

JAMES NUGENT, the first son of Mary and John Nugent, was born on a Sunday, the third of March 1822, at number 22 Hunter Street, off Byrom Street, in Liverpool. The old town was beginning its gradual transformation into the modern city, the gentler Age of Sail was giving way to the harsher Age of Steam, and a decade that would see great social and political reform, more tolerance of religious differences and Catholic Emancipation, was unfolding.

All the effects, both good and bad, of the Industrial Revolution were fully in evidence as the era of the Railway and the Steam Ship was born. In politics it was the time of the so-called "Liberal Tories", who had formed a Government under Lord Liverpool, to oversee an age of great technological advance, and social development. These reforms would pave the way for the new Poor Laws in 1834, which would come to play an important part in James Nugent's priestly ministry.

The Nugent family home in Hunter Street, was situated between the areas known at that time as Mile End Road (Scotland Road) and Shaw's Brow (William Brown Street), close to the commercial heart of the town. James Nugent's first years of life would witness great social and demographic changes, the rise of Dockland Liverpool, a dramatic upturn in the British economy. Although the earthworks for the new railways could be seen and heard, it was still a time of relatively quiet prosperity, in the regency period of King George IV and William IV, soon to make way for the colourful and eventful reign of Queen Victoria.

A time of unparalleled industrial progress and development, bringing unimaginable wealth, also meant a time of unimaginable poverty. In Liverpool, the 'river of a thousand delights' would be cruelly turned into an ocean of misery. There is no doubt that James Nugent was deeply influenced by the surroundings and the contrasting times in which he lived and his early years were spent in a close-knit, working-class community full of the atmosphere and activity of the shops and market stalls. His father, John Nugent, worked among the traders as a seller of poultry and vegetables. James's father added to his business when he acquired a couple of stalls in St. John's Food Market which opened the year that James was born. He had a comfortable start in life.

There was a thriving, bustling life around the docks, with sailing and shipping activity on the River Mersey that connected a network of inland waterways and canals carrying goods and produce in barges to and from the industrial and mining heartlands of Lancashire and Yorkshire. The advent of the Railways, the sights and sounds of the ocean, a prosperous market trade, were all good subjects for the vivid imagination of a boy like James Nugent whose dream of travelling drew him to the sea like a magnet. They formed the backdrop of his childhood.

His boyhood ambitions would later be translated into frequent crossings to America and Canada in a restless search for better opportunities and homes for the poor. The ocean would have been visible from his home on the rare, clear days in Liverpool, and he would witness the first transatlantic sailings from the dockside. The statue erected in 1906 in memory of his work, by his grateful fellow-citizens, shows James Nugent facing the direction of the river and the original town where once there had been only a tiny enclave of seven inhabited streets and 138 families. During his youth he watched it grow into a thriving and prosperous port.

Everything about Liverpool and its people became a powerful challenge to James Nugent as he grew up. One day his determined mind would focus on a mission of charity that would last for an extraordinary fifty years or more and take him on many a journey around the world. The decade in which he was born marked a new springtime in Britain's economic fortunes and an important crossroads in the nation's historic growth to greatness during a time of consolidation and progress.

Prosperity and progress on the one hand, poverty and neglect on the other, produced a mix of fortunes for the people of Liverpool at that time and it was at the painful interface of these contrasting fortunes that James Nugent exercised his ministry as a priest. The injustices that came from uneven distribution of wealth were felt more keenly in Liverpool than in almost any other town in Britain since it was at the forefront of the process of change and expansion. The population of Liverpool grew from around 80,000 in the year 1800 to 140,000 in 1820, to 356,000 in 1850 and, increasing at an even greater rate from that time, reached more than 537,000 in 1875. Massive immigration in the late 1840s accounted for the dramatic increase, although the true numbers are not reflected in the official figures. Nugent observed years later that Liverpool was quite unprepared for the influx of people from Ireland - it did not have the infrastructure to deal with it. Yet nothing could have prepared it for the scale of the poverty it was to inherit.

The Nugent's home in Hunter Street was part of the new housing development that was moving northwards from the town centre. The building of houses was relentless but not enough to keep pace in later decades with the unexpected demand. The house where James's parents had chosen to live dated from the turn of the nineteenth century and was, judging by the photographs of later years, typical of the dwellings of that time - a solid, cheerless looking, three-storey terraced house with a cellar visible through iron bars at pavement level and some stone steps leading to the front door. It lay between the busy thoroughfares of Richmond Row and Commutation Row, where John Nugent would later own a shop, behind Shaw's Brow where the pottery industry had once thrived. Today the outward signs of Liverpool's tradition of Philanthropy, Learning and Architecture can be seen boldly displayed in that part of the city, where St. George's Hall, The Picton Library and Museum, The Walker Art Gallery and the University Buildings now stand.

The city's great maritime life, past and present, can be seen in the Liver and Cunard buildings at the waterfront. James Nugent, like any of his Victorian contemporaries, would have been surprised and pleased to see today the structures that symbolise Liverpool's cultural and commercial heritage. He would grow up to play his own considerable part in shaping that heritage which has given Liverpool its special place among the cities of the world. It is appropriate that the location of Nugent's ordinary-looking birthplace should now be the exhibition window of Liverpool's extraordinary cultural inheritance.

James Nugent's first home, the cradle of his childhood, lay at a vantage point within a mile of the River Mersey. Perhaps even more important to him was the cradle of his religious upbringing in the residential, Catholic quarter of the town, where docks-related trade was brisk and work could be found for skilled shipwrights and carpenters, blacksmiths, plumbers and painters, and where the faith community, augmented by first-generation Irish immigrants like James Nugent's father, could grow strong. These advantages were given further impetus by the emerging parish life focussed on the near-by Catholic mission of St. Anthony's, Scotland Road, St. Nicholas's on Copperas Hill, St. Peter's Church in Seel Street, and the Benedictine Church of St. Mary's in town. By 1822 these Churches were already a significant feature in Liverpool's religious landscape and it was within these emerging communities of faith that Mary and John Nugent and their growing family lived their Catholic life.

It was at St. Nicholas's Church, now only commemorated by an obscured plaque on the side of the Post-Office Building, Copperas Hill, where James's mission to the stricken people of his native town really began. He was taken there by his parents for baptism on 17th March 1822. It was a church for which he would have a life-long attachment and passion, where, as he often liked to remind people, he was not only baptised but made his First Communion, was ordained priest and celebrated his Golden Jubilee of Priesthood. His extraordinary tenacity in regard to St. Nicholas's parish, is something often remarked on by his contemporaries: It was the anchor of his spiritual life.

He was baptised on St. Patrick's Feast Day. Dates were something important to him; they were milestones in his journey of life. It was the fourth Sunday of Lent, a season when the Church looks forward to a renewal of faith and the season which heralds the approach of Spring. It was also a day special to the Irish-Catholic community with which he had an affinity because of his father, and it would prove to be a highly significant date in the struggle for an identity among Irish-Catholics. No subsequent St. Patrick's Day was more significant than that first one in 1822 when his Christian mission began with Baptism.

The priest who baptised him was Thomas Penswick, who later became Vicar Apostolic of the Lancashire District. He was the first in a line of priests with whom Nugent came into contact during a long and happy association with St. Nicholas's. His Godparents were

Thomas Anderson and Mary White, who were friends of the Nugents and provided welcome moral support to James's mother who, although a local Lancashire girl, was a recent convert to the Catholic Church. Mary Anne Nugent had been brought up in the Anglican Church, having attended school at the local Anglican Centre at Christ Church in Hunter Street.

His parent's chose the name of James. It is a name that denotes a reliable man, a strong, natural leader. James is a name that resonates down the years with Catholic history, conjures up an image of fierce loyalty, of rebellion and The Jacobites. In Hebrew the name (Jacob) was that of one who struggled with God, whilst it also carries the meaning of 'flamboyant', 'a go-getter', one who will let nothing stand in his way, a supporter of good causes with an energy and lust for life. There would be ample opportunity for James Nugent to live up to his name in all these aspects as his life unfolded. He would fight the Catholic corner yet remain aware of the need to break down the barriers of religious prejudice.

As a boy, James may well have looked out on the scene that formed the setting of his Liverpool home and contemplated his future. He could not have envisaged at that time the extent to which his own priestly ministry would reflect the large and liberal nature of his environment. It would be large in the scope of his outreach to the suffering, liberal in his unstinting generosity to the underprivileged. In this James Nugent was to follow in the footsteps of some illustrious predecessors who had shown a great love for the disadvantaged people of their native town. He learnt, primarily from his mother, that 'Charity begins at home', and even though it does not remain there its greatest expression is in the care of those nearest to us, who we most easily overlook.

Large and liberal is an apt description for all the activity around the growing port at that time. A special empathy developed between Nugent and this area and as he himself observed: "I watched the docks grow up and I grew up with them". It may be said that the advantages of the port and river could be traced to the time when their potential was first glimpsed by astute King John and the strategic location of the sluggish pool and backwater as a place for trade, travel and colonisation was first recognised. Later it came into its own as a port of emigration and immigration, import and export, well situated for lucrative trade relations with the New World. Sadly, the flip side of this 'Gateway to The Empire' was the high incidence of transients and vagrants, of impoverished immigrants whose numbers swelled the place and gave rise to the description of Liverpool as 'The Black spot on the Mersey'. As such it was prime territory for Christian mission.

James Nugent was to step into a great sea of need and share the pains and triumphs of his fellow townsmen and women. When he was still very young, everything around him seemed to be driven by the relentless energy of the Industrial Revolution which had changed the culture and complexion of the whole land. More efficient but less healthy power sources were evident, disruptive and noisy applications of the Steam invention were seen in the new Railway that was cutting huge scars in the green and gentle Lancashire countryside. Throughout the 1820s and 1830s the Railway edged its relentless way, like a giant mole burrowing the earth, towards the centre of Liverpool, to the terminal at the old Lime Kiln Lane (Lime Street) not much more than a stone's throw from the Nugent's front door.

Looking back on the days of his youth, James Nugent liked to recall how he witnessed two historic 'firsts' in the new and exciting age of travel. One was the first passenger Steam Train leaving Edge Hill Station for its inaugural journey to Manchester, on what turned out to be a tragic as well as a triumphant day in the history of Liverpool. Onlookers, who would certainly have included enthusiastic supporters and vociferous opponents of the new form of transport, gathered at the side of what was in effect the first main line and witnessed the fatal accident that befell their local MP William Huskisson, the Secretary of The Board of Trade. Then as a youth of fifteen, James Nugent watched the first Transatlantic Passenger Steam Ship set sail from Clarence Pier on its maiden voyage to America. Canon Bennett points out in his biography that America became a lodestone for the Nugent Family, as it did for so many Liverpool families.

In early Victorian times the new Railway carried with it much more than the benefits of more efficient freight transport and passenger travel. In some people's opinion the railway had a religious dimension too. The Quaker, Joseph Sanders, preached about the benefits of the new technology, and saw the steam train as a means of connection between people and places, as a paradigm of the spiritual journey, the destination to God with the stations of life en route. Some of the attributes claimed for the Railway were fanciful and exaggerated but its practical advantages were undoubted. Within twenty years of Nugent's birth, the rail network would link Liverpool with London, Birmingham with Birkenhead and even Chester would be brought back in from the cold. There was work generated by the rail industry and many political 'spin offs', whatever the potential for human and spiritual development may have been.

The Railway network was a means of creating community, a great symbol of man's powers of invention and skill, like the internet of today. But like the internet it brought mixed blessings - prosperity and privilege, enjoyment and danger. At first it could be accessed only by the wealthier people and travel was still a luxury unavailable to the majority. Although the advent of Steam was bringing ever greater advantages, changing the way people lived and worked, the Liverpool with which James Nugent and his family would have been familiar in the first half of the nineteen century was still largely a part of rural Lancashire.

The gradually changing skyline that came with the building of the docks, foretold a different future. The Docks, the river and the streets, with names that proclaimed Liverpool's religious, rural and maritime past - Water Street, Chapel Street (an ancient chapel in 1361 had preceded St. Nicholas's Sailors' Church), Whitechapel, Dale Street and Tithebarn Street, were transforming the old town and the open spaces that had once formed the ampitheatre of James Nugent's childhood and turning them into an urban sprawl. In face of all the changing circumstances, the fortress-like docks created by one of the greatest of all Engineers, Jesse Hartley, gave the town a sense of permanence and a strength that would see it through adversity.

James Nugent knew the joys and the demands of being part of a large family, which was his first school of life. He was the first of nine children, three boys and six girls, born within a span of 26 years, so that by the time Joseph Francis, the last sibling, was born, James was already twenty six years old and had attained his prime objective of being ordained to the Catholic Priesthood. After James came a sister - Mary Anne, who arrived four years after him in 1826, then came a brother, John, in 1829, who also became a priest, and then Margaret in 1831, followed by Rosanne in 1834, Jane in 1837, Teresa in 1839, Lucy in 1841 and finally Joseph Francis in 1848. Being first in the procession of this little band of brothers and sisters, James Nugent was, from an early stage in his life, accustomed to a position of leadership. Later he would be found at the head of processions in the streets, as part of various reforming campaigns, and at the forefront of a developing Catholic consciousness which was the drive behind his mission in churches, streets and Temperance Halls. His position in the family also meant that he gained quickly the attributes and powers of a role model and father-figure, which were to be important in his later career.

The Nugent's House has long disappeared. It was demolished a century or so after the family lived there, by the bulldozer as part of the programme of slum clearance and the creation of the approach roads to the Mersey Tunnels. In its day the house was part of a thriving neighbourhood. The important role which the front steps (referred to earlier) played in the general culture and life of the area cannot be over-emphasised. For the families who lived there, the steps constituted a window on the world. They could be said to play in people's lives a role akin to the role played by television today. People, watched a living soap opera being played out around them every day. Being continually swept and cleaned, the doorsteps formed a place to gather, to exchange news, to entertain and be entertained, enjoy company, make friends and engage in gossip. The steps were a trysting place, an escape from the dull interior of the houses and, more than anything else, a symbol of home and family – centrally important concepts in Victorian life. The doorsteps stood for independence and privacy but also for neighbourliness and hospitality. Many are the old sepia photographs to be found in local history books of the later Victorian period showing family groups sitting on the cold steps, allowing us a tantalising glimpse of a shadowy world and way of life that has long disappeared.

There was an education to be had just observing and living in this mixed community. One day it would become more cosmopolitan, comprised of many nationalities, including Italians, Poles and others from several Eastern European countries who came to settle there, giving rise to the name 'Little Italy'. In John Nugent's time, when the population of the town was an estimated 242,000, the neighbourhood was composed mainly of first generation Irish immigrants like himself who had come across from the old country, well before the Famine Years and the

Hungry Forties drove many thousands more that way. After James's Father arrived in Liverpool, he married Mary Anne Rice on 13th of June, 1821, at Christ's Church Chapel in Hunter Street and set up his own business as an 'Egg and Fish Dealer'.

John Nugent had emigrated from his home in County Meath in Ireland. Along with many of his generation he had perhaps experienced the increasing unrest in his native land during the early part of the nineteenth century. An unsettled political and religious situation had made people leave for America and England. John Nugent could have gone westwards and the story may have been different. Instead he made for Liverpool, possibly intending to travel further, and it is probable that he landed at Clarence Dock, where most new-comers from Ireland arrived in those days. At least one other member of the family, his sister, Catherine, also came from Ireland to live in Liverpool.

Catherine Nugent, James's aunt, married Peter McKinley whose name is associated with St. Peter and Paul's Church in Crosby, north of Liverpool. Their names appear on an engraved stone memorial inside the Church today recording the fact that Peter McKinley, who was in the shipping trade, was a most generous benefactor who gave the money for the building of the church - a sum of £6,600. The Nugent family would maintain its connection with St. Peter and Paul's parish when James's parents came to live near the church, in later life. Mary Nugent is buried in the churchyard along with Catherine and Peter McKinley but John Nugent's name is absent, indicating perhaps that he was buried back on his native Irish soil.

So, in the 1820s James's Father found himself in what was a fairly respectable, safe and middle-class environment where numbers of his compatriots had already formed an identifiable Irish ethos. Irish pubs and bars, newspapers, and music made up a kind of imported

Irish culture, a home from home. Yet there was a distinctive Liverpool feel to it.

Hunter Street derived its name from a local Liverpool builder and tax official, Roland Hunter, who had constructed his own house there and who had lived in near-by Cable Street. Like many benefactors of the time he gave not only his name but also his wealth to the town, a wealth which in many cases came on the back of businesses that had grown directly from the Slave Trade. The smaller enterprises and businesses had to adapt or diversify to survive and there is evidence that John Nugent had to do the same. The family business grew modestly. Although Gore's Liverpool Directory first lists him in 1824 in a humble way as an 'Egg and Fish Dealer', with two stalls at numbers 11 and 12 St. John's Food Market, by 1831 it is recorded that John Nugent was trading from premises at 6 Gloucester Street. By 1840 the shop had moved to 15 Lime Street, though the market stall was still operating and by the year 1846 he is listed in more grandiose fashion as a "Fruiterer, Poulterer and Dealer in Game" in a shop at 9 Commutation Row. By that time the Nugent family would have grown in number to eight children and the Nugents were often on the move to larger premises. Various other addresses are given at Circus Street and Richmond Row, indicative of a rather nomadic family existence during this period.

It might have seemed logical that James would follow his father into the family business; he would almost certainly have helped John Nugent in the shop. Perhaps the continual change from place to place upset this pattern and a restlessness which members of the family displayed later in life may well have stemmed from this unsettled phase. Eventually some of the family would leave for a new life in America, but for the time being James Nugent enjoyed the blessings of loving parents, a good home, a secure environment, access to school and the prospect of work. He would one day try to give back to the poor some of the advantages with which he had begun life in his first home.

Although business was brisk in the seaport of Liverpool in the 1830s and 1840s, small independent market traders like John Nugent faced a tough challenge. Gradual control from the Trustees of the Dock Estate, later to become 'The Mersey Docks and Harbour Board', was forcing the smaller or less successful businesses to face the prospect of merger. The phrase 'King Cotton' denoted a thriving industry which cushioned Britain and Liverpool from adversity until the American Civil War when the variety of imported and exported goods had to be widened. The secret of Liverpool's success was its ability to adapt and be flexible in matters of commercial enterprise, dealing with a greater variety of products such as Sugar from the Caribbean and Tea from China. Liverpool was also uniquely placed to break the monopoly London held over trade with the Far-East, opening up possibilities with India and China through the East India Company, and had the added advantage of the Shipbuilding Industry. Liverpool may have been Britain's second biggest town but it was still in the shadow of London. The capital could re-invest its economic gains in a way that Liverpool could not. Liverpool's geographical position made it a trading post but not the permanent home of wealth creation, and it was a place where prospectors and would-be emigrants passed through en route to the New World.

John Nugent must have survived these shifting economic realities quite well. He was part of a growing community of local shopkeepers bound together by strong nationalistic and religious ties who could rely on the loyal custom of like-minded, fellow ex-patriots. John Nugent's view of Liverpool would have been quite different from that of his children, so dramatic were the changes within the span of one generation. James may well have had the experience of the market-place – a first informal education, but there is virtually nothing to tell us of his relationship with his father. The more decisive influences seem to have come from his mother. If we can discern anything of his father's impact on him it would be in his loyalty to Irish Catholicism, an eye for business, a spirit of enterprise and, of course, a loyalty to the family. Although we have not been left with many direct signs of how his father influenced James's outlook on life, it is very likely John Nugent wanted him to be educated and to succeed in business. There may also have been quite definite political opinions handed down from father to son.

The social, economic and religious developments of those years certainly had a formative influence on James Nugent. The programme of legislative reforms under the 'Liberal Tories' who represented the Government of the day, led first by Lord Liverpool and later by George Canning, helped to make the 1820s a decade of outstanding political development. It was a time when there was an unlikely combination of Conservatives with an eye for radical change. They heralded an era of enhanced trade, confident prosperity and greater religious tolerance, even though the beliefs that lay behind Catholic Emancipation had more to do with political expediency than with the gospel. It should be remembered that Catholic Emancipation came about slowly and grudgingly, under pressure to avoid the prospect of civil disturbance. The new legislation did not always imply any heartfelt conviction.

As George Canning succeeded Lord Liverpool, and in turn the Duke of Wellington (brilliant in battle but not in political leadership) took up the reins, the Conservatives spell in power came to an end in favour of The Whig Government at the 1830 Election. Lord Liverpool, as Prime Minister and the famous Robert Peel, at the Home Office, and their cabinet colleagues, had moved things carefully forward into a new climate of politics that would have strong implications for a place like Liverpool. It was, for the luckier ones at least, a favourable time, an exciting, inventive, ambitious, and auspicious time to grow up in.

James Nugent's young mind was sharp and his eyes observant. He may well have been forming questions for himself about the not so lucky ones. Business was booming and he could have felt confident about a good job in Shipping or in Business but the plight of the unemployed, the poor and uneducated, was unfolding like a stage drama before his eyes. He would have seen the violent protests, as well as the clear advantages which the arrival of the Railways brought. The power of steam led to the introduction of machinery and so to the decline in manpower, which meant a smaller manufacturing base for Liverpool and greater redundancy.

James Nugent watched Liverpool changing from a semi-rural area by the river into a sprawling town and he would have seen how it was becoming a centre for trade and transport, for immigration and emigration – a place of transition. People felt the pain of constant change, not only in the community and politics but also in the religious sphere where intolerance and prejudice was still rife. Political and Religious leaders were looking to find new ways of bringing the fruits of the Industrial Revolution to the lives of ordinary people, there was greater efficiency in the workplace, there was wealth creation, reform of the penal system and an improvement in health care, housing and education. But not for everyone: There were the Gamekeepers and the Poachers. On which side was James Nugent to be?

A group of children outside of their homes *(circa 1934)*

Chapter 2

The Gift of an Education

Although he often expressed a disdain for class distinctions, and would work very hard for equal opportunities in education and the workplace, James Nugent was born into and moulded by a class-ridden society. Some of his words and attitudes betray this. He would refer to 'the dregs' of society in regard to those who were the left-behinds in Liverpool's impoverished areas – it was not an age of 'political correctness'. Nevertheless, he always tried to use his advantages to promote the cause of the poorer people and he learnt at his mother's knee the value of care for his neighbour. Mary Nugent would prove to be a 'Good Samaritan' to many in need in the local community and she also had definite ideas about the sort of education she wanted for her children – the education that she herself had received. It was not going to be a Poor School for them!

It would be understandable if John Nugent expected his son to follow him in the family grocery trade or to go into business. He was moderately successful in his own trade and there were good prospects in the city. Hopes of a place for James with one of the local merchant companies looked like being realised at one stage when the firm of W.G. Maxwell and Company, King Street, was suggested. The aspirations his mother had for him began, as for all the others in her family, with a sound education.

James Nugent's upbringing was rooted in the practical experience of the life around him. The streets of Liverpool were his first school, but something more was called for. The things he learnt from the life and the people around him now had to be complemented by formal schooling. More than sixty years later he looked back with gratitude to the important influences of church, school, home and family upon him, recalling the time when he went to College, to the Seminary in order to train for the priesthood. With a hint of the singularity that marked his personality he reflected on his whole career:

"God has been specially good in giving me a long life. Few priests that I can remember – in fact I know of none – have laboured forty eight years in Liverpool and celebrated their Golden Jubilee at the altar where baptised, ordained and served as a priest. If I have done anything I have only obeyed the inspiration arising out of the conscious knowledge of things. My early life before I went to College was a practical one. I was brought in contact with men; was actively engaged so that the mind had been exercised in the actualities of life and I began my college career under very different conditions from the ordinary run of Church students. This possibly has shown itself in my career; addressing myself to the wants of the times, power of organisation, influence with young men and the working classes, a breadth of action, seeking to do good to all, not working within narrow lines but feeling the obligation of creating a better feeling among all classes by enforcing the duty of good citizenship; taking what was running to waste or becoming a social plague, utilising the natural power, ability and action of neglected children and fallen humanity and lifting men and women up from the degradation of ignorance and vice and making them useful rather than a pest to society." (Letter to a priest friend at the time of his Golden Jubilee, 1896.)

In and around the town of Liverpool, James Nugent would have had his first encounters with successful businessmen, hard-nosed dealers, philanderers, entrepreneurs, rough labourers, dock-workers, sailors, shoe-shine boys, flower girls, match sellers, vagabonds, thieves, merchants and factory hands. He would be familiar with the fine buildings, the Town Hall and its Officials and he would also have seen ragged children roaming the streets. Acceptance of people as they were became a vital feature of his priestly ministry and so did his desire to improve their conditions. Unlike the street children he saw, he had the advantage of a good start in life, a good home, a loving family and an education. He was always aware of these privileges.

Hunter Street had a strong religious history. There was a Friends' Meeting House there in 1796 when the Quakers moved from their premises in Hackins Hey, one of the poorest quarters of the town. There was also a well-known local School, The Hunter Street Free School, one of the few establishments of its kind in the country. In his younger days James Nugent would have been familiar with these and also with the Unitarian Chapel in Hunter Street, built in 1824 and later taken over by the Baptist Church. The Baptists were based in Great Crosshall Street and a key part of the mission and outreach to the poor of the town. James would also have known the Anglican Church of St Stephen on the corner of Byrom Street and Hunter Street, and Christ Church Anglican Chapel that had a School of the same name attached to it. They were landmarks in the area and it was Christ Church School that Mary Nugent had attended. Nearby in Gerard Street a first Catholic School had been built and run by the Benedictines from St. Mary's mission. Although it has been said that William Ewart Gladstone, the future British

Prime Minister, attended the Christ Church School there is no evidence to support this. Biographies of Gladstone indicate that he received his elementary education at St. Thomas's, Seaforth, which was a similar, private establishment, run by the Anglican Clergy.

Liverpool people shared humble beginnings but fared very differently. William Gladstone's father was a millionaire in 1820, a multi-millionaire in 1850 - such was the growth of prosperity in Liverpool during that thirty year period. He sent his son to Eton and was part of an élite group in Liverpool that gave rise to the saying – "A Liverpool Gentleman", "A Manchester Man" and "A Salford Lad", which reflects Liverpool's perception of itself but also the rivalry between these northern towns and the emerging differences of class and culture.

Having said that, Mary Nugent was not from a rich family. The family name of Rice is well-known in Liverpool. Her family may possibly have been from the near-by Mount Pleasant area where that name is recorded. Of her background we know little, except that she was a convert from the Anglican Church, had a strong, practical nature as might be expected of a "Lancashire Lass", and eventually, and perhaps most importantly, the mother of nine children. She married John Nugent in 1821, and was only eighteen years of age when James was born.

We know more of her from tributes paid after her death than we know from any contemporary accounts. She seems to have been a fine person, full of down-to-earth charity, ambitious for her children and, following her conversion, a devout Catholic. At the time of her death on 11th March 1887, the 'Catholic Times' newspaper, contained this tribute: "Through a long life she was ever the active and devoted helper of the poor……

unselfishness, gentleness and heroic energy stamped her character." Mary Nugent's work among local victims of the cholera and typhoid epidemics which devastated parts of Liverpool in 1847 and 1849, demonstrated her pastoral sense and zeal in caring for others, attributes which were communicated in full measure to her son. Like his mother he too would play an important role in that testing and sad time in Liverpool's history.

James felt his mother's influence very deeply and ascribed his own vocation as a priest to what he called her 'saintly' example. She would no doubt have taught James at home in the early years, as the custom was, and when he was about seven or eight she used her influence to obtain a place for him at "The Academy" in Queen's Square, a Church of England, Private School. The two brothers who ran The Academy were relatives of James Picton, the Rector of Christ Church, Hunter Street, where Mary Nugent had been a pupil. Through this connection she was able to ensure that there would be a start in life for James and so avoid the Charity School.

The benefits of this first formal schooling at The Academy were limited but probably the best available at that time. There he made friends with the sons of merchants and businessmen from the town, the majority not being of the Catholic Faith. Maybe the first experience of religious tolerance was given to him at The Academy and perhaps there the first real awareness of the differences between religions became clear. Liverpool was Protestant and Tory and this was reflected in its educational and business establishments. Nevertheless, James did well at The Academy and showed intelligence and promise. A school friend, Thomas Gibson, recalled that James was hard-working and always succeeded in being among the top three in his class.

In Mary Nugent's mind there had been no question about her son's continuing education, though she would look in vain for a good Catholic school in Liverpool, or anywhere else for that matter in 1830. There were Charity Schools or Poor Schools at Mount Pleasant and in Duncan Street, but only for the younger age groups. The Hunter Street Free School, an establishment first built by Stephen Waterworth the Sugar Magnate and later endowed by gifts from his family, was itself a Charity School. In 1823 it catered for 180 boys and 120 girls and remained in existence for several years. The Methodist Church too had its Sunday and Day School but for Catholics little choice was available after the Elementary level.

Catholic-based charitable organisations at this time had been responsible for building the Poor School on Copperas Hill - 'The Catholic Charity School' as it was called, built in 1806 before the Chapel of St. Nicholas was erected in 1815. It was one of the few of its kind and built near the former site of an old Copper Sulphate (Copperas) factory. On the Board of Management was Father Tom Penswick, a friend of the Nugent family. Funding for Catholic education was either meagre or non-existent. The Benevolent Society of St. Patrick - founded on St. Patrick's Day 1807 for the provision of care for children of Irish immigrants - was one of the few such Catholic organisations around.

Of course, apart from such charities and ad hoc groups there was always The Workhouse. Its very name was guaranteed to strike a note of doom in every human heart. First erected in 1772 the Liverpool Workhouse in School Lane (or Workhouse Lane) was quickly established as the largest and most populated of its kind in Britain. In time James Nugent would serve as Catholic Chaplain at the Brownlow Hill Workhouse, which would represent another milestone for Catholic development, but by then some improvement in the general standards of education was discernible and schooling and welfare for the Catholic poor had improved slightly. Father Nugent would become well acquainted with the joys and sorrows of the Workhouse.

Whilst provision for Education, or the lack of it, would dictate much of James Nugent's later ministry, evidence of the importance he placed on equal opportunities in education can be seen in his early regret about not been given the chance to go to University. Catholics were barred from a University place at that time; good old-fashioned English prejudice reigned in such Institutions. This feeling of exclusion rankled with him and became a factor in his efforts to create more openings for Catholics in Education and for equality of opportunities. No doubt he would have flourished at Cambridge or Oxford... but now other possibilities were presenting themselves.

At the age of sixteen James Nugent may not have had very coherent thoughts about what Priesthood meant, but he was given encouragement from the clergy at St. Nicholas, especially from Father Walker there who had become a good friend of the family. By the following year, 1838, the seeds of a call to Priesthood had taken root and in the February of that year everything was ready for his admission to the Junior Seminary at Ushaw in County Durham. Ushaw College, like St. Nicholas's Church Copperas Hill, played an important part in the life of the Nugent family as both John and Joseph Francis followed their elder brother there. Of the two, only John went on to ordination and became a priest of the Liverpool Diocese. His appointment as the first priest in charge of the mission of Blessed Sacrament, Aintree, happily coincided with James's appointment as the Chaplain at nearby Walton Prison in 1863.

The increase in speed and efficiency of travel, already mentioned as a key factor in Liverpool's ascendancy to greatness as a seaport in the 1830s, did not immediately benefit everyone. James Nugent would one day put the new travel advantages to good use in his journeys to America, but for now his sights were set in another direction, north-eastwards, to St. Cuthbert's College, Ushaw. In those days it involved a lengthy journey by stage coach, canal barge and even a trudge on foot across the moors. Rail travel was not really an option as the network was still only in its infancy and the Terminus at Lime Street was not yet fully operational. Edge Hill, then the nearest station for Liverpool had a major depot where most goods and produce for the local community were handled. It is likely that retail traders such as James Nugent's father obtained their supplies from there. Rail travel from there to Ushaw was not an option.

The Nugent family must have been aware that the chance of a College education was a rarity at this time for Roman Catholic youngsters. What is taken for granted today was then only possible for the privileged few. James would not have found it easy to have access to a Catholic education if he had not gone to the seminary at Ushaw in 1838, where he enrolled as a Church student. Unfortunately, few details about his time there are available. He arrived at the College on 7th February 1838, shortly before his sixteenth birthday.

The College Presidency at the time was in the hands of Fr. Charles Newsham who had been appointed in May the previous year, in succession to Dr. Youens whose presidency had not been a happy one. As we shall see, Dr. Youens' name became more happily and successfully associated with work for The Blind in Liverpool, and he later became known as one of the priest-victims of the plague, succumbing to typhus in 1848.

If Dr.Youens' presidency at Ushaw had not been the happiest, his successor enjoyed a very different experience. Charles Newsham, who had held the post of Vice-Rector under Dr.Youens, is considered one of the architects of the building we see at Ushaw today. He was responsible for expanding and modernising the original structure, for building a new chapel and a museum and other additions in the years between 1838 and 1858, which included Nugent's five years there.

The austere walls of the College, set like sentinels over the Durham landscape, matched the plain, unadorned interior of the College that would now become James Nugent's home until his departure from it on March 9th 1843. It seems that his course of studies was "broken up" (to use his own words) by bouts of illness and that there was an unexplained gap between March 1843 and the December of that year by which time he was moving on as a student at the English College in Rome. The eight years of seminary life were not uneventful, nor were they without their difficulties.

During the five years at Ushaw, James would see, as he had seen in Liverpool, a time of building and improvement. The introduction of gas light during that time was an innovation which brought both benefits and problems. The new source of lighting lent a smoky, gloomy atmosphere to the long corridors, yet it represented at the time a giant step forward from the rationed use of tallow candles. However, candles were still the norm during most of Nugent's time at the College. With the introduction of gas, improvised but unauthorised ways of boiling water for making tea or for shaving were devised by the more enterprising students but if this was discovered, it could lead to a delay in the promotion to Holy Orders or even to expulsion.

The imposing Entrance Hall and front stairwell leading to the President's Gallery were built in 1840 and the south-west staircase constructed the following year, whilst the foundation stone of the lovely chapel, designed by Pugin, was laid in 1844, the year after Nugent left the college. He would return many times to enjoy the use of the chapel and he was instrumental in sending many students from Liverpool to his old 'alma mater' to train for the priesthood. In many ways the training he received at Ushaw gave the inspiration for his firm belief in the importance of training and educating young people, which was to be a hallmark of his whole mission.

Despite the frugal conditions, and the separation from home for long periods of time – factors which caused many students to give up, James Nugent appears to have made good use of his time at Ushaw. It was during this time that two important talents were nurtured: a gift for public speaking and for producing plays. There is plenty of evidence in his later life and in some of his speeches that he had acquired a liking for and a knowledge of Shakespeare's plays and a good knowledge of other writers, and that he had a striking ability to mimic the voices and actions of people he met, using this as an aid in his talks and sermons. Later, in his notebooks, he alludes to Shakespeare's play 'Hamlet' ("amblitt" as he would one day hear the street urchins pronounce it) and makes references to 'Macbeth' or 'Richard The Third' and several other literary works, showing not only that literature, drama and opera were among his great interests but also that he would sometimes assume the persona of an actor. *(c.f. Prologue @Nobody's Children'.)*

He was fascinated to find young destitute boys and girls acting out plays in the streets as they begged their way through towns and villages searching for whatever food and shelter they could get and collecting coppers for their efforts. Necessity often brings out talent and inventiveness and Nugent was quick to recognise this in helping young talent to develop among even the most abject poor. He would also use his interest and ability to good effect in directing plays among the members of the St. Nicholas' Boys' Guild in the parish when he was first appointed as a priest in Liverpool. A talent and a liking for the stage, and for dramatic effects, would one day become useful in both the pulpit and on platforms where he spoke eloquently on the evils of drink, persuading men and women of all classes and creeds to take the pledge.

It was this special presence on the stage that would one day make James Nugent a much sought-after speaker at Dinners and Rallies. It caught the attention of his friend Gabriel Ellis whose first meeting with Nugent was at a Temperance Rally in Liverpool in 1882. He described a stooped figure wrapped in his black cloak, suddenly springing to his feet and in one bound attaining the platform, raising a hand to signal he was about to speak and proceeding to do so "in a voice at once articulate, sonorous and mellow." Nugent was then 60 years of age.

James Nugent always remained proud and fond of his
'alma mater' which had given him so much. Speaking on
the occasion of the College Centenary celebrations he
declared that there was "no greater privilege than for
someone to speak of his own mother," by which he
alluded both to his mother and to the College. Although
the years spent there have not been recorded as
spectacular in any way, there was a steady, quiet growth, a
mature outlook on the Priesthood and a pride in the
vocation to which he felt God had drawn him. More than
fifty years later when he had achieved considerable fame
in his priestly work, the 1896 edition of The Ushaw
Magazine, marked the Golden Jubilee of his ordination
with a glowing tribute to their distinguished former
alumnus. By that time he was already a legend in
Liverpool. As the article pointed out, he could be credited
with the foundation not just of one Institution, which
would have satisfied most mortals in their life-time, but
with several successful and enduring ones.

At Ushaw James Nugent came of age. He celebrated his
twenty-first birthday just a few days before he left the
College. In his own estimation Ushaw had set him on the
road to his true vocation, and provided him with the solid
basis of philosophy and theology, an adherence to a
pattern of daily prayer and a good knowledge of Catholic
Teaching. The Seminary where he spent the five years
from 1838 to 1843 was his first formal experience of a
Catholic School. It was a privilege not granted to many in
the days when schooling was neither compulsory nor
widely accessible and whilst his early days at The
Academy had provided a start, it was at St. Cuthbert's
College that he received the foundation for his remarkable
priestly career. He may have considered that he brought
with him from Liverpool an experience of life, but what

was given in the Seminary, whatever its shortcomings, was a discipline of thought and academic training to complement his practical experience in the market place.

One of the things Nugent derived from his College experience was a sense of Catholic history, especially of Catholic martyrology. The system of studies at Ushaw followed the tradition of Ushaw's parent college of Donai in France, which had been founded in 1569 by Cardinal Allen and where students for the Catholic Church had, per force, trained, in penal times. In England, Catholic priesthood was high treason at that time. The hapless students of Donai had been obliged to flee the College in the 1790s when Civil War broke out in France, their building being commandeered by French troops. Great courage, sacrifice and guile had been necessary for students and priests returning to almost certain death in their homeland. With a slightly more tolerant climate for Catholicism by the end of the 1700s in England, the Vicars Apostolic, who, before the Restoration of The Hierarchy in 1850 were the forerunners of the Catholic bishops, began to look for property at home where preparation for the priesthood might continue in safety.

At the instigation of Bishop Gibson, a key figure in the revival of Catholic seminaries, property was purchased at Flass Hall near Durham. It was to be the prototype of one of the first English seminaries and it led to the purchase of land at Ushaw Moor. Other similar Colleges, modelled on Douai, were built as time went on and as the demand for places increased. At the Centenary Celebrations for the College in 1893 mention is made of a Bishop Carroll, who, among other benefactors, helped to establish the seminary in its modern form. Among Bishop Carroll's gifts to the College was the installation of a swimming pool and as shortly after that he was made a bishop, a local wit remarked that Carroll had "given the College a bath and in return the Pope had given him a See". The Vatican still retained a close interest in the efforts of the Vicars Apostolic to promote the Catholic Church at home through the provision of such training colleges.

Looking back on those frugal, student days at College, James remembered how they "drank their breakfast out of tin cans and ate their dinners off pewter plates." He recalled this whilst speaking in the elegant surroundings of Liverpool's Adelphi Hotel at a Gala Dinner and must have enjoyed the irony of the situation as he compared those far off days with the "present days of improvement and comfort". Whatever adversity was endured in those earlier times – including cold winters and icy nights in draughty dormitories - James Nugent certainly took advantage of what Ushaw had to offer. He was an able student and mastered Latin, which was essential, and progress was related to the level of proficiency in it. It was one of the elements in his ability to proceed to Rome in 1843 for a further phase of studies.

Chapter 3

Rome, Lancashire and Plague

A mystery surrounds James Nugent's state of health at this time. He had survived the rigours of Ushaw winters and rationed food. We know from contemporary accounts that breakfast was meagre - milk and bread, eaten in haste and standing as if at a Passover, for the sake of speed. Yet there were breaks in his studies that are unaccounted for; presumably he suffered from either physical or mental exhaustion. He had left Ushaw in the March but did not go to Rome until 8[th.] December, 1843, when he began his studies at The English College (The Venerabile) and at The Gregorian University as a student for the Diocese of Lancaster. This meant a gap of nine months. He himself makes reference to his "broken up course of studies" but whether this implies that he left Ushaw in March of 1843 because of illness, is not clear. It would not be the last time that a breakdown in health caused a temporary halt in his progress.

The reference to the "broken up course of studies" comes in a letter written to a friend in Liverpool, John Rankin, and was written from The English College in Rome in May, 1845. Happily, the whole letter is extant. As it is a letter both informative and revealing of events of those years and tells us a lot about Nugent's character, his intense interest in all things 'Catholic' and all things 'Liverpool', it is printed here in full. His correspondent, John Rankin, later became successful in the Shipping Industry and had an office in Liverpool, in Manchester Street.

Nugent was anxious for news from the parish, though he does not mention his parents in the letter. In a long missive, replying belatedly and apologetically to his friend on May 16th 1845, he

offers advice about the advantages of training for the priesthood
in Rome and demands immediate answers to all his enquiries.
The hallmarks of his emerging character are certainly there! It
was the first sign of his belief in the importance of recruiting
more seminarians and the value of training abroad. The letter,
written nearly fifteen months after his arrival at The English
College, shows that he expected to be in Rome for at least a
further three years. Once again providence took a hand and led
him in a different way. His bishop, George Brown, was anxious
to have priests back quickly for the growing mission at home
where he was working to establish the new diocese of Liverpool
and so he recalled his students home early to meet the demands:
James was not destined therefore to stay on and become
qualified to teach at the seminary as some may have expected.

In the precise but naïve style of youthful years, he wrote
as follows:-

My Dear Friend,

*I suppose long before this you will have relinquished
every idea of hearing from me and will have set me down as an
ungrateful and good for nothing fellow. It is true that at first sight I
may appear to merit the appellation, but I trust that before I have
finished this letter I may be able to show you that I am not quite so
much at fault. When your letter arrived, we had, just the evening before
returned from our country house, Monte Porzio where we had been
spending a very pleasant vocation(sic). It was rather fatal for your
letter that it did not come a few days sooner, for that evening we had to
enter upon a spiritual retreat of ten days, and as we omit all other
duties during the time of retreat, even so much as that we do not
exchange a single word with each other all the time, so of course I had
not an opportunity of answering your letter immediately. When the
retreat had terminated, school opened for the year. I have, so you no
doubt may have learned, commenced the study of Theology a year before
the proper time. Now I was anything but prepared to enter upon the
theological course owing to the previous broken up course of studies I*

had at Ushaw and for being sick at home for such a length of time. So that I found it as much as I could to keep pace with the several professions, and in fact I find the same difficulty at present, but not to such a degree as I experienced at first. You will clearly see form this why I was prevented from writing and I assure you it was as much as I could do to write home every six weeks. However I have come to the resolution to be more exact in my correspondence, so, craving your indulgence for the past, I dismiss the subject, and commence my letter.

Here, I have been in the Eternal City nearly eighteen months, and the time has passed like a shadow. It seems to me only so many weeks. These Romans have their different public festivities and amusements so well arranged, and following each other in an admirable order that a year passes in Rome before you know what you are about. My health has been most excellent; so far everything is as comfortable and agreeable as I could possible desire in a College. The only thing that affords me any uneasiness is that I shall be at the end of my course too soon. For this time, three years, if all succeeds well, and it is the will of God, I shall be in England a priest. At present I am in the Minor Order and next November I may be sub-deacon. It frequently makes me humble when I reflect seriously on the matter, that in a short time, and with such an indifferent preparation, I shall have to fulfil the important and responsible duties of the priesthood. However, I trust in the Divine Mercy and the most powerful intercession of Our Blessed Lady that I may receive the requisite dispositions and graces. I hope you, my dear friend will frequently remember me in your kind prayers and that you will, from time to time, say a Hail Mary for me, to our Blessed Lady that she would obtain for me the grace to become worthy of so high and exalted a calling. It affords me very great pleasure to hear that you have a prospect of coming to Rome and I hope and trust that such may be your happy lot. The advantages of a Roman education are manifold, as your friend Mr Murphy no doubt has told you. Besides the opportunity a person has in studying Theology in Rome, there is another of still greater moment and it is this; you are at the fountainhead of catholicity where you can (imbibe) that true spirit that ought to animate each of us. Here you get a noble and exalted idea of our holy religion, for wherever you turn your eye, it rests upon some object or other connected with religion. This city is filled with innumerable shrines of illustrious saints, all of which combine to fill one with fervour and devotion. If it is your intention to come to Rome, my advice would be that in the meantime you should endeavour to gain so much competent knowledge as possible of the Latin language, for all the lectures we attend are given in this language and all the books that we study are in the same. You should see the great necessity of knowing Latin before you come here for you would have to commence philosophy when you come here, for they never take any that are not ready to begin with that school, and so as all the studies are in Latin you would either have to know it before you come here, or learn it after; now I know that Dr Grant the present Rector of the college has a strong objection to anyone coming here that is not conversant with that language, - so, if it is your intention to come to Rome you must endeavour to give all the spare time you have, to the study of the language. I suppose it would be a year, or perhaps two, before you could have the office, - now if such is the case, you could be studying a little every day and obtain sufficient knowledge of Latin to commence the course of philosophy. But your friend, Mr Murphy will be able to give you all the information you require, as to how to employ your time until you go to college. I assure you that if you can get to come to Rome, you will be very comfortable and happy. Everything I know would please you. The only difficulty is that Dr Brown would have no vacant place for nearly two years. However, you could come here at any time, if you could afford to pay £50 per annum. Any further information that I can give you on this matter I shall always be most willing to send you, if you require it. It delights me to hear of the great spread of Catholicity in Liverpool, and the great devotion the people have of late displayed. I was very glad to hear about the Missions that were given at Copperas Hill, during Lent. Be so kind as to let me know if they had a great effect upon the people, and how the chapel filled, etc. I suppose that during this month you have had the month of Mary at Copperas Hill; - do they give a short discourse every evening, or do they read anything from a book? Have they had it this year at any of the chapels, besides Copperas Hill? From these questions you will see how anxious I m to have all the news, so I beg of you to write to me, by return of post (at least as soon as possible) and send me all the Catholic news you can think of. You must never delay writing to me on account of the postage for our good Mother, the college pays the postage of all our letters, even if I had to pay for them myself, I should never allow that as a reason why I should not hear from my friends. You say in your letter that you never received the set of beads that I made mention of, in my letter; indeed I do not wonder at it, for they never left Rome! The reason why you never received them was that when I brought them to Mr Murphy he had all his things packed up, and his bag was fastened, so I did not like to make him undo his things to put them in. However, they are in store for you. You may rely on receiving them shortly after the next Easter season. If there is anything else you would like to have, on your sisters, send me word, and I will send it if possible by Dick. How are Mr Murphy and Dr Kelly getting on? I hear they are doing wonders are they good preachers? I never remember seeing Dr Kelly to know him. Mr Murphy was in the college about four months with me, but I never had the opportunity to hear him preach. Now, I must put a great number of questions to you:- Who is going to be the third priest with Murphy? How is Blundell getting on? How is Mr Hill? Who is Isaac married to? How is Milner? What has Mrs Connolly's son done with himself since he left Ushaw? Any news about Dr Butler? I hear he has settled everything with Dr Brown? Do you know the two young men at St Edwards – Messrs Walter and Brettargh? They are good friends of mine. Are they building a new convent at St. Anthony's? You must excuse my great inquisitiveness, but I know that you are delighted to send much about Catholic affairs. I sent my likeness home a few days ago, by a young man that was leaving here on account of ill health. You must call and ask them to let you see it, and let me know what you think of our dress. It is the complete dress with the exception of the cornered hat. I thought it would be better to have it taken with the cap – in the house. Is there any chance of your sister returning again to our holy religion? Let me know how she feels as to the devotion of our Blessed Mother. I hope you will, on your part, cultivate as much as possible, in ardent affection towards the mother of all good gifts, for, whatever favour or grace you stand in need of, if you ask her fervently to obtain it for you, she is certain to do it. When I see you, I have to tell you how I was miraculously preserved from a sudden death, and which I firmly believe was through the protection and powerful intersession of the Blessed Virgin. The short of the case was that driving in Cardinal Acton's carriage, with the good Cardinal, and two others of my fellow students and the Cardinal's chaplain, the two leaders (horses) became restive and turned towards a deep descent on one side of the road, and succeeded, in turning down the descent, the carriage in a most wonderful manner, upset on the side of the hill about 25 or 30 feet from the road. What makes it more wonderful was that there was a deep precipice below, and the carriage overturned on the side of the hill, and although we went down the descent above 30 feet, there was not a single person the least hurt. The carriage and one of the horses were a little injured. All this we attribute to the guardianship of the Blessed Virgin, for as soon as we saw the danger that threatened us, we invoked her aid. At the time we were going to a celebrated shrine of the Blessed Virgin, about 25 miles from Rome. The particulars of this I must reserve until I see you. However, I hope that you will even evince a warm devotion to our Blessed Lady. I must now bring my letter to a close, begging of you that you will favour me with an answer as soon as you possibly can. Give my kind regards to all your relations, and to Mr Murphy, Mr Nightingale, and all the Reverend Gents. By the bye, what is Mr Parkinson doing? Remember me to all my friends.

Anxiously awaiting your answers. I am your ever attached and devoted friend,

James Nugent.   English College, Rome.

Whilst in Rome, away from the scene in Liverpool and desperate to keep himself up to date with events, James Nugent would have been at least partially aware of some of the undercurrents at work in the local Church back in England. In his letter he implies an acquaintance with Cardinal Acton, who was an English aristocrat and at that time a member of the Diplomatic Service at the Vatican. Here was perhaps the first influential figure of high rank that Nugent met. Cardinal Acton was directly involved in the controversy surrounding the St. Francis Xavier College and Church in the centre of Liverpool. As early as 1840 this issue had come to the fore and had already reflected something of the tension between the local bishop and the Religious Orders in a "power struggle" over pastoral strategy and Catholic mission in the town. Secular Clergy were struggling for the right to control their own Church affairs as the movement towards the restoration of the Hierarchy was growing. Religious Orders, especially the Jesuits and Benedictines, had been prominent in education and urban pastoral mission for some time whilst Bishop Briggs, Vicar Apostolic for the Northern District, had attempted to give some balance and harmony to the situation. His successor, George Brown however, described as "no friend of Liverpool" was apparently no friend of the Jesuits either.

Bishop Brown opposed Jesuit plans for a new College and Church under the title of St Francis Xavier, always known from then on as simply 'SFX'. He was supported in this by the redoubtable Father Wilcox, parish priest of the neighbouring mission of St. Anthony's, Scotland Road, who naturally had a vested interest in avoiding such a project. Battle lines were drawn between Secular and Religious clergy: It was a battle for the right to run the local church by means of the resources and inherent ability within in the local community, free from undue pressure or interference from Rome. Pope Gregory had taken personal charge of English Catholic affairs in the wilderness years before the official Hierarchy was restored and it was a break from this "direct rule" that Bishop Brown wanted. He did not want a breakaway church but a mature relationship between the universal and the local Church - loyal to Rome but desiring freedom to do what was appropriate for the local people. Bishop Brown was also perhaps aware of the financial implications of a "Religious Mission" such as SFX.

The Jesuits, courting the blessing and authority of Rome for their new Mission, tried to persuade Bishop Brown that any new church of theirs was not going to be a parish church and so the threat of taking away vital revenue would not come into it. Letters passing to and fro between Bishop George Brown and the Jesuit Provincial, Father Bird, reveal a plethora of issues, including details of Canon Law, loyalty to the people, loyalty to the pope, and the way forward for Catholics in Liverpool. Bishop Brown still feared that a major new project under the control of the Jesuits would jeopardise the parishes of St. Anthony and St Nicholas. In turn the Jesuit Fathers believed that the needs of the centre of Liverpool were already so great that existing churches were not sufficient to cope with them and something more was needed. They saw their position as a friendly offer of help at a time of expansion and need.

In the end, the powers that be in The Vatican prevailed upon the Bishop of Liverpool to accept the Jesuit proposals. On 17th April 1842 Propaganda Fide, the Sacred Congregation in Rome responsible for these matters, issued a decree to that effect and Mgr. Acton, who soon afterwards became a Cardinal, had been instrumental, with his English connections, in this decision. His interest in setting up Jesuit-based education for all Catholics in England was well-known. As an acquaintance of Cardinal Acton and as a future student with a stake in this matter, James Nugent would certainly have come under his influence. Though he may not have known it then, Nugent, as a young priest working in Liverpool, would find himself caught up directly in the issues surrounding Catholic Education in the town.

Departure from Rome in 1846, after 3 years of studies, would not have left any further opportunity for an academic career, but James Nugent had already proved himself a capable student and no one ever expressed doubt as to his piety or his suitability for ordination. Only the earlier health scare had marred his excellent track record. He himself may have been disappointed, certainly surprised, at his recall by Bishop Brown before the summer of 1846. He in fact left the seminary in March of that year (again an unexplained gap, except that Easter may have been the agreed leaving time) and returned to Liverpool, awaiting Ordination which was planned for the 30th. August. It was Bishop Brown who would lay the ordaining hands upon him on that momentous day in the Church of St. Nicholas, Copperas Hill. As far as records show, it was probably the first ordination there of a priest for the newly-established diocese of Liverpool -another 'first' for James Nugent.

If in later life he reflected that he had started College with a more practical experience of life than most of his fellow students, James Nugent also knew that he owed much to the seminaries he had attended. After eight years of academia this experience was tempered with a sound education in what his generation called the Humanities and Divinities which only a College education could provide. He would have learnt Latin, studied liturgy and Scripture, Philosophy, Church History and Canon Law in the usual pattern of seminary life. His experiences of the market place may have been important but his life was now to be enriched by a routine of prayer and study and, as can be seen from the letter to John Rankin, it was in Rome that he began to take into his life an unerring devotion to the Mother of God to whom he felt he owed his physical and spiritual survival.

The deployment of clergy to the parish missions in England at this time had been a problem for the Vicars Apostolic. They were limited in their powers of decision-making by control from Rome and the absence of recognition by the State at home. New dioceses were being created and boundaries were being drawn up so that the large mission area of Liverpool, which had come under the jurisdiction of the Vicars Apostolic of the Northern District and was now in the pastoral care of George Brown (soon to be Bishop Brown), stretched from south of the River Mersey to the Scottish border, across county boundaries. Help was sent wherever it was needed and new missions were being founded both by secular and religious clergy. It was an unpredictable and open-ended situation that faced a new priest.

It wasn't to the heart of Liverpool but to the centre of Blackburn that the newly-ordained Father James Nugent was first sent. In fact he was not so much sent there by the bishop as hi-jacked by the parish priest. His appointment to St. Alban's in Blackburn was as a result of being "picked up", to use his own words, by Father Peter Kaye, the Parish Priest of St Alban's, when they met at a clergy gathering at St Mary's in Chorley. Presumably, this impromptu arrangement had been ratified by the bishop at some stage, though Nugent does not say so and the appointment clearly took him by surprise.

No other Roman Catholic parish existed in Blackburn at that time and the Catholic population was focussed around the church of St Alban, a building just 20 years old when Nugent arrived there in the autumn of 1846. A new building had replaced the earlier one, at Larkhill in 1826. One of the clergy officiating at the opening of the new Church had been Father Tom Penswick, the priest who had baptised Nugent at St. Nicholas's Liverpool in 1822 and who went on to become the Vicar Apostolic of the Northern District. The 1826 building would eventually be replaced by the church that stands there today, opened in 1901 for a much larger Catholic community. James Nugent would return to his old parish in October of that year, when he was nearly 80 years old and 'famous', to take part in a fund-raising bazaar for the new church. Such connections, that threaded his priestly career, always remained very strong.

At St Alban's the youthful Father Nugent was remembered for two things: his boyish good looks and his eloquent preaching. These were two qualities that proved to be useful and charismatic elements in his ability to win friends and support from the earliest days. There were other priests with him in Blackburn; fellow curate Father Haggan, and Fathers Joseph

Smith and Henry Newsham. Because of the large and growing population the Vicar Apostolic clearly saw it as a place to put resources and personnel and it was a busy place for the clergy serving a large part of the industrial heartland of Lancashire. Most parishioners either worked in or were associated with the mills, mines or factories that had grown up in the wake of the Industrial Revolution.

The town of Blackburn derived its name from the 'dark water' that was the River Darwin and which in earlier days had been a quiet tributary of the Ribble but had gradually become a busy conduit of trade and commerce in the heart of Lancashire. The Leeds and Liverpool Canal ran through the town, providing a vital link for the transport of factory and mining produce transported to the docks at Liverpool and for ferrying raw materials to the factories. As such it was a tangible link for Father Nugent with his home town 30 miles away. In fact, whilst working in Blackburn his thoughts were often with Liverpool. He was aware of reports of the developing crisis there as the disastrous year of 1847 unfolded and the tragic tales reached him of the suffering of immigrants from Ireland. The plight of thousands of destitute Irish families, arriving in Britain in the wake of the Famine, attracted the sympathy and response of many; nearly every community had Irish connections.

Parts of Lancashire, like Blackburn and Wigan, would have had their own experience of indigenous hardship, and the effects of Famine and the high incidence of Plague were all too evident there. The first mention we have of what was to be a life-long work of fund-raising for good causes is of a collection Nugent organised in St Alban's parish for the Irish Fund. It raised a total of £78.12.8 sent directly to Liverpool to aid the plight of the Irish poor. The money was equivalent to over £20,000 in today's terms; a notable achievement in a short time. He was flexing the muscles of his organising skills, his powers in appealing for money and imaginative planning which would characterise his later work. This collection also signalled his strong interest in Irish affairs and his support of Irish welfare. Father Nugent, in his first curacy, had already succeeded in winning hearts and minds and rallying support for those in need. At the same time he had drawn up his battle lines in the complex world of Irish political and social life.

In its industrial hey day, Blackburn was the biggest weaving town of its kind anywhere in the world. Some of the leading mill owners were very wealthy people, many amassing a fortune from patented machinery used in the mills and factories, most famous among these being Hargreaves' 'Spinning Jenny'. Competition and rivalry increased as profits increased. The copyright to machinery was jealously and fiercely guarded, and it was not uncommon for mill owners to break up their own machinery when foreign investors or visitors arrived, to prevent them copying the patents and attempting to create cheaper products in their own country. It was an extremely competitive climate in Industry and vast profit was gained at a great human price. Nugent and his priest colleagues would have known the serious effects of worker-exploitation and inhuman conditions that affected the daily lives of many parishioners and local families. The same indicators of potential strife had been evident in Liverpool.

Cotton and coal provided primary sources of work for women and children as well as men. The related textile and manufacturing industry meant they could find employment but were also subject to exploitation. Young children were employed as tappers, wagon pushers and messengers underground in the mines, in dangerous conditions that were injurious to their health and careless of their safety. Few safety principles were adhered to or even thought of and long hours of drudgery were the lot of many girls and boys as young as nine years of age. These relentless and inhumane pursuits of wealth were to come under the scathing critique of Karl Marx who, in his 'Das

Capital' powerfully exposed the dangers and corruption of working conditions. Nugent, it seems, at least made sure that some of the capital being accrued from industry went to charity, even though there is no clear evidence of his being involved in political action as such.

Humanitarian concern about the unjust conditions of human labour was real but slow to be accepted. Reform was inimical to those who stood to gain so much profit from the situation. Many of them had no scruples about using children as a means of obtaining an income from the mines and factories. "Poor infants sacrificed at the shrine of avarice", Richard Oastler called them in 1830, lamenting the cost in human sacrifice of such profiteering. It was a sentiment echoed by Father Nugent in his speech on 'Nobody's Children' half a century later in Liverpool when he referred to the "poor children of the streets" and witnessed 'crowds of dirty, naked, shoeless children......exposed to every vice". Calls for reform were opposed on the grounds of loss of wages, loss of wages meant a poorer quality of life for people, and so more poverty would be the consequence. This classic argument continued through the century with materialism, benefits and the human standard of living all being weighed in the balance.

Yet reforms did come. In 1847, as Nugent's ministry was beginning, Fielder's Factory Act established the ten-hour day for women and child workers to add to a measure already in force that prevented those under-13 years of age from working more than six and a half hours. Certain other abuses however took longer to curb - it was still common up to 1865, even after the so-called 'Climbing Boys Act' (despite the title this was not a circus act but an Act of Parliament!), to see boys under the age of sixteen cleaning chimneys, and often meeting with fatal accidents.

The use, or abuse, of children in the workplace meant their effective disenfranchisement from education because they were too tired to attend lessons in school. They had no legal rights and insurance against injury was unheard of. Blackburn was not alone in experiencing a large infant mortality rate since disease was often related to poor working conditions. A report into factory conditions in Britain, commissioned in 1833, brought home to those in parliament the true scale of the horrors that existed. A man of Nugent's sensitivity was no doubt deeply influenced by these issues and as he went around the area in his first year of priesthood and began to formulate his own ideas, the seeds of future projects were sown. Equally, he learnt to know the importance of money as a means of power and its potential for good as well as for evil and saw that it was those who wielded this power through money who were the ones accountable. Money itself is morally neutral but its use in the hands of others is what makes it good or bad.

Henry Tate, who was to become synonymous with the Sugar Empire, was a native of Blackburn. He had begun life in the grocery retail trade, like James Nugent's father, and by 1855 Tate was the owner of six large shops in Liverpool. But he would sell this enterprise for a stake in the even more lucrative Sugar Industry, including the huge refinery at Liverpool on a site next to the docks. The lives of Nugent and Tate must surely have crossed from time to time in Blackburn and elsewhere. The young Father Nugent was ever watchful for potential benefactors from whom he could extract funds for his charities. Like his father, he could "do business" with people, influential or inconsequential. Canon Bennett's book on Father Nugent makes mention of his friendship, during the Blackburn days, with a Doctor Morley, who was the father of John Morley who gained prominence as a politician in Liverpool. Nugent got to know father and son well. He told John Morley that this association with his father was one of the great pleasures of his time in Blackburn, showing that in serving the immediate needs of those in his care he found time to become acquainted with those who were perhaps of a professional class or status.

Meanwhile, the great crisis in Liverpool in 1847 had the bishop sending for clergy from all over the scattered Lancashire parishes to come and help. Yet it was not everyone's inclination to leave rural idylls and rush to plague-ridden towns and both medical and spiritual resources were stretched. A hard year of Famine and Fever had begun with an important appointment in the medical profession. William Duncan had for some years been working in Liverpool both as a GP with a practice in Toxteth and at the Royal Infirmary(at that time located at Shaw's Brow) and he had already gained a reputation as a pioneer of health care. On January 1st 1847 he became the country's first Chief Medical Officer, based in Liverpool. Other similar appointments soon followed in other places in Britain. Meanwhile, the secondment to Liverpool, a town in crisis during that fateful year of '47, would bring its own impact on the young priest in Blackburn as he returned to his native town and home parish to lend a hand.

The influence of Father Peter Kaye, parish priest of St. Alban's, on James Nugent was considerable. Peter Kaye is described as being "of old recusant Warrington stock" which conjures up a picture of a formidable, determined and dour approach to the Catholic cause. This is exactly what he brought to Blackburn. He became parish priest at St. Alban's in 1844 having been a product of Ushaw and the English College in Rome, which may partly account for his 'picking up' James Nugent to help him in his parish. He was a tall commanding figure, well-dressed "in knee breeches and leggings" and walked with a stately bearing. Born to command he was as humble as a child and kindness itself to the poor. His sermons were described as "marvels of conciseness, simplicity and silvery-tongued eloquence and never lasted longer than half an hour ". He was considered to be a "conciliatory" man who did not make his strong Catholicity a burden on others and so won the "admiration of all denominations." This tribute to Peter Kaye reads uncannily like the descriptions of James Nugent in later years and there can be no doubt that this, his first parish priest, played a vital part in the formation of an impressionable young curate.

Under Father Peter Kaye at St. Alban's Nugent witnessed the growth of Catholicity and much new building. There was the building of a new Chapel of Ease in 1847 which later became the new parish of St. Anne's in 1851. There was also the steady build up of Catholic educational provision in the town, for which Father Kaye secured the help of the Notre Dame Sisters and The Christian Brothers. Catholic Guilds and Societies were re-established and began to flourish, such as the Guild of St. Joseph and Our Lady. Fund-raising was a constant feature of life in St. Alban's and throughout the town, so it was a busy and fruitful time which gave James Nugent much food for thought and inspiration for his future work.

Whilst industrial Lancashire was not immune to plague and poverty it was in Liverpool that Nugent first witnessed these horrors first hand. At the church of St. Patrick, which suffered most from the loss of clergy who succumbed to fever, he would preach, fifty years on from the tragedy, a moving sermon in tribute to the Martyr-Priests and recall his own personal involvement. By then a venerable monsignor, aged 75, he would recall the priests' sacrifice as they died from contracting typhoid in the course of their ministry. He could speak of it as if the experience was still fresh in his mind.

Catholic History has recorded with pride and sadness, (a pride and sadness shared by other denominations in Liverpool), the fall of so many priests in the course of their pastoral care of the sick and dying. Father Peter Nightingale, of St. Anthony's Scotland Road, who died on March 2nd. 1847, was the first to fall victim. Then on April 26th. William Parker, senior priest at St. Patrick's for ten years, died, followed on May 1st. by Dr. Kelly, at St. Joseph's church, who had joined Liverpool diocese only a short time before from the Irish College in Rome. On May 26th. it was the turn of Dr. Appleton an influential and much respected Benedictine priest of St. Peter's Seel Street. On 31st May, Dr. John Gilbert of St. Mary's Church succumbed to the fever and on June 16th. it was the turn of Fr. Richard Grayston, Rector of St. Patrick's, one who had physically picked up the bodies of the dead and placed them in coffins for burial. He died leaving St. Patrick's without a priest to celebrate Masses or Services for some time. Next, on 23rd. June Fr. James Hagger of St. Patricks died and on 26th. June Fr. Vincent Dale, O.S.B. from St. Mary's, also sadly died directly as a result of the plague. On 22nd. August news came of the death of the heroic Fr. Robert Gillow and on 30th. May the following year, 1848, another local hero. Dr. Youens, died in a further outbreak of the disease, bringing the total to ten.

Many other names may be added to the litany of those priests who suffered as a result of ministry during the time of the fever, many of them recovering from the symptoms and going on to give great service. One such was Fr. Bernard O'Reilly who later became bishop of Liverpool. Along with him in this perilous battle to save and reconcile souls were Fr. William Gillet and Fr. Thomas Kelly of St. Anthony's, Fr. Edward Walmsley of St. Joseph's and Fr. Wilkinson, a Benedictine Monk at St. Mary's parish.

With Father Gillow, James Nugent spent one memorable day and night in 1847 answering 43 sick calls. One visit vividly recalled was to a cellar of a house where a mother lay dead on a heap of shavings, a baby at her breast and two young children playing on the floor. Not long after this time of trial and all the scenes of death, James Nugent was mourning the loss of his friend Robert Gillow.

There was outrage in Liverpool. Those with responsibility for the sick were appalled by the devastation and the conditions that had brought the events about. William Duncan, born in Seel

Street in 1805, had a hopeless task. Like Father Nugent, Duncan was appalled at the conditions of poverty in his native town. Cholera epidemics had occurred regularly over the years, usually toward the end of summertime when rubbish had built up and festered and disease had been rampant in the close streets and within the 'blind' windowless courts and back-to back houses where people lived crowded together. There was little or no sanitation in these hovels and some of the courts had only a single water pump in the middle of a shared yard to serve all the inhabitants of the court. It was usually the only source of water available for washing and drinking.

Valiant efforts had been made a decade earlier by Catherine (Kitty) Wilkinson and her helpers to improve cleanliness and general standards of hygiene by the opening of the Laundries and Public Baths. These had also provided much needed employment in the town for many of the girls and young women. Benefits came from these establishments but they could not in themselves prevent the spread of disease. William Duncan was convinced that 'bad air' and stale or rotting food was the cause of the frequent illnesses in children and the recurring epidemics of Cholera were thought to be due to the miasma that ensued. There was at that stage no medical knowledge about germs and viruses as causes of disease. Duncan protested to the Town Council and the Magistrates that something be done quickly about the sanitation problems. His views were not taken seriously at first. He predicted further outbreaks of cholera and typhoid fever. Liverpool had the sad distinction of having more child deaths per capita than any other town in England: 229 of every 1000 babies died under the age of one; this cold statistic does not make clear that the deaths of most infants were attributed to lung and chest infections which had already left them weak.

In 1843 William Duncan had delivered a series of lectures to the Liverpool Literary and Philosophical Society on the causes of the high mortality rate. Overcrowding, he said, contributed to the dangers of bad air and poor sanitation. The back-to-back houses and filthy courts left no chance for people caught in the flood of the epidemic once it took hold. Liverpool had at that time fifty-seven and a half miles of streets of which 32 miles had totally inadequate sanitation and sewerage systems.

When Duncan's talks were made available to a wider audience through their publication in a pamphlet, the real situation became generally acknowledged and pressure mounted on local authorities to do something about it. Meanwhile Parliament was preparing to push through legislation in the form of the Public Health Act of 1848. The moving force behind this was Sir Edwin Chadwick in London who had headed the Poor Law Commission enquiry into the state of Britain's poor and whose pioneering work brought the stark reality of the problems to light. An earlier Act of 1842 had called for an end to the use of cellars as living quarters but many of these continued to exist, in an appalling state, six or seven years later. In the north, the vast numbers involved in immigration from Ireland and Wales, fleeing famine and poverty, swelled the problem of public health and hygiene out of all proportion. That year, 1847, some 300,000 people arrived in Liverpool in the first six months alone, of which more than 70,000 remained in the town crowded into 3,000 cellars. This chilling statistic has often been repeated but it never loses its impact.

Liverpool Town Council had anticipated government legislation with its own local Sanitary Act in 1846 and it was from that the power came to appoint a Medical Officer to oversee the problems of public health in the town. The Medical Officer would have powers to intervene and order improvements to ventilation and sanitation in churches, schools, lodging houses and any other public buildings where people lived and worked. Duncan had talked himself into the job. He was, in any case, the best qualified to do it, knowing the area well and having the expertise and personal touch to set reforms in hand. He expressed the belief that house-to-house visiting was pointless, but the medical profession was also a pastoral one and visits were important morale boosters for the sick even if not cost-effective in the crisis that had developed.

Besides this, no clear census had been taken and individual house calls were the only means of gauging the situation fully. As ever the question of money inhibited initial progress. Duncan was offered an annual salary of £300, plus whatever fees he acquired from the continuation of his general practice. This met with loud objections from some members of the Council and medical profession and after protracted debate about where his remuneration should be drawn from, he was eventually employed to do the immense job as Chief Medical Officer of Health at a salary of over £700 per annum. It was on 1st January 1847 that the Secretary of State for Health made the appointment official.

Today, television allows us to see what is happening in the world as events unfold. but in those days there could be no perception of the scale of the drama that was overtaking the unwary victims, nor the extent of the effects on Liverpool. As always, with hindsight, the signs could have been detected. Three years on the run the potato crop in Ireland had failed, stricken by a fungus blight. From 1845 to 1847 the overall effect of this for sixty percent of the population of Ireland who were farmers or lived in the countryside, was catastrophic. Only by the third year when the 'Kitchen Soup Act' brought organised relief to the starving, did a concerted aid effort begin. By then the people were on the move. It was too little too late. Yet, it should not be forgotten that care of the afflicted people in Ireland had been the concern of many benefactors for years before this disaster struck.

1849 saw one of the worst outbreaks of cholera Liverpool had ever known, though not quite as bad as in 1847. However, by then some lessons had been learnt. Duncan still felt insufficiently equipped to stem the tide of the disease. The 1849 epidemic was traced to India, to a family that had travelled across the continent of Europe as far as Scotland. They had boarded a ship at Dumfries and from there had sailed to Liverpool. Within hours of their arrival the disease had begun to spread like wild fire and the thousands of vulnerable, malnourished people, already huddled in cellars and courts, were an easy prey.

Nugent would have been all too aware of the devastating effects of the fever in 1849 as by then he was based full-time in Liverpool. In Vauxhall Road area alone there were 572 deaths recorded in one week, out of a total of 5,245 who had succumbed to the disease. Emergency 'Cholera Hospitals' were opened in Queen Anne Street and then even more locally in Vauxhall Road and Ansdell Street, as victims were dying on the way to the treatment centres. Two ships were commandeered as Hospital Ships on the Mersey as the overcrowding in the special hospitals became chronic and staff were stretched beyond their limits. For some months Liverpool was in disarray.

Then, in November, the epidemic was over. The after affects had to be faced and the appalling loss of life and human sadness assessed. The tragedy brought into play the administration of both religious and statutory organisations and future legislation and wholesale changes to housing conditions began to be addressed. It is a lesson of history that a catastrophic event is needed to bring about effective action. There were to be further outbreaks of Cholera and Smallpox but not on the same scale. Duncan's view that house to house visitation by doctors during the epidemic was futile was given the lie by Father Nugent and his fellow clergy who did not hesitate to make sick calls their priority. The administration of the Sacraments, care of the dying, support for bereaved families, all took first place in their ministry and took their toll on their health.

Whether William Duncan and James Nugent ever met is not known for sure, but they shared many of the same ideals. Duncan died at the relatively young age of 58, on 26th May 1863. Despite the limitations of his knowledge of the causes of the epidemics and the restrictions placed upon him by over-cautious authorities, his work and that of his colleagues was of vital importance in changing attitudes and led to legal reform in regard to matters of public health.

Meanwhile, in the March of 1848, Father Nugent had begun work at the parish of St Mary's in Wigan. It was to be only for a brief period of about nine months. He was sent there as a replacement for the parish priest who had contracted the fever that was prevalent in that area too. Fever seemed to dog everyone's footsteps at this time. At one point Nugent would write in his note-book the chilling words "Fever Raged". It was not by any means confined to London, Liverpool and the main urban areas. Whilst few major towns escaped it entirely, the country people suffered too. With the death of the parish priest at St Mary's during the brief period of James's ministry there, It must have been rather a fraught few months with a lot of sadness and upheaval in the parish. Nugent might well have asked himself if his work as a priest would ever be free of the scourge of plague?

During his time in Wigan, as in Blackburn, Father Nugent was able to see once again the tangible links with his home town, through trade on the Leeds and Liverpool Canal and the waterways that formed the transportation system for cotton and coal from the mills and mines of Lancashire to the docks. Here in one of the oldest towns in the country there was the now familiar story of wealth and poverty, power and oppression in the community. Wigan people have a justifiable pride in their history, Wigan being the town that was the scene of the last battle of the English Civil War in 1651. Haigh Hall, home of the earl of Crawford, was sited near the town and the imposing building, constructed between 1830 and 1849, would have been part of the landscape familiar to Nugent. He would have been equally aware of the no less important but far less pleasing architecture of the Gas Works, constructed in 1848. Like Liverpool, urban life was one of contrasts, highs and lows, rich and poor. From a Catholic stand point the people of Wigan could be proud of their record of recusant families within the town, and also of a strong tradition of education, focussed most notably in the foundation of Wigan Grammar School.

As a vital trade route for the industrial north, the town of Wigan had burgeoned when the road system, especially the old Trunk Road (now A49), came into being. This also helped to gel together parts of the new diocese which had always been disparate, poorly connected and therefore hampered by slow communication. There were many parallels for James Nugent with the former scene of his priestly ministry in St. Alban's, Blackburn, and these days of his youth and vigour were partly taken up with the care of a large, and responsive Catholic population; the confessional box would be busy, with priests in full flow hearing confessions, and Sunday congregations would be strong, and the busy round of house visits, the care of the sick, made huge demands on time and energy. As a young curate he would have found plenty of work in St. Mary's, but circumstances arose that led the Bishop to appoint Father Nugent to the task of setting up a new mission at St. Patrick's, Wigan, and so for a very brief period he went there, going down in the annals of the parish's history as its founder and first Rector. It would be the first of many things of which Nugent was the acknowledged founder. Despite the shortness to date of his parish experience he was obviously regarded as the man to inaugurate and inspire new projects.

The pattern of life and the experience so far was to change his outlook on pastoral needs. Towards Christmas 1848 he was aware of the possibility he would be returning to Liverpool and this time it would prove to be full-time. The first day of the New Year, 1849, (New's Year Day being a day of good omen for him,) he began his long and distinguished service as a priest in Liverpool. On that day he moved to the presbytery in Warren Street, next to St. Nicholas's church, a church that would soon take on greater prominence as the Catholic Pro-Cathedral. It was a momentous time, when the new diocese of Liverpool was to be officially begun, the restoration of the Hierarchy was being prepared for and he himself was looking forward to a 'Second Spring' in his own personal ministry.

Chapter 4

Children of the Second Spring

"In the little world in which children have their existence, whosoever brings them up, there is nothing so finely perceived or so finely felt as injustice."

(Charles Dickens: 'Great Expectations')

The sad and vivid memories of his time amongst the Liverpool plague victims of 1847 must have remained with Nugent all his life. They would certainly have been still clear in his memory when he returned to the Liverpool scene in 1849. The New Year may have heralded a new start for him, and an exciting challenge, but the painful legacy from that earlier experience and the need to minister to the immense pastoral needs of the people with the limited resources for Catholic schooling, made it a mountainous task. Arranging Catechism classes, ensuring attendance at Mass and the Sacraments, the visitation of the sick in an area of poverty and a hugely increased Catholic-Irish population, made arduous work, requiring dedication and stamina. Father Nugent seemed to be blessed with both.

Those who have chronicled Nugent's work around this time attest to the fact that he threw himself into the work with an extraordinary energy and sense of urgency. This was due in part to his impulsive nature and to the great desire to make a start in tackling the needs he saw around him. Events sometimes conspire to produce a sense of destiny; he was the first priest ordained at St. Nicholas's for the newly-formed diocese, in the church where he was baptised and made his First Communion, in his home parish, in his home town, on the threshold of a new

chapter in the Catholic life of Liverpool. From what we can
guess of his personality and sensitive nature he appears to
have had a strong sense of this destiny himself. He was in
what were largely uncharted waters for Catholic action
and pastoral work, circumstances which, in the vigour of
his youth, undoubtedly gave him a sense of history in the
making. Before long the town would become his parish
and the parish become his world in an all-consuming,
practical, Christian mission.

Perhaps the most important factor in Father Nugent's
decision to make the street children his special concern
was his restless energy that took him, night and day, on
walks around the town. Sometimes accompanied by his
friend Father John Carr, sometimes by the local
Stipendiary who was said to be overwhelmed and
saddened by the social needs he saw, these walking tours
revealed the extent of the problem; the homelessness, the
perilous conditions of some of the children who could be
found around the docks and in shop doorways looking for
warmth, food and shelter, the street crime and the abject
poverty.

Father Nugent wanted to know his parish and what
type of ministry it called for. He wanted to know the social
conditions and the nature of the life the people lived. It
was, in any case, the work of a curate to visit the parish
and focus on the people's pastoral needs, administering
the sacraments as he made house-visits. He already had a
head start at St. Nicholas's with his first-hand experiences
of human misery there two years earlier when he found
himself, together with Father Robert Gillow, caring for the
victims of the twin tragedies of Famine and Fever.

The example and efforts of the clergy who were part of
that first mission, especially around St. Nicholas's church -
which became the Pro-Cathedral after 1850 – is in itself an
inspiring chapter in the history of the diocese. The
courageous work of evangelisation formed the basis of the
parochial and pastoral life we know today. At St
Nicholas's, Father Robert Gillow and later also his brother

George, were among the pioneers of a mission that would have far-reaching effects on education, on pastoral care and on the pattern of devotional life centred on the town parishes under the authority of Bishop George Brown and then Bishop Goss. Members of the Gillow family had already proved themselves to be significant figures in the recent history of Catholic life and in the education and training of priests for the future mission in Lancashire.

The collaboration and friendship Nugent had known with Robert Gillow was one of the abiding influences upon his priesthood. Father Edward McGlynn, whose concern for the social needs of the parish reflected Nugent's own priorities, was also a member of the group of clergy at St. Nicholas's Copperas Hill, resident in the presbytery at Warren Street. Priests such as these responded together to the new pastoral needs with a shared concern that was a significant element in their success, though it quickly became evident that James Nugent was not, at heart, a team man but more of an individual with his own special agenda.

In 1850, he was joined by Father John Carr, who came to St. Nicholas's after ordination that year and who was to become one of Nugent's closest friends and helpers. Meanwhile, Father Robert Gillow had been instrumental in helping to set the tone of the parish in a period of twelve years before Nugent's arrival there. Gillow had first gone there in 1836 at which time St. Nicholas's Church was under the control of a lay committee with proprietary rights and they seemed to deliberately make life as unbearable as possible for the clergy there, even to the extent of refusing any coal for fires in winter. It was a good job they had experienced the training as students at Ushaw to prepare them!

This proprietary lay-committee system was scrapped by Bishop Brown in 1844 ahead of the setting up of the new diocese. Despite the restrictions, men like Robert Gillow set the tone of what was to be the culture of Catholic life from that time on. The devotional practice and pastoral routine of the life of the parish community was created at that time. Solemn High Mass celebrated each Sunday morning and Benediction of the Blessed Sacrament in the afternoon and again in the middle of the week, formed part of the pattern, but there was a practical side too. Fr. Gillow had initiated a Conference of the St. Vincent de Paul Society at St. Nicholas's and the growth in membership of this Society elsewhere would have a vital part to play in the provision of care for the poor in the unfolding needs brought by mass immigration.

In addition, Father Gillow had established separate Guilds for the young men and women of the parish and this was instrumental in linking the prayer life of the parish to the charitable work of the area. The 'Liverpool Mercury' newspaper described him, at the time of his death on 22nd August 1847, as a man remarkable for his attention to the sick, the poor and the children in need of education: and his heroism during the time of the fever in 1847 has already been noted. It was earlier in that same year that on one night, 16th. June, James Nugent could recall he and Robert Gillow dividing between them 43 sick calls. The parish priest of St. Patrick's (Father Grayson) had died that day of plague and the demands on the remaining priests were overwhelming. But it was Robert Gillow's brother, Father George Gillow, who one memorable day quietly and bravely volunteered to go to St. Patrick's Church when an urgent call for help came and several priests had succumbed to the fever as they tended the dying inside the Church. The unspoken question in all of their minds must have been: "who would be the next one?"

The prominent place St. Nicholas's Church came to have in the diocese meant that Nugent quickly met key figures such as Father John Wallwork - who later became Secretary of the Chapter, and Canon Walmsley whose work with the social services became an important part of diocesan pastoral plans. September 1850 marked the time when the English Catholic bishops were recognised once again as an official body, as an organisation in their own right, free to govern and administer the affairs of the local Catholic Church as they saw fit. There followed a hectic time of reorganisation around the country as new dioceses were formed.

The Restoration of the Hierarchy brought an end to the use of the title 'Vicar Apostolic' and it was replaced by that of 'Bishop' as in the Church of England. In 1850 George Brown became the first bishop of the new diocese of Liverpool, which was a natural progression since he had already done the arduous groundwork of building up the necessary structures in the Northern District. He wanted all hands on deck and this had prompted the early return of some students from college, to be ordained in readiness for the mission at home. But the Bishop's health had suffered as a result of his labours and the first years of the new diocese would be difficult ones in which hard decisions were required from a man of failing strength.

The parish of St. Nicholas, at this key time, was under the competent care of Father Worthy. Later he became a Canon of the Diocese and, mainly for health reasons, went to serve in a parish in the Spa town of Buxton in Derbyshire, but not before he had set his seal on some memorable, pioneering work in Liverpool. As Rector of St. Nicholas's he had promoted important pastoral changes and was yet another major influence on James Nugent. His appointment as parish priest was in succession to the highly regarded Doctor Youens who had first promoted the work for The Blind and created opportunities for education in the Catholic community. Sadly, he, as we have seen, was another victim of the plague.

Dr.Youens' death in 1848 was a tremendous loss to the Catholic community. He had helped to forge many new initiatives and brought many benefits, working closely with the authorities of the town to found The Catholic Blind Asylum, a lasting testament to his dedication. He set the benchmark at that time for care of the Blind, stating that they deserved the support and understanding of all.

At St. Nicholas's there was a wonderful tradition of charitable work to live up to and a lot for Nugent to learn from. As successor to Dr. Youens, Father Worthy, who had a special interest in promoting Catholic education for older children, would help Nugent to found a Middle School in Liverpool and so together they made a significant contribution in response to the acute social needs that prevailed in the town. Both men believed passionately in education as the premise for all social improvement.

The young Father James threw himself into the challenge of ministry at St. Nicholas's parish with a vigour that few could match. A wide variety of activities soon built up around him. The Boys'Guild was his special responsibility and with this began his life-long association with the care of boys, their education, formation and spiritual care. As with everything else, he took his work seriously. When he took over the Boys' Guild in 1849 it was struggling to survive, but he put new life into it and transformed it into a well-drilled and confident troupe of youngsters capable of performing simple concerts and plays and boasting a fine band of amateur musicians. It became a group with a purpose, with a pride in itself, reflecting very strongly Nugent's own belief in the reforming power of music and drama.

The embryo of a more systematic Youth Work could be seen in these early efforts, and Nugent was always a strong believer in the formation of the young through activity and purposeful work: "work is the elevating power" was his philosophy in life. He shrewdly recognised that when people saw a thriving organisation they were more inclined to give money to it and raising money was going to be constantly on the agenda. The contributions collected in the streets or at the back of church were used for uniforms and equipment for the band; each parish or organisation seemed to have its band with its own identity, its badge of membership and its proud drummer boy.

The support and approval that Nugent attracted for his work with youngsters went side by side with his success in restoring their sense of dignity and purpose - drawing out the children's own latent talent and ability. He made direct appeals to people's pockets and, even more significantly, to their consciences. Before long, under his skilful hand, the Boys' Guild was transformed into a flourishing organisation for the parish. There grew up a popular Debating Society, another of Father Nugent's passions, and a Reading Club, by which he put great store as an essential educational tool. As a student at College he had delighted in debate and public speaking and conveyed this to the children in his charge, just as he encouraged in them a taste for literacy, art, drama and music. St. Nicholas's became famous for its children's choir which sang at many occasions in the diocese. In these early days of his ministry he won the undying respect and love of the youngsters he helped, and their gratitude was shown publicly when the time came for him to leave the parish and the members of the Boys' Guild and the choir presented him with the gift of an expensive Roskell pocket watch – something which they had all saved up to buy.

St. Peter's Church in Liverpool, (always a town with music in its soul,) was the venue of a Music Festival every three years. After 1837 it was staged at Saint George's Hall which had a fine Concert Room. Nugent, whose love of music is evident from his personal note-books, which he used for jotting down ideas for sermons but also opera lyrics and quotes from Shakespeare's plays, found expression for this interest in his later work for Temperance. He knew how to draw upon the traditional love of music that was part of life in Liverpool.

St. George's Hall would become a favoured venue for 'Cultural Evenings' and 'Variety Concerts'. Events of a national nature could now be held in places like St. George's. The Young Christian Men's Society, for example, convened there and this was an organisation in which Nugent took a keen interest from the beginning to the end of his priestly life. Girls also had their parish organisations and opportunities for creative use of talents, music being a medium accessible to all.

There was, as yet, less opportunity for the girls in a male-dominated Society and Church, in a culture that focussed primarily on a career in domestic service and homemaking skills. Criticism of this stereotyping of women's roles would eventually bring about a more equal and enlightened approach. Investment in opportunities for women in society was neglected at the expense of provision for men. Whilst James Nugent accepted the prevailing view in this, his contribution to the spiritual and educational well-being of girls and young women was evident when he opened a Ragged School, which in theory was for any needy child on the streets.

The Ragged Schools were very informal places. Without any conscious discrimination on grounds of gender, race or creed, they aimed to provide for as many children as possible. It would also become clear a few years later, in his strenuous efforts to bring Orders of Religious Sisters to Liverpool to teach and train girls, that Nugent had long-term education in mind. He was ahead of his time in this. We must be careful about judging attitudes too harshly as it was something inherent in Victorian Society that trades and practical occupations were generally seen as a male preserve.

The Church reflected Society, in this male-dominated ethos of the day. It favoured the promotion of the Catholic Men's Society, for example. The Liverpool branch of this organisation owed its origin mainly to the formidable Dean O'Brien who was another of the priest-heroes of Father Nugent's early days. He was one among many clergy who saw that Catholic Liverpool was growing along with the growth of trade and commerce. The value of an organisation of Catholic Men within the context of a local parish community was recognised. But women of the parish too had a crucial role to play in the resurgent life of the parish and not just in the home. This would be an emerging feature in the years that followed.

In spite of the calls on his time during the fever months of 1849, Nugent managed to find the time and energy for the founding of the Ragged School in a dilapidated and reputedly haunted building in Spitalfields. It was a run-down place between Dale Street and Whitechapel on the site of a former Silk Works. In some ways, the foundation of the Ragged School set the tone and direction of his entire ministry. As he walked around the town he became anxious for the hordes of small children, girls and boys, who ran wild and half-naked around the town at night without shelter, with very little food, sleeping rough, amidst dangers posed by the unscrupulous and immoral characters of every kind all around them. By day they were scarcely less vulnerable. They were often seen as a nuisance by the people of the town, scavenging for food in the dustbins and gutters, waiting outside pubs and corner shops for scraps of charity, looking for some fleeting warmth from inside the pub and bars, moved on and treated roughly by drunks. They were everywhere, but especially along the dockside and Father Nugent's heart went out to them; he pitied their emaciated bodies, their young faces, drawn and pinched by the cruel winters or the cold winds that blew off the River Mersey. He noticed how many of these "poor children of the streets" had grown old before their time.

His description of them in his speech entitled 'Nobody's Children', given to an American audience in the mid 1880s was harrowing and moving. (It is printed as prologue to this book).

The Ragged School was never seen by Nugent as anything but a temporary solution to the problem of child vagrancy. He may well have been aware that there were mixed views about education which often paralysed the authorities from taking coherent action. Some opposed education of the poor on the premise it would lead to discontent and revolution. For many the purpose of education was almost wholly that of preparing the next cohorts of youngsters for the industrial society, whilst others saw an added religious dimension. The religious element has to be put in context too, as often it was a weapon of suppression; one Ragged School having inscribed over its portals the warning taken from Scripture: "All liars shall have their part in the lake that burneth for ever!" In fact, a clash emerged between the ideal and necessity of work and schooling in its own right, a dilemma we can detect in Nugent's own approach, and it was this, in part, that led to the widespread establishment of Sunday Schools among middle-class communities.

Throughout this period there were very few thinkers who perceived education as being for personal formation. Teaching methods were primarily those of rote learning and the monitor system, allowing a larger number of children to 'learn' as they sat on their long benches in their oblong-shaped rooms.

There were seven Ragged Schools in the area when Father Nugent founded his in 1849. A decade later there were thirty-two. A few other schools already existed in the area, the so-called Poor Schools and other Charity Schools, mainly under the driving force of Non-Conformist, Baptist and Anglican churches. They were private enterprises, often a tool for Evangelism or even Proselytism. There was one notable Catholic one under the care of the Jesuits at St. Francis Xavier in Birchfield Street and another run by the St. Vincent de Paul Society at Everton Brow. Meant to be non-denominational in theory, they were in fact symbols of the religious divide. A Ragged School in Hodson Street became the focus of religious tension on one occasion when the Anglican Warden tried to coax children from near-by Holy Cross Chapel with the prospect of food. This type of proselytising did not go down well in the Irish quarter of Liverpool and the OMI Fathers at Holy Cross raised support and money for a Boys' School and Girls'

School to be opened in Fontenoy Street to counter this trend.

At the laying of the foundation stone for the new Fontenoy Street Schools on 31st. May 1852, James Nugent was the invited speaker and, in typically triumphant mood, he promised a great future for Catholic education, announcing the role of the Notre Dame Sisters from Belgium for that purpose. Yet whatever the ideals behind the plans for education, the Ragged Schools were little more than refuges for the children and a cause of religious tension.

Nugent had announced on that occasion that The Sisters would take charge of the Girls' education and begin to transform Catholic school provision. In the few, pathetic, establishments to be found in the areas of greatest deprivation there was little or no organised system; it was a case of responding to needs as they arose, with meagre resources and little sense of direction. Earlier, in 1833, central Government had given a £20,000 building grant for schools on the proviso it was matched by private and voluntary subsidies - a familiar note here that parallels our own times. Behavioural problems engendered by long deprivation and neglect, the stigma of rejection, the lack of self-esteem among a growing population of street children, made for a most difficult time for those prepared to take on this challenge.

From the time Father Nugent set up his Ragged School until the time of the Government's Education Act in 1870 it was quite literally a more or less ragged, make-shift educational provision for both teachers and pupils in England's poorer areas. Things improved as the 19th.Century advanced in all areas of investment in health, safety and school provision. School books and equipment were provided by the Government, but just as things were on the way to better times, events conspired to drag progress back. The Crimean War in the middle of the century slapped a bill of £78 Million on the country and led to a contraction of many services.

Typical of the urchins seeking admission to the Ragged School were the waifs and strays who had wondered around the buildings at the Liverpool waterfront. They were unkempt, wild, smelly, cunning and often desperate with hunger. There was an assumption that they were the neglected children of the immigrant Irish poor, still suffering greatly from the effects of the Famine. This was not entirely accurate. The street children were not all of Irish descent, as Nugent was often at pains to point out, nor were they all from the most destitute families. Sadly, child neglect was not the monopoly of poor or immigrant families.

Photographs of Victorian 'street arabs' show pitiful little children and youths, aged anywhere between four and fourteen, in rags and sackcloth, without shoes or socks, in ill-fitting trousers and frocks which were tied up pathetically at the waist with an old piece of string and on their heads a filthy cap or bonnet. They lived on rubbish dumps and foraged in dustbins for scraps of food. Those who had some form of occupation, such as the boot-blacks, lived a precarious life, subject to cruel kicks and rebuffs. In their hollow eyes Nugent could see that neither their suffering nor their plight was all of their own making and when he made a widespread plea for help he stressed the potential for future improvement even among the most abject of the children. The newsboys, shoeblacks, and fuzee–sellers (fuzees being long matches that stayed alight longer in the street, and as one boy said "went off like a Vesuvius") the ballad singers, diminutive street entertainers and informal traders who "ran with sore feet, with naked limbs and unkempt hair about the streets from midday to midnight" to quote Father Nugent, became his special concern. He soon realised that a Night Shelter was needed, but permission for that was some way off.

He was also anxious for the children's spiritual well-being since many had fallen away from their faith – if they had one - and many others were falling into a spiral of petty crime leading to the increasing threat of arrest by the police and to imprisonment. In London the problem was on a greater scale. A report dated as late as 1868 recounted the figure of 100,000 children roaming the streets unchecked "in fair training for prison life and finally for Penal Servitude". The youngsters were a prey to unscrupulous people who exploited them for work and treated them as worse than dogs or vermin. For the most part they were abandoned, orphaned children, many of them of mixed ethnic backgrounds. Where there was no immediate prospect of returning them to their natural family they were always a likely prey to slavery, abuse, prostitution and criminal activity.

There were a few organisations and individuals who were making efforts to rescue some of these unfortunate urchins from the streets and away from the perils that beset them. The original purpose behind the Ragged Schools was clearly not sufficient. They became subject to the scrutiny of external inspectors, unrealistically coming along making an issue of maintenance, safety and educational standards. Nugent was said to be angry about this. Not only did the inspections hamper his plans but they also seemed to undermine what he regarded as his rights in the matter. Interestingly there is no indication at this stage of what restrictions Bishop Brown had placed upon him, except that Brown thought him over ambitious. Up to this point he seems to have been a free agent, but the situation would be different later, under Bishop Goss.

It is doubtful that bishop Goss would have approved of the cost and time required by this project. Restoring a ruined building cost a lot of money and one cynical comment of such enterprises described Charity workers in this way: "in dilapidated Warehouses they sought to protect some virtuous ones and reclaim multitudes on the road to ruin". Father Nugent did not usually stop to heed the critics. He and his friend Father Carr pressed on. They would work together again some years later when they were both in the Isle of Man, and they remained firm friends throughout life, inspired by the same ideals of education and reform.

They had set about obtaining the money to make the building in Sptalfields watertight, useable and as welcoming as possible. It was far from ideal when the first bedraggled 'pupils' shambled in through its doors but it was at least a better alternative to being in the street all day, and was a start in reclaiming the souls of children who were otherwise "running to waste in the gutters" as Nugent put it. Integral to what he and his helpers were about was the desire to win back souls to God, to rescue the most vulnerable and, perhaps forgivably, retrieve Catholic children from the danger of what we might now call lapsation. Suffice it to say, there were always enough reasons to justify Nugent having a go in the unpromising conditions prevailing at that time.

The Spitalfields Ragged School was demolished around the year 1879 to make way for town improvements and was later the site of the offices of Midlands Railways. Its initial popularity soon waned in favour of a wider provision of child care and the advent of new schools.

Case studies exist which bear out the precarious and sad existence which many small children, some as young as four or five, experienced. James Carling and his brothers (described in the book 'Liverpool - The Irish Connection') found themselves on the streets when a cruel step-mother drove them out. They earned coppers as errand boys, crept into shops for food and into the theatres and Concert Halls in exchange for a few pennies. It was through his familiarity with the theatres, sitting up in the gods, that Carling learnt to quote Shakespeare and poetry. He developed a reputation as a pavement artist by which he earned his meagre wages, together with his brothers, Willy, Johnny and Henry, dodging 'the Peelers' who always threatened them with prison or the workhouse on a charge of disturbance of the peace. James Carling particularly came to rue the day he set foot in Bold Street, a no-go area for the pavement artists. Luckily for him he was one of the many fortunate ones who, released from detention, found his way into Father Nugent's care in St. George's Industrial Schools in West Derby Road, of which Nugent was Headmaster in the mid-1860s and which Carling attended from the age of six to fourteen. In later years he always spoke with great regard for his former Headmaster.

A Mrs. Holmes had been an invaluable help to Father Nugent acting as housekeeper at the Ragged School. She was exactly the matronly figure that was needed and she proved to be one of Father Nugent's greatest allies. With her interest and support he had managed to keep the school running but she could not continue the work later when the idea of a Boy's Refuge and Night Shelter was mooted. The work would increase significantly as breakfasts would have to be provided as well as second-hand clothing, books, entertainment and finally supper. It would be too much for one person. Yet whatever sort of Institution Nugent had in mind – and his mind raced ahead with different projects all the time, – his guiding principle in regard to these most unfortunate of children was "their plight is their misfortune not their fault". They deserved better.

The scene that could be found in any major town or city was the same as that described in the July 1905 edition of The tablet which drew attention to the sad contrast of poverty and wealth in many cities at the turn of the century: "the shoeless street arab turns his somersault beside the carriages of the prosperous". The genius of James Nugent was that he could convert the tragedy of the streets into a more hopeful theatre of human talent and resourcefulness. He could turn the pageant of the life of the poor, the pathetic antics of the boy conjurors and the sad circumstances of the smallest girls and boys selling matches for a living, into lives of decent and responsible citizens, giving them a new way of life they had never even dreamed of. *(c.f. the Prologue of this book).*

As time went on and the organisation of the Ragged School showed up more and more the need for a Boys' Refuge, it became obvious that a Night Shelter was needed and Father Nugent began to look around for a suitable location. There was little in the way of appropriate or affordable buildings. Although this seemed to be his overriding intention he was already moving in a different direction with the Middle School idea and it would be some years before he opened the Night Shelter in Soho Street. The Ragged School was an experience he would never forget. It was a sign of his individualism and vision which began to set him apart as a priest with a special charisma. It was also a project which brought Father Nugent into a happy and fruitful association with the great Canon Major Lester, an Anglican whose work for the rescue and education of the poor endeared him to Nugent as a life-long friend and collaborator.

The suggestion sometimes made that Nugent's reforming work was a series of sudden jumps and unconnected ideas has, I think, been proved false, but it can be seen at this stage in his life why people found him inconsistent and not always able to consolidate what he had done. Concern expressed by some that shelter and education were the duty of the state not the individual must be seen along side his efforts to secure cooperation from the local Council. The plans to obtain the services of Religious Sisters from the Continent to educate the girls was also a sign of collaborative thinking. Nugent's vision was not only for the social welfare of children but for their religious welfare too and that was something the local Council was not providing.

The Girls' Orphanage, which Nugent referred to as 'The Catholic Orphanage Asylum', was one of the special concerns in his mind at this time. It had originated in 1816 as a privately- run house at 96 Mount Pleasant. Some fifty girls were given accommodation there, but in 1845 its location was changed to Falkner Street where it came under the care of The Sisters of Mercy, who had arrived in

Liverpool two years before, and where the number of orphan girls is recorded as sixty-five. On 31st July, 1851, Nugent realised an ambition when the Sisters of Notre Dame, newly arrived in the town, took over the care of the Orphanage as part of their new mission which was to grow in an extraordinary way from that time.

The scope and status of the Orphanage took a leap forward as it was accepted, in 1869, for certification under the Industrial Schools Act of 1866, and, as part of the Government legislation that ensued, the building was extended and refurbished, with two new workrooms and a larger dormitory housing 110 youngsters. The Falkner Street Orphanage was to remain in place until 1927 when it became the site for the Women's Hospital. The record shows that over a period of some forty-nine years over 750 orphan girls had been looked after, and in Nugent's words had been "clothed and fed and the means of earning a respectable livelihood placed in their hands". He proudly noted that "of the 750, 71 have died, leaving a surity of their salvation, and 13 have entered on a Religious Life in various Orders and many of the remaining number still keep up a correspondence of nearly fifty years standing with their old home, though they themselves are in all corners of the globe". The report is interesting as indicative of Nugent's own priorities but also of his focus on statistics and trends that gave substance to the ulterior purpose of the welfare of the orphans, their spiritual well-being and the importance of their being kept in the family circle. The Catholic Reformatory Association in later years would take this further in providing homes for orphan children in Canada and America.

During this time too a second Girls Orphanage Asylum was opened, in 1854, at 32 Soho Street and named 'St. Elizabeth's Institute' under the management of a Miss Gordon. This Home was later transferred to Breckfield Road, in the year 1861, where a Mrs. Roskell was its President and Canon Walmsley, the Vicar General, was its Director. Meanwhile, the Sisters of Charity ran a further

Orphanage in Mason Street in the 1860s and the indications are that Father Nugent kept a watchful eye on all of these establishments, though he took a more active involvement in the Falkner Street building. The Orphanage work would become the focal point for one of Nugent's greatest accomplishments – bringing the Notre Dame Sisters to Liverpool.

Chapter 5

The Catholic Institute

A National Catholic Institute already existed in 1853, but the inspiration that led to the opening, in October of that year, of The Liverpool Catholic Institute, (usually abbreviated to C.I.), came in response to a combination of needs Father Nugent had witnessed among the people of his own town.

The acute sense of deprivation prevailing at the time, the lack of statutory provision for education, health care and other social benefits in his own neighbourhood, struck Nugent with a sense of great injustice and spurred him to action. Canon Bennett's observation that Nugent's early school experience at The Academy, Queen's Square, had convinced him of the need for more Catholic schools and equality of educational opportunities, at a time when only the Poor Schools and Charity Schools were available, may also be a crucial factor here.

Others have detected another, even stronger, motive, which was a deliberate attempt to counter what he saw as the purely secular curriculum of other educational establishments in Liverpool at that time, in particular the Liverpool Institute. The C.I. may well have been inspired by an effort to redress the imbalance he saw in the Liverpool Institute and to fight the Catholic corner for a better deal in education. In some people's opinion this was the real driving force behind Nugent's mission. Redressing the balance, or even outdoing the opposition, was a powerful incentive for much of his work, though it was only part of the story. The paradox is that the C.I. was intended as an 'all-comers welcome' sort of place, and Nugent hoped it would be a place of learning and exchange for people of all religious persuasions , in effect an ecumenical institute.

The Poor Schools in Liverpool, like the ones situated at St. Nicholas's, Copperas Hill, and in Pleasant Street, were obviously inadequate, especially as the Catholic population in that area had increased dramatically. The National Catholic Poor Schools' Committee had been set up seven years earlier but, controversially, the Vicars Apostolic had separated child education from the work of the National Catholic Institute. Leading Catholic figures like Dr. Youens and Mr. Charles Townley represented Liverpool on the Bishops' Committee and helped to pave the way for regional Catholic schools. However, school attendance was not compulsory prior to 1871, and before then efforts to fund education were voluntary, ad hoc and reliant mainly on charity and local philanthropy. Poor Schools were a symbol of crisis management: a desperate attempt to contain and control the population of waifs and strays that roamed the streets unchecked and around which Father Nugent had cast his fatherly arm. These unfortunates had prospects only of a life time of crime, as Nugent later came to realise for himself when they entered prison and came under his professional eye.

In Standish Street, in the centre of town, a temporary Church School had been built to serve the parish of Holy Cross – a mission founded by the Oblates of Mary Immaculate in March 1849 that became a central focus of community life for the Catholics of Liverpool for a century and a half. A combined school room and church accommodation was characteristic of the buildings in those days of Liverpool's growing Catholic mission. New churches were still frowned upon and had to avoid the appearance of a church building. It was at Holy Cross on 25th March, 1849, that the young Father James Nugent found himself invited to preach, (or perhaps he had invited himself), on the launch of the new mission, just three months after his arrival at St. Nicholas's parish. His preaching skills were already well-known.

The occasion of his sermon at Holy Cross that day was a turning point in his early ministry. He was shocked and concerned by the numbers of undernourished, under-privileged children he saw shuffling in to the parish school room. Whilst his heart went out to them, his mind was busy with practicalities. Who could be found to teach them? Where could suitable Catholic teachers be found to cover not only the immediate needs, but also the long-term future for such a growing number?

The age-group he particularly identified as needy was that of the 9 – 15 year olds, whose physical and moral welfare he believed to be most at risk. It was from this that the idea began to form in his mind of a Catholic Middle School that would train and equip this vulnerable age group with an education and the chance of useful work in the community. The solution he saw to the problem of teachers lay in his former experience in Blackburn where his parish priest, Peter Kaye, had successfully enlisted the help of Religious Orders for parish work and teaching. Like his mentor Peter Kaye, Nugent knew that his own education at a Catholic Seminary had been a privileged time and he had grown up to appreciate the value of a broad, thorough schooling, based on the faith values which his family and the seminary had shared with him.

In the absence of qualified staff for Catholic Schools nearer home, he began the search for teachers from abroad and looked to the Continent of Europe, where Catholics had not been subject to the same religious persecution and where, as his time in Italy had shown him, there were many flourishing schools and convents well staffed by Religious Orders. After all, England was missionary territory and needed a missionary approach. He set about gaining the approval of his Bishop, George Brown, to approach the Sisters of Notre Dame de Namur in Belgium to see if they would agree to come to Liverpool. George Brown, whilst not getting on too well with his impetuous priest, and eyeing him with some caution, agreed with this proposal and had in fact already seriously considered it.

The Sisters' special purpose and skill lay in education and offered the poor the opportunity that was otherwise denied them. Their convents were also financially well endowed since many of the Sisters came from wealthy families and were of independent means or even aristocratic background. They did not make education fees compulsory, and they tried to make schooling accessible to all. This fitted well into Nugent's own philosophy and he perceived these Sisters to be ideal for the job. From that time on he was eager to persuade the Mother General to release the sisters for work in Liverpool as soon as possible.

By the March of 1851 his plans had come to a happy fulfilment and it was in that month the Notre Dame Sisters arrived in Liverpool. They set up their first home and training school straightaway at Islington Flags in the town centre. The vision of Father Nugent and his bishop – a man now seen to be under considerable stress, working hard to establish the new diocese – was one of the examples of forward thinking that would take the fledgling Diocese forward. It gave the lie to the criticism of some of Father Nugent's opponents that he only addressed immediate needs, rather than long-term solutions, or that he was concerned only about schools for boys and not for girls. Religious Orders like the Notre Dame Sisters were a vital ingredient in the long haul that was the task of rebuilding Catholic Tradition in England and re-instating some measure of parity in the education of boys and girls.

The arrival of the Notre Dame Sisters in Liverpool, as elsewhere in England, was principally to bolster and enrich Catholic Schools and train future teachers, but a general remit to serve the poor was a vital aspect of their dedicated service. They had to restore morale and confidence in the Catholic community at a vulnerable time. Liverpool was prime territory for this type of work, as Bishop Brown and James Nugent recognised. Providence seems to work through the meeting of minds, and it has been frequently recorded that the local bishop would be on the point of writing to the Superior of an Order or Congregation at the precise moment when the Superior was about to write to him and offer help. The Sisters of Mercy had already established themselves in Liverpool from as early as 1843 and the arrival of the Notre Dame nuns from Belgium in 1851 was followed by that of the Good Shepherd Sisters in 1854, the Sisters of Charity of St. Vincent de Paul in 1863, the Bon Secours Sisters in 1867, the Little Sisters of the Poor in 1871and the Sisters of the Immaculate Heart of Mary in 1876. The litany continued in 1891 with the 'Selly Park' (Birmingham) Congregation - The Sisters of Charity of St. Paul the Apostle, whose work in nursing and child education was outstanding and they were joined by the Sisters of the Mother of God and later by the Sisters of Nazareth in 1897. Archbishop Whiteside later introduced to Liverpool the Christian Brothers to staff the Boys' Schools. Both the quantity and the titles of these Orders coming from France, Belgium and Ireland, are an indication of the type of pastoral and spiritual care that was deemed a priority in England at this time.

The challenge the Notre Dame Sisters faced was enormous. They were to take charge of the Poor Schools as well as the work of Higher Education. In the straightened circumstances of Liverpool at that time – chronically over-populated and stretched to the limit – the Sisters had to take under their wing all the needs that presented themselves, and within a short space of time too. They had a blank canvas but not an unlimited pot of money to draw upon, and whilst they enjoyed support and encour-agement from most quarters their presence was not universally accepted. They had to cope with the scepticism of both laity and clergy who felt it was an admission of defeat to look for outside help and that it reflected badly on the local Church's ability to manage its own affairs. This would not be the last time Father Nugent's enthusiasm and drive would gain him both supporters and opponents in the same project, even among his own clerical fraternity.

One of the first projects the Sisters took on when they arrived in Liverpool was the Catholic Female Orphanage in Falkner Street. The building there, designed by Augustus Welby Pugin, had been under the care of the Sisters of Mercy since 1845 but, as we have seen, its humble origins dated back further to 1817 in Mount Pleasant, where a lay Committee of the local parish had started it. At the end of July 1851, the Sisters of Mercy had finally to accept that they must give up the work which had grown steadily in the intervening years, and agreed to hand over to the members of the newly arrived Notre Dame Community. In this way the property at Mount Pleasant, which had previously housed the first Girls' Orphanage, was bought over to become the base for the future Notre Dame centre of Catholic Teacher Training.

The pioneering role of the Sisters in this respect can be too easily forgotten when the history of Education is recalled. Their role was nothing less than vital in providing not only a kick-start to religious education after the wilderness years of Catholic life in England, but also in sustaining it for the next 150 years. Father Nugent was able to draw on his earlier experience in the Lancashire town of Blackburn to realise the potential of the Sisters and he was completely un-phased by doubters and detractors. He was generally un-phased by anything. His usual tactic was to carry on regardless in the face of opposition which seemed only to serve as a catalyst for further action.

Meanwhile, other developments in education were coming to his attention. Among the many places with which Father Nugent's name became identified was Soho Street in the centre of town. In time he would help to establish a Boys' Refuge there, but before that Soho Street was already well known as the location for the grand sounding 'Preparatory Classical and Commercial Day School' which had been opened in October 1842 by the Jesuit Fathers. This school, at number 36 Soho Street, later developed into St. Francis Xavier College, already referred to. It would play an important part in the educational and

Catholic provision in Liverpool. Just a few months later, in December 1842, a Boarding School for Boys was founded at St. Domingo House, Everton, and was given the name St. Edward's College - a forerunner of St. Joseph's Junior Seminary at Upholland, founded nearly forty years later. The Solemn Mass for the Official Opening of Upholland all those years later, on 26th. September 1883, would mark the beginning of one of the most important developments in the life of the Diocese. The training of priests, always such an important part of Father Nugent's ministry, meant that the Diocese could produce its own clergy for the home mission and look to the future confidently.

Long before the progress in middle school education that made places like the Junior Seminary at Upholland possible, the yawning gaps in the education system for the majority of youngsters remained all too evident. The Middle School project, providing for children from families of lower income and not designed to set children on the road to academic glory, was important in Nugent's scheme of things. It grew out of his instinct for what today we call social inclusion.

As always, he had looked for suitable premises for his project. He was now working hard to purchase a house in Rodney Street and by January 7th. 1850 was able to publish Notices for the opening of a school there. It was only a year after his arrival in Liverpool, and having secured the patronage of Bishop Brown for the new venture, with the invaluable help and encouragement of his parish priest Father Worthy, things moved quickly ahead. With the appointment of Monsignor Cook as President of the new School and Nugent himself as Vice-President, an impetus and confidence was given to the project.

It is hard to know where Father Nugent was finding the time for this increasing list of pastoral projects and the strength to carry the mounting work load. Parish commitments alone would have occupied all of most people's waking hours. He had his sights set firmly on some form of Institute that would be the flagship of his educational plans and in which the Notre Dame Sisters were to play a key part. Things moved rapidly now in regard to the main objective of setting up an Institute for Higher Education to complement the Middle School in Rodney Street. Fund-raising, as ever, was the first and last element in any of his enterprises and many of the parishes mobilised to canvass businessmen and merchants of the town for their crucial support.

Financial support always seemed to be forthcoming when Father Nugent was on the case. His persistent nature – no doubt a source of irritation to many - was becoming legendary. Donations or pledges of money were constantly and vigorously being sought by friends and supporters of Nugent among the Private Companies as well as among the ordinary people. Collecting boxes were a regular feature in cafés, pubs, shops, railway stations and doctors' waiting rooms.

One of the biggest and most imaginative sources of public funding came from the inauguration of Sponsored Lectures. These were usually held in the Concert Hall in Nelson Street, near Lime Street Station. This type of event for fund-raising and publicity was to become a hallmark of Nugent's mission. With a natural flair for the stage and public oratory he was in his element organising lectures and producing concerts or 'stage-managing' events. At a time when general literacy levels were very low, the presence of a well-known Speaker, coupled with the prospect of a free Concert, proved to be irresistible and Nugent was well aware of this. Speakers and entertainers were drawn to the Concerts from various walks of life, whilst political and religious figures from the town, and from other parts of the country, were invited. Sponsorship by the big commercial firms and wealthy businessmen was actively sought, so that within two years or so of the opening of the Rodney Street Middle School sufficient funds had been raised to buy the desired site for the proposed Institute in near-by Hope Street.

It represented an immense achievement and the fruit of long collaborative effort when on the 29th March 1853 the

Foundation Stone for the Catholic Institute was laid by a pleased but failing Bishop Brown. By the end of October that same year, 1853, within a period of just six months since its foundation, the building of The Catholic Institute was complete. Father Nugent, as its first Director and inspirational founder, wasted no time in establishing the reputation and popularity of his new project. Again drawing on previous experience, he saw the value of attaching staff of good calibre, and also prestigious, well-known visiting speakers, to the Institute.

A prominent member of staff at the birth of the C.I. was a Mr. Grant, brother of the first Bishop of Southwark and a founder of the Association of Providence of which Nugent would later become an enthusiastic member. In his desire to give the Catholic Institute as high a profile as possible, Nugent thought big in regard to those he should invite to the opening. Why not begin at the top, with the leader of England's Catholics? Cardinal Wiseman was due in Liverpool to give a lecture and happily accepted the invitation to visit the Institute while in town. He was anxious to see the project for himself, having made Catholic Education one of his principal concerns.

The years ahead would see the C.I. produce many good and prominent leaders to serve the Catholic Community, though, as we have seen, Nugent never intended it to be the exclusive domain of Catholics. The C.I. was 'catholic' in the sense of offering an open door to all. Nugent wanted it to be a place where everyone might benefit from its facilities and services. In a sense it was a proto-type of the Community College of our day. This wider scope gave him greater leverage also in his fund-raising. There was a library, the facility for Art, Drama and Debate, there was teaching of basic subjects like English and Science, in which Nugent himself took a leading part, and there was also an Institute Magazine to advertise and record the virtues of the new establishment. All of these were ingredients in an exciting new venture at the service of the whole community.

Shortly after the informal launch which accompanied all Nugent's subsequent new projects, Cardinal Nicholas Wiseman arrived in Liverpool to give a public address at the Philharmonic Hall in Hope Street on "Catholic Life and the Arts". Nugent arranged, with the support of Bishop Brown, for the Cardinal to officially open the Catholic Institute the next day. It was an historic visit, the first visit of the leader of English Catholics since the Restoration of the Hierarchy three years earlier and Liverpool's first sight of a Cardinal. His visit helped to focus wonderfully on the purpose of the C. I. and the place Nugent was giving it in the development of Catholic life. For Nugent it was nothing less than a great moment of triumph. The big occasion of the opening was further enhanced by a nice touch from Father Nugent. With his impresario's skills, and alert to the benefits of good propaganda as well as a little well-aimed flattery, he had rehearsed some of the boys from St. Nicholas's parish in a production of a play Cardinal Wiseman had written, entitled, "The Hidden Gem". The boys performed it in front of their distinguished visitor that day with great success.

Nicholas Wiseman was not the only high profile figure to visit the Catholic Institute in the early years of its existence. Nugent's long-standing admiration for Father John Henry Newman, and the desire to enhance the profile of Catholics, caused the idea to form in his fertile brain of putting the C.I. under the patronage of St. Philip Neri and establishing it as an Oratory on the lines of Newman's Birmingham Oratory. Nugent believed that this tradition, which John Henry Newman had embraced as the spiritual anchor of his own life, would be the best model for the new Institute. The badge and logo of St. Philip was on all the publicity material, magazine and letterheads of the new Institute because Nugent had already made up his mind about this, and when he did that he usually succeeded. His pursuit of the idea of an Oratorian-style community in Liverpool became, like many of his schemes, something of a private obsession.

This was his Achilles Heal. Nugent did not sufficiently avert to the fact that the Oratory link would not be favoured by Bishop Brown or his successor, Alexander Goss, who would soon express misgivings about the way the project was being financed. He was of the view that Nugent was being far too hasty and ambitious for his own good. But Nugent was on a roll. Zeal for the project, and the spin-offs from it, led him on in spite of objections. Storm clouds lay ahead for the C.I. but in these first years of his energetic mission he was not looking too far into the future, concentrating instead on the current successes and how to capitalise on them.

He resolved to make the most of the opportunity of John Henry Newman's much advertised and eagerly anticipated visit to Liverpool for a series of Lectures on the subject of Christianity and The Turks. Newman travelled each week from Birmingham for the Lectures. His analysis of the developing situation in the Crimea and its implications for the Christian world had attracted widespread interest, and the Crimean War in 1854 represented the most serious conflict for Britain in 40 years.

The Crimean war began as a relatively minor dispute about guardianship of the Holy Places in Jerusalem. The Russians believed it was their duty to sustain this care-taker role on behalf of the rest of the world. As so often in poor Jerusalem's violent history, the Sovereignty question came to provoke prospects of war yet again. The Ottoman Empire had declined in its supremacy; its weakness being exploited by other powers. Britain on the other hand seized on the potential imbalance of power in Europe and did not want its own Empire endangered. The British joined forces with the French and others to prevent Russian ambitions going too far, and there ensued one of the most ill-prepared military conflicts of the 19th Century. Among the key names and places still well embedded in popular memory are Sebastopol and Balaclava where the action was most concentrated. When the British put all their military eggs in the one basket of the Port of Balaclava they were surprised and overwhelmed by a massive counter-attack from the Russian Army.

Like many people in Europe, Nugent took a keen interest in these events, and in Britain interest built up greatly during the year leading up to the outbreak of the War in 1854. The articles and reports in 'The Times' kept the attention and it perhaps dawned on Nugent at this time how powerful was the influence of the media in both information and propaganda. He may already have begun to consider what he could do with a newspaper of his own in which to disseminate Catholic teaching.

Nugent gave a warm welcome to his prominent guest speaker, not only because of the theme of the Talks and the interest it had engendered, but also because it again served his purpose of giving an even higher profile to the Catholic Institute. Newman was a celebrated convert to Catholicism and this much publicised conversion, attracting both antagonism from some and admiration from others, had brought widespread interest in Newman so that his visit to Liverpool was a coup, and fitted well with Father Nugent's plans for the Catholic Institute. A place of broad education, attracting brilliant minds and holy people, offered to as many people as possible, open to every denomination and supported financially by wealthy prominent benefactors, looked to be an unstoppable success. In addition – the church of St. Philip Neri was selected as the link and chaplaincy base for the C.I. and Nugent was keen to form an Oratorian community there. He would not let go of the subject, yet for a variety of reasons it did not develop into an Oratory on the lines Nugent had hoped. Only the Church of St. Philip Neri retained the title of 'The Oratory' and Nugent put his brainchild, the C.I. under St. Philip's patronage. The main opposition came from Bishop Brown, and Nugent's intentions in appealing to Newman were thwarted because of the lack of this vital support.

Newman took a cautious view, like Bishop Brown, of Nugent's fast-moving plans but did not want to pour cold water on his good intentions, especially when these involved the Oratory. There may have been more success in developing the Oratory idea had the bishop supported it from the start. The future Cardinal did however give money to the Institute and promised Nugent faithfully he would ask a blessing for it from the Pope. Whilst in Rome in 1856 with his great friend and confrére Ambrose St. John, Newman made good his promise and brought back both a papal blessing and some relics of St. Philip Neri for the Institute. It was, in some respects, a peace offering.

James Nugent has been compared to John Henry Newman and the two have taken their respective places in the modern history of Catholicism. Yet Nugent and Newman were very different. They were their own men with their own distinct contribution. Nugent's fame was somewhat overshadowed by the older man's prestigious position. A more useful comparison would be between Father Nugent and Father Faber since Faber, also in the shadow of Newman, was the catalyst and enthusiast who saw his role as one of agitating for more Oratorian foundations. John Henry Newman was a more cautious man, with a deeper current of thought and a more measured approach, and was able to see the wider picture if not the distant scene. An interesting study in its own right would be the relationship between these three outstanding figures of Catholic Church history.

It is clear that The Catholic Institute became a useful platform for much of James Nugent's ministry from that time on. From its foundation in 1853 until 1863, James Nugent took up residence at 26 Hope Street, from where he directed the mixed fortunes of the new venture with qualified success. Nugent never lost his desire to establish an Oratory, nor did he easily forgive or forget the lack of support from Bishop Brown who he believed had prevented this development and refused to release funding for it. There is no doubt that the issue soured relations with his bishop but later developments reveal a measure of cooperation that made for joint efforts on behalf of Liverpool. Bishop Brown had his reasons and in some ways he was right to be cautious. He had to consider the needs of the whole diocese and what would best serve the whole Catholic Community rather than just the select few.

Whilst the C.I. gained many admirers and many a grateful youngster passed through its doors, and went on to find a good career as a result, there was a down side to the enterprise. There were those who came to look on the Institute as an imposition of culture and of class that did not sit easily with the poorer sectors of society. The criticism often made by Father Nugent's opponents was that he did not take sufficient account of the consequences of such an ambitious scheme and that he exacted a standard and a level of commitment that many could not meet. The difficulty he experienced in accepting this was the cause of many a personal crisis for him in the years that followed.

It would be a severe test of his resolve that those he might have hoped to have as allies were actually opposed to him. He now had to draw on the commitment of other pro-Catholic and Non-Catholic allies to sustain his plans. Prominent among them was the important figure of John Denvir, as we will see. Denvir claimed to have provided the slogan "Save the Boy" which set in motion for Nugent a campaign that was a foil to the critics who had complained that the C.I. was too "middle-class". The "Save The Boy" campaign was to open up the whole issue of child welfare and education in Liverpool.

Nugent's response to pressure was to work even harder than before. In the first ten years of the life of the C.I. he consolidated and initiated some of his ideas and projects for homeless street children and remained absorbed in parish work, though no longer living at Copperas Hill. The beginnings of his breakdown in health in 1858 might have been predictable at this time, the effects of overwork having already played a part in his life. The people who advised him to slow down were usually the same ones that asked him to do something more! He was known to be a willing horse who would get things done, arbitrate in difficult dilemmas, write to this person, visit that person, speak at this meeting or at that. His tendency to over-work went hand in hand with the high expectations he placed on himself as well as on others, but he was not a man to slow down easily and in any case he was now in too deep to stop. It was not so much the amount of work as the underlying worries the work produced which took their toll. There must surely have been worries engendered by rumours of financial difficulties at the C.I.

Buoyed up by the initial success of the C.I., Father Nugent forged ahead with his work for the poor and the education of Catholic youngsters. The campaign that later brought the cry "Save The Boy" to the lips and to the agenda of the whole Liverpool community may be said to have its origins in these early moves towards equality and justice in the Catholic community. James Nugent believed strongly that the long-term approach to the problem of poverty lay in education. There were to be many opportunities to see this proved right in the years that followed. The ideology behind the Catholic Institute – the education and formation of the young who could take their proper place in society alongside others – was the ideology that underpinned his whole mission.

Catholic Education in Liverpool owed its origins to the Benedictines and the Jesuits, and to individual champions like Father Henry Gibson, who came to the fore at this time. A decade earlier Father Gibson had worked effectively in the background, along side the Catholic Club which had the avowed purpose of defending and promoting Catholic interests against Protestant inter-ference. From within the local parish missions Henry Gibson laboured to provide a foothold for basic Catholic instruction for the children in the Poor Law Schools. When they left these Schools, Father Gibson tried his best to find work for them and at times he even opened up his own home to boys whose wages were so low they could not afford even the cheapest lodging houses. If the propriety of this is totally in question in today's society, at that point in time he only wanted to preserve them from the influence of the low life in the Lodging Houses, from street life and aimlessness.

In this sense Gibson was Nugent's immediate predecessor in pioneering Working Boys' Homes in Liverpool. It is interesting that twenty years after these first tentative efforts by Father Gibson and his Anglican colleagues, Nugent was to set up his Boys' Refuge in Soho Street, an indication that the acute problems remained two decades on and in fact had got worse, mainly as a result of the one period when the influx of poor from Ireland changed the situation for ever. No matter how many times the statistic is given it does not lose its impact on the imagination; in 1847 alone, 300,000 Irish immigrants arrived in the port of Liverpool. That an Organisation, entitled "The Association of Providence" was necessary at this point in the century is a sign of the dire situation Liverpool then was forced to address in face of the plight of its poorest people. Nearly twenty years later it was recorded in the accounts of the Boys' Refuge for 1867 that 48,205 suppers were provided and over-night accommodation made available for 2,913 needy youngsters in that year. This criterion of poverty may find a pale reflection in the Free School Meals indicator of today.

Two years later, in the Midnight Census taken on New Year's Eve, 1869, it was found that some 713 homeless children (541 boys and 172 girls) were begging on the streets. This did not reflect the scores of other undetected waifs and strays. Such figures represented only the tip of a vast ice-berg of wretchedness and pauperism among children. The difficulty was to harness the greater provision for education with the practical need for shelter and food, and these two missionary quests formed the nucleus of what James Nugent and his friends were all about in these extraordinary and challenging years.

Father Nugent, donning the mantle of Henry Gibson, learnt to use the links with the Catholic Club to bring political pressure to bear on the local Council for change, especially in educational provision, and also to make use of his links with wealthy businessman to secure funding for the ever-growing work of The Association of Providence. The beneficial outcome of Father Nugent's ambitious programme for the Catholic Institute had led him inevitably to consider even greater projects.

Typical Street Scenes *(circa 1928-1935)*

Chapter 6

Catholic Times and Turbulent Times

In 1860 Father Nugent embarked on a venture that some would consider foolhardy. He was still technically in charge of the CI, despite all its problems. To enter then into the fraught world of the Media at a time of great political and religious turmoil may seem almost suicidal. What some people might consider madness, Nugent saw as an important challenge to be undertaken. When he decided to get involved with the Catholic Press the journal he would have known and read was the 'Lancashire Free Press' which had been launched in 1859 under the editorship of Stephen Meaney who had come from working on the 'Liverpool Journal'(Liverpool Daily Post). It was new therefore when James Nugent came to it and he would have endorsed its editorial policy to "honestly and fearlessly vindicate Catholic interests at home and abroad" and would have applauded its stated intention never to let any "vulgar abuse" or "degrading personalities" degrade its columns. He described his motives in taking on the enterprise as being "for the public good" having seen the vacuum in Catholic publications and the derth of decent religious journals.

The 'Lancashire Free Press' was, by all accounts, well printed and presented in eight large pages and selling at 3 pence. Meaney's tenure of office as editor lasted less than a year. He incurred considerable debts in that short time and had to be replaced. A new editor took over and the name was changed to 'The Northern Press' incorporating the Liverpool General Advertiser. It proclaimed itself as the organ of the Catholic body in the north of England and non-party-political. Nugent was to find Stephen Meaney a thorn in the side during the years that followed as he rejoined the 'Liverpool Daily Post and teamed up with its editor Michael Whitty who was to be James Nugent's bête noir. Meaney's activities were more serious in the years ahead and, two decades later he became leader of the Fenian Movement.

At some point in 1861 Father Nugent had bought the company and was advertising for shareholders in what was called 'The Northern Press Publishing Company'. He was not financially responsible for the paper until 1867 but he was already its acting editor. In 1869 the heading of the newspaper was extended to include the title 'The Catholic Weekly Times' and three years later was simply called 'The Catholic Times' under the ownership of Nugent. He used his salary (£300 per annum) from the Prison where he had become Chaplain. There was to be a further change in 1876 (The Catholic Times and Catholic Opinion) but all this chopping and changing stopped in 1933 and it reverted to simply 'The Catholic Times' and so has remained to this time. Several prominent people have been editors in the intervening years but Nugent's immediate successor was Father John Berry, who Nugent hoped would succeed him generally in his other work. Things turned out differently.

The helper he enlisted as manager and acting editor at the beginning was John Denvir, a strange bed-fellow but someone with the interests of the paper at heart, and obviously capable as he ran the whole business on his own for some time when Nugent went on an extended visit to America in August 1870. Denvir would also prove himself a valuable ally of Nugent in looking after the Boys' Refuge that started in soho Street. As manager of the paper he later recruited fellow-Irishmen John McCardle, and James Finigan and found a staunch adviser in Father James McSwiney, a Jesuit priest based at St. Francis Xavier's Church in Salisbury Street. With their help Denvir increased the sales and popularity of the paper and was the driving force that kept it not only in existence but profitable and widely read. In thirty years the circulation figures rose eight-fold from 9,000 to 73,000 and had a national status, claiming to have at one stage the biggest circulation of any comparable Catholic newspaper in the world.

As a monthly supplement to 'The Catholic Times' Nugent also published 'The Catholic Fireside' and this proved popular with Catholic households, so much so that it became a separate publication, though under the same management as the 'The Catholic Times'. The 1879 May 31st. edition of 'The Catholic Fireside' printed a tribute to Father Nugent, then aged fifty-seven, in which he was surrounded by scenes depicting his various charitable labours over 30 years: his temperance work, his care of emigrant families, his work with abandoned and abused mothers and their children, his pastoral and parish work of reconciling sinners and his care of prisoners, his charity towards widows and orphans, the formation of young men through the guilds and the concerts and, of course, his work at the printing press giving employment and training to the boys of the Refuge.

The newspaper paid honour to Nugent for more than a quarter of a century of distinguished service in these ways, an achievement that had also been recognised, a few weeks before, by the townspeople of Liverpool. On April 17th. 1879, The Recorder of Liverpool had presented Father Nugent with a cheque for £1000 to reimburse him for the costs of a holiday abroad. This holiday had been an extended convalescence after an exhaustion-related illness in 1878. The people of Liverpool had come to appreciate that his exhaustion and retirement from the scene for those few months was due to his exertions on behalf of the community. Naturally, 'The Catholic Fireside' was fulsome in its praise of him, singling out his work for Tee-Totalism that had gained such ground and brought many benefits during the previous seven years.

Nugent made good use of 'The Catholic Fireside' to fill what he saw as a vacuum in good and decent literary output and to counter some of the pernicious or unsavoury material that many people were presented with by the Media. It was a corrective measure therefore which tried to bring good, wholesome Catholic teaching into the home in a light-hearted and informative way. The cost of the publication was subsidised by advertising and by sales of the parent paper 'The Catholic Times', and its price in 1879 was given as one penny. Nugent aimed to keep it within range of most people's means, though there was a greater problem — illiteracy. Often 'The Catholic Fireside' would be read aloud, where it was intended to be, at the firesides of Catholic families. It bore an ambitious heading as its mission statement: "May Faith, Hope and Charity ring through the world from earth to sea".

The March 31st edition of 1879 contained a lengthy account of John Henry Newman's contribution to Catholicism, thirty-five years after his famous conversion. Nugent never lost an opportunity to appraise the work of his hero Newman for the benefit of the wider community. Again, some may detect an attempt to capitalise on what for many Anglicans would have been a cause of resentment or embarrassment. Yet we may see it more as Nugent simply taking the opportunity to strengthen Catholic resolve by putting forward the example of prominent figures in the Church. There was no more prominent figure at that time than Newman; he was known to be on the verge of being named a Cardinal.

This same edition of the 'Fireside' gave a summary of Bishops' opinions about the new publication. The views of several Irish bishops were quoted — indicating the wide circulation Nugent had won for it. Bishop Gilooly of the diocese of Elphin said: "I shall not fail to commend it to the clergy". Whilst in England the Bishops of Hexham and of Birmingham respectively are quoted as saying: "No doubt it will do a great deal of good" and "for quantity it is wonderfully cheap, for quality it is promising". The sense of caution, if not exactly dismissal, in these comments, seems clear, though Nugent printed them as proof of the success and a sign of triumphant vindication of his paper. Comment from the Bishop of Liverpool is notably absent.

Despite a health set-back, at this time a potentially serious breakdown, James Nugent was obviously enjoying great popularity and was on a roll with his publishing business. He later added 'The Catholic Family Almanac' (later called the Quarant'Ore Guide) to his portfolio. This continues to be published today as a 'Diocesan Directory'. At the same time, as business flourished – perhaps as a result of Denvir's skills in publicity, and other able assistance - Father Nugent found himself coming under increasing fire from the rival newspaper 'The Liverpool Daily Post'. Its editor, Michael Whitty, though a Wexford man and a fellow Catholic, disliked Nugent, thought him a showman and deceitful and was scathing about 'The Catholic Times' likening it to 'Punch'. He looked for ways of discrediting Nugent whenever he could. He sought to exploit a weakness of Nugent in his lack of accounting and in the fact that the printing press for 'The Catholic Times' and associated publications was in the Boys' Refuge where cheap labour was obtained from among the boys.

Michael Whitty made it a matter of public attention that the press equipment had been bought by Nugent with money meant for charitable purposes, but Nugent would have none of it. He had already stated that he was using his Chaplaincy salary and that the printing press, worth over £700, was purchased with money given him as a personal gift for his use. Meanwhile Whitty accused Nugent of having employed a writer specially to write vitriol against him. The disputes festered for some time and represented one of the less savoury episodes in James Nugent's career, though he did not use his newspaper to attack his archrival in public.

Michael Whitty's death in the June of 1873 put an end to the spats but the two newspapers continued to co-exist in some rivalry for sales and popularity. Whitty's considerable contribution to Liverpool society should not be overlooked in the troubled relationship he had with

Father Nugent. He had been instrumental in his day in establishing the foundations of the modern Police Force and Fire Brigade in England before he returned to his first love of journalism and came to find himself pitted against James Nugent in the more minor conflicts of the Press.

Press-related troubles continued in a different way when in that same year of Michael Whitty's death, 1873, the appointment was announced of Bishop Bernard O'Reilly as third bishop of Liverpool in succession to Alexander Goss. The letter Nugent printed in 'The Catholic Times' in February 1873 was not well received by the new Bishop and created a frosty atmosphere between them thereafter, without preventing the two men from collaborating in a lot of good work for the diocese. (part of the infamous letter in question is printed as an appendix to this book).

It goes without saying that throughout the time that Nugent was editor and owner of the paper there were a great deal of other, much weightier matters than these internal disputes to contend with. Notably, the coming in of compulsory education in 1870 interested Nugent considerably as it meant the lessening of the tensions involved in Charity Schools. There were also many editorials relating to national Catholic pronouncements and activities and of course Nugent used the paper to promote many of his own charitable services. He used it to advertise and promote the 'Save The Boy Campaign' and the Temperance Society which grew into The League of the Cross for Total Abstinence and carried with it all sorts of meetings, fund-raising and the weekly Concerts. All this continued along-side his arduous prison chaplaincy duties, reformatory work, the Boys' Night Shelter and the work of the Emigration Committee.

'The Catholic Times' was an organ of news and information, but it was also a vehicle for change and not infrequently for political and religious change following informed debate, especially when local elections came around. He struggled to keep the paper non-party political in his long thirty year association with it. Yet he did not hesitate to use the editorial power he had, and the publicity potential of the Newspaper to back certain candidates in various local constituencies as the occasion required. Through the paper he gave consistent support, for example to Charles McCardle for his pro-Catholic and pro-Temperance stance!

Whilst dealing in his inimitable way with Stephen Meaney and Michael Whitty in the embattled world of the Press, Nugent had, with some reluctance, accepted the position of Catholic Chaplain to Walton Prison - an historic appointment in that it was the first such posting for a Catholic priest. It was a watershed in his personal outlook on life, and a crucial turning point for his future priestly ministry, but it did not mean he had relinquished his job as Editor.

The influence of the 'The Catholic Times' newspaper continued to be strong. Even in Father Nugent's last year or two of life it proved a useful support to him in his charitable projects. A journalist writing in the 'The Catholic Times' in 1903 reported the event of the Catholic Truth Society meeting in Liverpool and Nugent's speech at St. George's Hall. When his long intervention caused the visiting Cardinal Logue to call for him to stop, Nugent in the full gravity of his disapproval retorted: "Ah be quite man! I would not let my own bishop tell me I was talking too much".

Thirty years before, on 22 March 1873, Nugent used his editorial privilege and command of language to give an ironic and probably ill-judged assessment of the new bishop, Bernard O'Reilly: "from what we know of him we can foretell a most useful and solid episcopal career, We do not expect a brilliancy or that energy and vigour of thought, habit and language, which distinctly marked his lamented predecessor … but a calm, peaceful sway….." Here was an example of how Nugent had over-stepped the bounds of diplomacy and used the privilege of his editorial position unwisely!

Squalor and overcrowding is self evident *(circa 1934)*

Part Two (1863 – 1905)

Chapter 7

A Time to Serve

On January 1st. 1863 Father James Nugent went to Walton Prison, the Borough Gaol as it was then called, for twenty-three years. Luckily for him (and for us!) it was not for a custodial sentence but as Catholic Chaplain that he went there. In 1883 he would look back, no doubt with a mixture of emotions, at what he called his "twenty years penal servitude". Considering he had first gone with great reluctance, which was unusual in him, those long years of prison ministry must have surprised him. They were years that brought untold blessings, sadness, insights and experience that enabled him to develop his pastoral skills and his knowledge of the criminal underworld.

It was a strange but highly significant change of direction or perhaps, more accurately, the providence of God that led him into this phase of his life. 'The Catholic Times' was still occupying much of his time – although he had a growing army of apprentices and helpers in the boys at the Refuge, and he had set his sights on beginning a new mission in the south of Liverpool, in the area of Sefton Park, where he considered the pastoral needs of the people to be acute. He had voiced this idea to Bishop Brown but the bishop had other ideas, and when the Borough Prison Reform Bill was debated in Parliament in 1862 the possibility had been opened up for the first time of appointing Catholic Clergy as prison ministers. Nugent took some persuading that he was the right man for the job and the persuading was done by Bishop Goss and his Vicar General, Canon Cookson, a formidable duo, who may have pointed out that the position carried with it a substantial annual salary of £300. Whether this tipped the balance or just sweetened the pill for Father Nugent we do not know, but he was eventually prevailed on to go to Walton at the beginning of the New Year, 1863.

Note the date – another January 1st. another new start. Typically his term as prison chaplain would end on 31st. December 1885. The exactitude of the dates was characteristic of Nugent, he always needed to complete the year, to round things off, to make a fresh start at the appropriate moment; his preciseness in this was not evident in everything he did. He was still regarded by Bishop Goss as being too hasty and impetuous in the many activities he had undertaken. Goss had got him away for a long recuperation and he perhaps saw the advantage of a new appointment. He could not have foreseen the extraordinary way this work was to unfold.

If Father Nugent was at first a reluctant candidate for a job for which everyone else seemed to think he was most eligible, he threw himself into the new task with customary enthusiasm and energy. He soon found that despite the arduous commitments of the daily round of prison work he had a freedom, almost carte blanche, to develop ideas and plans related to the work and outside the prison walls. He had a busy mind and he quickly acquainted himself with the prisoners' circumstances, their character, background and spiritual needs. He saw the importance of ministering to their families and he was anxious to provide for the catechetical instruction of Catholic prisoners. Later on, his post as Prison Minister would also give him access to the Workhouse where he applied these same concerns. He was encouraged in the first year or so by the fact that his brother, John, had been appointed as first Rector of the mission at Blessed Sacrament, Walton, and the two brothers sometimes offered Mass in the barn that was the first church there.

In carrying out his new tasks he did not completely relinquish his hold on other things. The Catholic Institute was picking up again, ironically, after he ceased to be the Director of it. It was on a new footing and the shadow of financial irregularities which had hung over it had been lifted. The strain of trying to maintain the success of the C.I. told severely on Nugent's health and, though reluctant to let go, he perhaps sensed it would be better off in hands more adept than his in management. A good staff had been put in place there, including three priests: Henry O'Bryen, Peter Laverty and Henry Thrower. Nugent had handed over the role of Principal to Father Henry O'Bryen in 1861. It was no longer his 'baby' but he kept an active interest in it, gave lectures there and cast a supervisory eye on things even if a more distant one. Just to be sure though, he had put the whole enterprise under the patronage of his hero, St. Philip Neri, and secured the connection between the C.I. and the Chuirch of St. Philip's in Catherine Street which would be the chaplaincy base and from where the parish priest would have an active role in the spiritual care of the Institute's students.

Aware of the possibilities that a salary of £300 could mean, James Nugent began to look ahead to the advantages of his new position. Some have seen in him a calculating man. This may have some justification but his calculating mind hardly amounted to selfishness or self-aggrandisement. He could make use of the extra capital for his charitable projects like the Boys' Refuge, the Girls' Orphanage and the work of the Notre Dame Schools. The money did not always bring him peace of mind (does it ever!) Certain members of the Town Council and the other Churches were bitterly opposed to the idea of the Catholic Chaplain receiving a salary at the expense of the rate-payers. Something of this resentment would surface several times in the years that followed, evident a long time later when the cry of "Rome on the Rates" was heard, in a scarcely disguised anti-Catholic attitude to the school buildings programme.

Nugent's salary was not drawn from the ratepayer but from Court fees. It represented, in those days, a considerable sum of money and it soon ceased to be an issue when it became clear that Nugent was putting it to good effect. He himself reflected that it was his experience of the plight of young criminals in Prison which, as he said, "prompted me to deal with crime in its infancy" that led to the setting up of a trust for reforming ex-prisoners and finding new situations for them when they transferred from prison back into society. He would use some of his own money to help in this. Even more important than rehabilitation was the means of preventing youngsters coming to prison in the first place. He was a great believer in the old adage "prevention is better than cure" when it came to juvenile crime. He looked for ways of diverting certain individuals from prison or the workhouse and so often took on the role of advocate in the courts. This would be one of the services that his successors would continue in the Society he later founded.

Inside and outside the forbidding prison walls, Father James Nugent embarked upon a ministry that was to set him apart in the history of the Catholic Prison Service; a pioneering role which would set the pattern for other such appointments around the country, and the start of a long tradition of excellent service by Catholic clergy. Once again, Nugent was at the centre of history in the making. Walton, the Borough Gaol, was one of the largest of its kind in the country and had the highest 'population' of male and female prisoners. Nugent's own calculations soon confirmed the fact that it was the only prison in the country where female offenders outnumbered the males. His natural interest in statistics (a very Victorian obsession) developed gradually into a phenomenal knowledge of prisoners and their ways, of prison life, and the criminal mind, which he frequently put to good effect in speeches and in reports he gave to Select Committees for Prison Affairs in London. All this was before the psychological insights into the criminal mentality had become possible. Often Nugent's views were rejected or little understood by the prison authorities. He was ahead of his time in his insistence that criminal tendency was induced by circumstances and environmental influences, not something innate.

The system of Prison referrals was crude at this time, with far too many convicted and imprisoned without proper trial and of course without the benefit of legal representation. For the poorer classes in particular it was often a case of a summary trial, regardless of the nature of their offence and usually without any regard to age. Nugent found himself the spiritual father of a host of young offenders, men and women who came to the Prison off the streets, not appearing once but many times before the courts. Chronic offenders and recipients of repeat sentences, with no opportunity, means or even will power to get out of the cycle of crime, concerned Father Nugent greatly.

That the streets were the school of crime was now something he was more acutely aware of than ever, from his vantage point within the prison system. There was little that could be done to "deal with crime in its infancy" whilst this intolerable situation continued. Lucky ones went to the workhouse; the more unfortunate ones were deported for a life of hard labour abroad. Perhaps Nugent's instinctive empathy with the luckless juvenile offenders was increased by the knowledge that he himself had been lucky in his family and upbringing, with all the advantages of a good home and loving parents. Perhaps too, his own initial reluctance about being prison chaplain gave him a sympathy with the hapless victims who came within the prison walls. He not only learnt to put this reticence aside but seized with both hands the opportunity to help the inmates at Walton and in the Workhouse at Brownlow Hill.

The fact that James Nugent took full advantage of his Prison Chaplaincy experience can be seen in the wide dissemination of his speeches on "Incorrigible Women" and "Nobody's Children", which were reflections on his prison work and the nearest thing we have to a memoir. He was pressed at one point to write his prisons memoirs but this he knew would infringe prisoners' rights and be an inappropriate betrayal of confidence. Both as Confessor and counsellor in the prison he must have heard many a sad and immoral tale which he was always extremely circumspect about at a time when few people cared about prisoners' rights and confid-entiality.

His concerns about female offenders and what to do about them became a major factor at this time. Some may have questioned his naivety but few doubted his sincerity and enthusiasm for this difficult aspect of pastoral care. He argued vehemently for longer, tougher sentences to replace frequent shorter ones, recommending time for rehabilitation, education and appropriate training for women prisoners so that they could face the outside world. To whoever would listen he preached this message and backed up his opinions with statistics about repeat offenders.

He began to form a knowledge of "every variety of character and disposition" and of "every form of human weakness" in this practical school of the study of mankind (and womankind). In the many places where he spoke or preached he made good use, with his "personal bearing and his vocal power" of the insights gained into the mysteries of criminal life at Walton Prison. A refreshing lack of condemnation or judgementalism characterises Father Nugent's comments on prisoners. Among his most memorable phrases would be the words "take them gently by the hand" and "speak a kind word to them". However, there was an iron fist inside that velvet glove. He talked up the strengths rather than the weaknesses of his charges, especially the young ones, and he had a genuine admiration for the quick intelligence and artful nature of some of his prison flock. At the same time he had an uncompromising attitude to reform, to moral renewal, hard work and character building. Insistence on these meant that he was at once respected, admired and even held in awe by prisoners and prison staff. Kind words – but hard sentences, this was the typical double-edged sword of his campaign against crime.

As we have said, statistics fascinated him and he noted the rate of convictions - 10,530 in one year, "of which '6,707 fell to my charge." Apart from giving us the percentage of Catholic prisoners in Walton Gaol at that time this reference in his notebook tells us of his sense of propriety. He was responsible for them, his sense of being a crusading pioneer, so central to his whole life, came through clearly in his prison work, but people were never just objects or statistics. As always, he put his 'earnest efforts' as he called it into this work, going on believing that prevention was indeed better than cure and that striking at the root of the problems in society was more important than devising brutal punishments. Young offenders were, for this reason, his special concern. He was genuinely shocked by the number of female prisoners and the high rate of re-offending, but what was more important than stating the information about numbers inside the prison were the measures Catholics must take to improve this dire situation on the outside.

It was an aspect of James Nugent's ability that he was able to look deeper than most people into the underlying causes and circumstances that led to a life of crime. He kept meticulous records from his own observations and from newspaper cuttings, taking careful note of statistics over time that enabled him to compare the figures and trends from different years and bolster some of the arguments for reform that he put forward. In face of scepticism he was fearless before Government Ministers!

He recorded, for example, that in 1854 there had been 4,097 adult female prisoners in Walton Borough Gaol. Over a period of twenty years this had increased by more than 50% to 6,504. Again, in 1854, first time female offenders numbered 1,341 but the figure had decreased over twenty years to 1,136, a decrease of over 8%. The trend downwards was gratifying but what really caught his imagination was the huge disproportionate rise in repeat sentences for women from 1,754 cases in 1854, to a staggering 4,107 cases in 1874; a rise of around 140%. There was one woman who had been sent back to prison 130 times.

Picture James Nugent pouring over his copybooks. Probably few people were as interested as he was in such figures at that time. His oft-repeated assertion that re-offending and repeated sentences were out of all proportion by 1874 and showed a lamentable failure to grasp the problem, was only slowly acknowledged by others. With the unenviable record of having one of the biggest prison populations in the country, Walton Prison's situation was something James Nugent was at pains to highlight to others. He relayed the figures for the period 1st October 1865 to 30th September 1876 when a total of 13,317 people were committed, of which 6,501 were males and 6,816 were females. This represented a unique situation in Britain at the time.

There is no doubt that Nugent's fastidious monitoring of trends and statistics helped to highlight the plight of Liverpool's prisons and served to advance reforms in the prison system, though we cannot claim too much in this respect. As Catholic Chaplain, the first one in the country, his place was relatively minor. It was the use of his experience though, for the benefit of a wider public, that was so remarkable. Public addresses, at home and in America, about inappropriate sentencing and better understanding of offenders, was something for which he became well-known. He caused a stir with some of his views, such as the assertion that the "Incorrigible Women" were made so by the sentencing of the Courts and not by their own choice.

Such views were becoming noticed and formed the basis of change. The belief never left him that longer prison sentences would give time for the men and women in prison to be educated and reformed for a useful role in society. Many came back to prison again and again because it was preferable and safer than the street. The reasons they were in jail in the first place – drunkenness, prostitution and drink-related crimes of violence and burglary, had underlying causes that needed to be explored and addressed. The sheer scale of the problem obstructed this from happening. Pragmatism was the order of the day and pragmatism dictated shutting them away; 'out of sight and out of mind'.

In a remarkable development of his role Father James Nugent became the mouthpiece of these forgotten ones and the voice of a voiceless generation of young offenders. The job of Prison Chaplain would largely have been a routine one, despite all these interesting and groundbreaking developments. The daily round of the prison wings and his own personal regime of daily Mass, prayer, visits to families and advocacy work in Court, occupied most of his working day. On his appointment he had moved from Rodney Street to number 1 Hornby Street, to a house that was part of the accommodation for Prison Officers. It was from here that he operated as Chaplain and although separated from the Prison itself he lived "within the shadow of its walls", as he put it.

The Prison Chapel became his place of spiritual focus; very different from what he had proudly built at the Catholic Institute. The Prison Chapel was a sombre, impersonal sort of place with separate cubicles for each prisoner and a gallery on three sides where Prison Officers could patrol, armed with truncheons and whistles, watching over their charges from on high. Freedom to worship was rather cruelly compromised by these restrictive measures, but this was typical of Victorian prisons. Celebrating Mass, or speaking words of encouragement to the in-mates must have been a challenge indeed in those circumstances. He would need to draw on all the eloquence and liberal use of gestures for which he had become known if he was going to compete for their attention.

He recorded in his notes special moments of reconciliation or of insight gained from the criminals he met. He recalled meeting a young lad of 20. On entering a cell Father Nugent's eyes looked not at a criminal but a sparkling and humorous eye and a

" face which did not bespeak a bad heart"'. Here was a human being in front of him who had a history, a story to tell. In fact this one had come to Liverpool as a nine year old as a friendless boy drifting around the streets. His case history showed that at the age of fifteen, in a lot of trouble – larceny and theft – he had been transported to Australia for five years penal servitude. It was evident that five years exile had served only to disillusion the boy more and no rehabilitation had taken place.

Father Nugent reflected on his ministry to the youngsters noting the lad's own words "It's no use spending your money and time upon us old guns Reverend...... If you can keep (kids) from being thieves up to the age of sixteen you will find very few take to it after that." Part of the lad's home spun philosophy from the streets was that the pull of others was too strong, few homeless and deprived youngsters could resist the attraction of crime and few would be allowed by their peers to go straight even when if they wanted to. Father Nugent recorded the young man's words with a tinge of sadness: "Dishonesty is a hard crust to eat, Father."

Encounters like this convinced James Nugent that it was the circumstances that led to the criminal mind and not anything inherited or congenital. It was this that persuaded him to approach the offenders in his care in the way he did. He was no soft touch but he looked into the real heart of the prisoners and not just at their criminal record. Quick to condemn vice, he was even more anxious to condemn its causes and the Christian perspective of 'hating the sin but loving the sinner' was something he endorsed. No wonder he recorded many years later what he thought might be a "surprising" statement that "there is no more practical school to study mankind than within the walls of a prison".

From the vantage point of his prison work James Nugent could look back with even greater appreciation to the vagrant children he had rounded up in the streets of the town and who had come to find a home in his Refuge – Nobody's Children he had dubbed them. In London at this time there were over 100,000 of them, in Liverpool there were 48,782 between the ages of 5 and 14, according to the census of 1861. He continued to keep notes in his personal journal of the sadnesses and the high points of his prison ministry, though never revealing names. Perhaps this practice of journal keeping helped him to come to terms with the experiences around him. He saw potential prisoners in the poor, friendless children who knew no other school but the school of crime on the streets. He observed how many of the orphaned children "swarm unheeded about the crowded thoroughfares and along the long line of docks, desolate and homeless wanderers without a heart to love them or a hand to guide them. Poor children of the streets!" He observed them growing up "in the lap of misery as flowers grow amid the mire". He saw a two-fold evil in their lives – vice and sorrow, and even more disturbingly he recognised that "these neglected ones are the seeds of a future generation."

One day Father Nugent was called on to help with a female prisoner who was out of control. She was known to be a trouble maker who had frequented the prison even though she was just under 18 years of age, and had used bad language repeatedly and violent behaviour towards the prison authorities. Prison property had been destroyed and so she had been put in solitary confinement – the dark cell. As Father Nugent came to the door she was kicking it and shouting abuse. Gently he suggested that she whisper instead of shouting. He was perfectly calm. His features, firm and kind, had an effect on the girl. Stopping in her tracks she looked in amazement at the Chaplain in his black soutane. Suddenly she burst into tears. He sat with her and waited until she was more composed, her face swollen with anger and tears. What's wrong he asks softly, after a pause. "Oh Sir, she says, you are the first person that's ever spoken a kind word to me in my life". Something in his manner had quietened her, an unfamiliar feeling of acceptance which in time he was able to build on and so gain her confidence. The only language and treatment she had known was violence and she had met with harsh treatment all her life, but now she had encountered unexpected kindness, hence her tears and the reconciliation that might follow.

It was during this busy and fruitful time in the prison that James Nugent proposed the idea of a Certified Prison Industrial Home. It sprang directly from his view that prison did not serve the interest or needs of many young offenders but rather put them at a greater disadvantage. The reforms of the prison service had not kept pace with some of the many other social reforms of the time. He envisaged a place, removed from the prison ethos, that would serve to rehabilitate and educate young people and equip them with basic skills. Whatever elementary training such a place might offer, the result he foresaw was greater confidence, self-respect, self-reliance and self-control, plus a better chance of a job somewhere. Though he had come to recognise the legitimate role of prison for many offenders, he saw it as totally inappropriate and harmful for certain types of youngsters whose only crime was that they had not had love shown to them when they were children. His view that the Prison regime only hardened the criminal tendencies of the young was not shared by many. The reforming zeal of the likes of Elizabeth Fry had not reached everyone in the prison service.

James Nugent's encounter with the young man who spelt out the harsh lessons of the streets convinced him that there was potential for many if they were taken into care earlier, away form evil influences. The success of the Ragged School, even if short-lived, had shown that a start had to be made sometime and preferably with the very young. It had also shown up clearly the scale of the problem and the derth of educational opportunities.

His mind always seemed to be moving several steps ahead. The idea of an Industrial Home, accredited to the Penal Institutions and regulated by the Church, was not new but it was an innovation for Catholics. In such a separate place the referred offender could be given useful tasks like cooking and baking, cleaning, needlework. The little industries within the Home would be beneficial both to the person and to the community and by far the most beneficial of all would be the laundry. The laundry would become an essential feature of all the Homes Nugent established for girls under the care of Religious Sisters. In such a place and with the right people to care for them he believed erstwhile offenders would flourish into respectable citizens. Changed circumstances would lead to a changed character.

On 15th. February 1865, the newly-appointed Stipendiary, Stamford Raffles, called a public meeting at St. George's Hall, Liverpool, at Father Nugent's request. It was to be the first of several public meetings in what came to be known as the 'Save The Boy' campaign. It was this campaign that brought Father Nugent to centre stage in the fight to help homeless children in Liverpool. Having decided that it was necessary to halt crime in its infancy he was determined to make a concerted effort to improve conditions for the most vulnerable in society.

In a remarkable bid to produce a united front, he succeeded, with the help of Bishop Goss and representatives of all the main denominations in the town, in bringing all sides together on the one platform in a common cause. Bishop Goss was no doubt surprised to find himself sharing the stage with the most vociferous Orangeman in Liverpool at that time, The Reverend Dr. McNeill, together with other leading Protestant figures such as Charles Burrell. There in attendance too was Dr. Martineau, a Unitarian Church leader and well-known preacher. There were Protestants, Catholics, Free Churchmen, Jews and members of other Religious Faiths, all prepared to do battle together against the common foe – child poverty.

With the aid of John Denvir, Nugent cleverly stage-managed the campaign, linking the slogan 'Save The Boy' with an appeal for 'A Million Pennies'. He used 'The Catholic Times' to very good effect in bringing the campaign into people's homes and catching the imagination of thousands in the town, and well beyond the town, so that they all rallied to the flag of 'Save The Child'. With good reason Nugent often proudly recalled this episode in later years in addresses to audiences in America and Ireland.

James Nugent's philosophy that the street children's plight was their misfortune and not their fault, grew strong through his prison experience. He harnessed this belief to the crusade that was now unfolding, a popular crusade in which everyone had a part. He showed that all had a vested interest in saving the next generation from a wasted life, a life "running to waste in the gutters of our great cities". He called on all to fight crime and turn potential criminals into potential citizens. It was a brilliant campaign, in which he had the vital support of Bishop Goss and the expert help of men like John Denvir. It proved more difficult to unite political parties than to bring together the Churches, yet here too he met with a measure of success and growing support, since members of the political parties and Town Council recognised that it was politically expedient to back such a public and popular movement. Nugent appealed to people's consciences and to their hearts. He also appealed to their religious sensibilities as he was not slow to use the pulpit on Sundays to proclaim his message. 'Save The Boy' had a strong resonance with the saving of the soul and not just the body. The strategy worked and the money rolled in.

Meanwhile, in his on-going battle to gain more concessions for Catholic paupers in the Workhouse he was fighting the Select Vestry, an elected group of twenty four local citizens who controlled access to the Industrial Schools and other Institutions. He opposed the discriminatory measures that deprived Catholics access to instruction in places such as the Workhouse. He would have partial success as time went on and a more enlightened approach emerged. There was a constant tension for Nugent between his very open campaign for the child, free from denominational bias, on the one hand,

and fighting the Catholic corner on the other. It was a difficult tight-rope to walk and one which only he would have attempted.

Prison work continued to be the backdrop for much of his reforming work and the base from which he operated. He was a man who saw a connection between things. In his experience, the deprivation of home life from the start led on to neglect, which gave way to street crime, theft, drink and greater crime, imprisonment or even deportation. Somewhere in all this he desired to break the cycle and inject the remedy of education and reform. Of course efforts were being made by a variety of people, local Municipal Council members as well as individual politicians, volunteers, philanthropists, and benefactors. But the problem was vast and complex and there was little co-ordination in the efforts for child welfare. James Nugent is described as leading the way at this time, certainly in the Catholic community in the city, but there was no shortage of voluntary help. He was the catalyst that enabled things to happen and he inspired other people to get involved.

His work at the prison was supplemented by frequent contact with the Workhouse at Brownlow Hill. This, like the prison, had been put out of bounds to Catholic clergy or to Catholic teachers. There was still a lot of paranoia about undue Catholic influence, and the fear of indoctrination was rife. Religious affiliation was never James Nugent's first thought when it came to helping the needy, but the Catholic education of those in his care was very crucial to his mission. The Brownlow Hill site was becoming greatly overcrowded and conditions worsened throughout this period. It was largely due to Nugent's initiative, once he had gained access for Catholics to the Workhouse, that families were reunited on Sunday afternoons and were allowed to go out and get some fresh air. He ensured that cases were reviewed regularly to see if any families could be brought together again permanently rather than be split up.Concessions came slowly and grudgingly.

Part of the difficulty with Workhouses was that they were always a reactive attempt to meet an impossible task. Since the late 18th Century the number of paupers and vagrants had increased dramatically, their numbers swelled by the expulsion of tenants of smallholdings by the land-owners. The bedraggled army of left-behinds from the War of the Roses, and those who succeeded the generation which had been dispossessed by the demise of the monasteries in an earlier era, swelled the number of outcasts that came into the towns. As a result there were far more of the bereft, the misfits and the itinerants in England's high-ways and by-ways.

The Workhouse was a rough attempt to deal with this and, in some ways, an attempt to stamp on it the seal of austerity and authoritarianism so characteristic of the Workhouse ethos. The Poor Law Commissioners in their report of 1837 said: The Workhouse should be a place of hardship, of course fare, of degradation and humility.... It should be as repulsive as is consistent with humanity." They seem to have succeeded in this aim.

As one of the officially appointed priest-Confessors to the Workhouse Father Nugent made every effort to make up for lost time and to ensure a better deal for the Catholics there. The alleviation of physical needs was the starting point for an improvement in spiritual care. To have the chance to attend Mass as a family, having a meal together, relaxation and exercise, away from the overpowering workhouse environment, was something he encouraged as much as possible and he sought changes in the law to achieve it. Despite the title of his report 'Incorrigible Women' Nugent never considered anyone truly incorrigible. Better treatment he believed would bring dividends.

The Workhouse was a difficult Institution to penetrate. For a long time it had presented itself as an impregnable fortress of social control; Protestant in religious outlook, authoritarian in ethos, barred to Catholic Clergy. A board of Governors was responsible for its management and even though the Poor Laws of 1780, 1834 and eventually 1871, successively lightened the heavy hand of gloom in the Workhouses, they remained oppressive and depressing places. They were marginally better than a homeless existence in the streets and at least provided shelter and basic food. Between the years 1834 and 1871 the children formed the largest group of institutionalised paupers – a situation that had been greatly influenced by the laws that made street begging illegal. The Poor Law revision of 1834 created a far more obvious role for the Law Enforcement Officers as a sort of "social police".

Descriptions of the fate of children in Victorian Workhouses are always harrowing, even when improvements slowly came about with the progress of the century. A typical Institution housed groups of up to ten people in a suite of three rooms. There was a separate infirmary or sick bay at the top of the building (presumably, in theory, away from contamination and bad air above the traffic). A bath was a once a week event, new bed linen was provided once a month. Other parts of the building were set up with special purposes such as workshops where boys could be taught simple trades, like bricklaying, tailoring and wheel making. A block for women and girls was used to teach sowing and dressmaking.

In the Workhouse, where, as one contemporary inmate said, "everyone goes to bed hungry" and where human spirits were generally at a low ebb, James Nugent and his Catholic colleagues had a difficult task. The best that could be done was to try to raise spirits, keep people occupied and 'on task', keep them focussed on their religious doctrines and take exercise and fresh air. Nugent insisted on the rights of Catholics to attend Mass and see their priest and their families. Even Sundays in the Workhouse, when dinner included 4ounces of cooked meat and extra bread, were special. Fleeting pleasures in the midst of dire poverty must have seemed like pure grains of gold or a glimpse of heaven.

Nugent found valuable help in two sisters of the Roskell family, Annie and Elisa, and in two of Father Gillow's sisters who took on the task of befriending the families in the Workhouse and offering some Catholic Instruction. Such allies were the secret of Nugent's limited but real success in the care of the poor in prison and the workhouse. Such dedication and care was integral to the parish, and the parish was one of the few organisations willing to help.

Chapter 8

Reform and Training on Land and at Sea

Nugent gave his best efforts to the care of homeless boys and addressed the problem of juvenile delinquents, and these were the focus of the reformatory movement in Britain at that time. Consequently he has been criticised by some who believed his work was so focussed on the care of boys that it failed to offer an equal provision for girls. At the same time there have been those quick to point out that Nugent favoured Catholic children more than other children and so was guilty of a religious bias. Both criticisms arise from a tendency to compare Nugent's time with ours and a failure to appreciate the ethos of the society he lived in. We must see the full scope of Father Nugent's reformatory work.

Comparisons have sometimes been made between Nugent's work in Liverpool and that of Dr. Barnardo's in London. There are obvious parallels. Both made underprivileged children their main concern and both had to battle against criticism. In the 19th Century there were as many detractors wanting to undermine good causes as there were good causes. Stories of Father Nugent turning away Non-Catholic children or failing to refer them to their own denominational institutions, whilst claiming to be non-discriminatory on grounds of creed, nationality or social background, were often a fiction made up by opponents. Dr. Barnardo's Homes had to face similar allegations. From our modern standpoint of equal opportunities and social inclusion we tend to make false judgements about earlier eras and for that reason, as the saying goes, 'comparisons are odious'. Today, the issues surrounding denominational schools have not gone away but are often under discussion and time will tell if the climate is right for change. One common factor between our own time and that of Nugent is his desire to nurture and strengthen in young people an understanding and love of the traditions of their own Church and Faith whilst respecting the right of others to do the same.

The history of Catholic reformatory work in Liverpool may help to put this into perspective. The Christian mission has always been subject to misrepresentation and no system is perfect. The best intentions can be misinterpreted and mistakes can take away from the general purpose for good. Nugent experienced this many times in his career. Sometimes projects were not properly thought through and came unstuck, sometimes there was a lack of proper management and sometimes he was let down by other people. Whatever criticism Nugent may have had to deal with in his time it was a wholly superficial view of him to say that he neglected the pastoral care of girls in his charitable projects. From the very beginning the education and welfare of girls was every bit as important to him as that of boys and this became more evident with his increasing concern for the plight of young women in Walton Prison when he became the Catholic Chaplain there. In what was arguably his greatest speech entitled 'Incorrigible Women' (printed as an appendix to this book) he highlighted the special problem of women prisoners, especially of repeat-offenders, and outlined ways of helping them.

The efforts to secure the help of Religious Sisters to provide education, training, and formation for girls, not only for domestic service but for other worthwhile work in the community, demonstrated Father Nugent's anxiety over the proper care of girls and his wish to find long-term solutions to the question of their education. This central aspect of his work went hand in hand with his ideas for reformatory provision arising from his prison experience. Above all he encouraged any measures that looked at preventing young women and men from being sent to prison with inappropriate sentences. "Prevention is better than cure" was his guiding principle.

The 1854 Reformatory Act in Parliament had gone some way to ensure that boys under 16 years of age might be spared a custodial sentence and referred to Reformatory Institutions instead. A Government grant for each boy referred to recognised Institutions made the idea an attractive one to the Courts and Nugent was a supporter of these new laws. It was to the male population that jobs at sea or trades in industry and agriculture were usually available and naturally Father Nugent looked for ways in which boys could be helped to access these jobs. Whether or not females came off second best in Father Nugent's estimation, it is a fact that his support for the idea of a Catholic Reformatory, on land or on the River Mersey, in the shape of a Reformatory and Training Ship, arose out of the acute need for accommodation and appropriate training for delinquent youths.

The problem of delinquency among Catholic boys had increased in the decade or so before, and the Bishops had expressed concern about it. One factor may have been the great influx of the late 1840s and the effects on the children of the immigrant and exiled generation. Nugent would later draw on his experience with the Training or Reformatory Ships to illustrate effectively his message at the heart of the "Save the Boy" Campaign, giving spirited renditions to his listeners of the scene of a drowning boy being saved by one of his shipmates. Although it may be argued that he never campaigned under an equivalent slogan to "Save The Girl" the spirit of the whole campaign and the Appeal was in fact intended in a general way as one in favour of "Saving The Child".

Whilst attending an important and ground-breaking meeting at the Public Hall in March 1863 in Wigan, his former stomping ground, James Nugent found strong support for the idea of establishing a Catholic Reformatory in the town of Liverpool. Since his brief time as parish priest in St. Patrick's Wigan he had kept an interest in events there. He told the gathering that Catholics "formed a large and significant body of the working class in England" and that they were "subject to the vicissitudes of trade and from this circumstance they must, of necessity, present a large proportion of the crime". The link between circumstances and crime was a point he never tired of repeating, rejecting the view that the criminal condition was something inherited at birth and stressing that it was influence and circumstances which bred it. This was still not a generally accepted view at that time. He went on to express the regret that over the years Catholics in general had not put their full weight behind the movement for reform or familiarised themselves with the true extent of the problem.

Nugent always prepared meticulously for meetings and came armed with hard facts to back up his comments. On this occasion he recorded that he had twenty-seven boys in Walton Prison under the age of 15, of which twenty-six were Catholics. He attracted great cheers from his audience when he declared that he was not one to cloak the true reality of the boys' plight and the sad state of affairs because, "the sooner they (Catholics) bestirred themselves with manly energy to grapple with the difficulties that surrounded them the more would they be respected and the higher would they hold their heads in a civil point of view." He urged, as he had often done already in other speeches, that Catholics take their stand as citizens making it clear to the public "they had no other object than the common good." He believed that Catholics had a crucial role in forming citizenship and still had to prove this to a sceptical, often antagonistic, public. He proposed a collection (of course!) at that evening's meeting for the setting up of a Catholic Reformatory and an annual levy to sustain it. Funding was always the last part of any appeal in Nugent's campaign speeches. Gradually, the idea of a reformatory ship on the Mersey began to form.

The use of ships anchored offshore as training vessels was already well established in a place like Liverpool with its maritime heritage. The idea seemed to commend itself naturally. A Training Ship was perceived, by some people at least, as both useful for training a boy for a life at sea and as a general discipline for juveniles who might qualify for other jobs as responsible citizens, whether on land or at sea. Reformatory schools and 'colonies' were already widely recognised by the mid-1860s as part of the overall reform programme, using the land on Farm Schools, as alternatives to ship reformatories. Yet something caught the imagination when it came to the idea of a training vessel, even if it was not suitable for everyone. The Anglican Church in Liverpool had organised one such ship, 'The Akbar'; the introduction of a similar vessel for the Catholics was something Father Nugent had been considering. 'The Akbar' that served as the Training ship for the Protestants would soon find a sister ship in the form of 'The Clarence' anchored off New Ferry.

The leader of English Catholics, Cardinal Nicholas Wiseman, on a visit to Liverpool in 1858, enquired if a visit to the 'The Akbar', which was anchored off-shore in the Sloyne Estuary, could be arranged. He was taking a keen interest in Father Nugent's innovative ideas for Catholic education and remedial training, and the idea of a Reformatory Ship for Catholics appealed to him. 'The Akbar' had proved to be a reasonably successful venture, though it had not been without its problems, and the seeds of an equivalent plan for a 'Catholic' ship gained ground (or perhaps held water!) with the crucial support of Liverpool's Bishop Goss. He had decided to take forward the work of his predecessor, Bishop George Brown, in strengthening moves for a branch of the Catholic Reformatory Association in Liverpool. Father Nugent was to become its Secretary, and it was bishop Goss who headed the drive for fundraising in Liverpool, Lancaster and Salford dioceses. The sum of £2,211 raised from this first trawl for funds was sufficient to be able to go ahead with the reformatory work.

Awareness of the problems that gave rise to the need for

the Reformatory Association was increasing quickly. As early as August 1860, Bishop Goss had stood on the stage of the Concert Hall in Liverpool's Nelson Street, outlining his ideas for a 'Catholic Training Ship'. He did not hesitate to point out that Liverpool's principal source of revenue came from the sea and the river, and it was in the town's interest to support a project that would one day equip more young men with the skills of the sailor or Merchant Seaman. At meetings of the Chapter, which comprised the Bishop's group of Consultors, opinion about the Clarence project was cautiously favourable but the Chapter asked that land-based reformatories were also considered. The Birkdale Farm School was one example some years later (this became The Thomas More School). Financial backing from the Blundell Family helped the Farm School project along. Such endowments made an idea into a reality. Still more support was forthcoming for 'The Clarence' project when it became clear to the Borough authorities that such a vessel would take juvenile male offenders off the prison roll. The benefit would be widely felt as boys could be referred from prisons as widespread as Liverpool, Chester, Manchester and Salford.

It seems the Bishop's powerful plea in Liverpool reached the ears of the Admiralty in London, perhaps with a little help from Liverpool's friend Cardinal Wiseman, and from there came a donation of £10,000, specifically for the refurbishment of a frigate for the agreed purpose. 'The Clarence', a ship built in Pembroke and in service as a gun ship since 1827, was now within the grasp of the Reformatory Association Committee. Nugent's dream looked like being realised after all and the appeal at the Concert Hall in Liverpool in 1860, which officially launched the project, raised £800. Yet despite initial enthusiasm, there would be a gap of three years before 'The Clarence' itself could become a visible reality on the river.

The Clarence, an 84-gun Line Battle Ship registered at 2,279 tons, had been named after the Duke of Clarence who had launched it when he was First Lord of the Admiralty. He could not have envisaged then that it would become a household name in Catholic circles and still be remembered a century and a half later in the name of one of the Schools of the Nugent Care Society. Its arrival in the area on the appointed morning, towed down the river following its journey from Davenport to Sandon Dock for refitting, was an event that attracted considerable excitement and interest from a large group of onlookers. Father Nugent might have been put in mind that day of the time he had watched the first Steam Ship leave the Clarence Pier for America when he was 15 years old. This for him was an even more important piece of history in the making.

The refurbished ship could accommodate 250 boys but until it was ready the boys were put on board 'The Akbar, at the Catholic Reformatory Association's expense, or at the Farm School in Newton-le-Willows. They had not got long to wait and the first boys went on to 'The Clarence' on 15th August 1864, no doubt with a mixture of excitement and apprehension. Whether they knew it or not they were guinea pigs in an experiment that would have very mixed results.

It was never expected that the Reformatory Ship (Nugent preferred to call it a Training Ship) could house all the young delinquents and offenders referred from the various institutions. For this reason the Farm Schools remained an important part of the overall reformatory provision and Agricultural establishments, of a kind that had existed for some time on the Continent, had been used to provide an antidote to the crime-related problems found in the city where bad behaviour seemed to be encouraged by the environment in which boys lived. The 'Farm Schools' gradually became an accepted part of the over-all provision for youngsters in this category, and, though not without their drawbacks, they were often supported by generous endowments and the help of local landowners like the Blundell Family.

There had been a tradition on the Continent of Europe for the great Monastic Communities to make provision for criminal reform. The discipline of life-style and the underlying ideals of the religious vocation went hand in hand with a belief in the forgiveness of sins and correction of life-style. The care of the marginalised and the outcasts of society was part of the vocation of many Religious Communities. In the early 1850s, as the delinquency problem grew and attitude to crime and to prisoners hardened, the idea of reformatory work grew in England too. New possibilities for a hard pressed Reformatory Association were considered. The 'Colonie Agricole' Movement in France found a favourable reception with the Abbot of Mount St. Bernard's, Abbot Burder, who welcomed the idea of a reformatory colony at the Abbey in Leicestershire. The Cistercian Abbey of La Trappe, in France, had successfully introduced the idea of an Agricultural Colony there and Abbot Burder was enthusiastic about bringing the idea to his own Community.

Agricultural Schools already existed in some parts of the country as an alternative to the penal institutions and workhouses in the towns. Juvenile Delinquents were, understandably, frowned upon by polite society, detested by the police and mistrusted and avoided by almost every one else. There was a growing generation of outcasts and disaffected youngsters attracting notice. Getting problem children out of harm's way, far away from the environment that led them into crime, became a priority for local authorities. Passing the problem on to someone else was often the ulterior motive.

By the early 1850s the idea took shape in Abbot Burder's mind to create a reformatory in the grounds of the Monastery of Mount St. Bernard. It may have appeared a surprising location for a reformatory school and certainly not all the monks of the Community were convinced of its practicality or its virtue. Yet the monks of Mount St. Bernard worked the land and the cattle farm in the surrounding area as part of their daily rule of life; they followed (as they do today) a regime of work and prayer. It was true that they could offer something important to these unfortunate youngsters whose lives had been devoid of all discipline, love, family and religious faith. Didn't the charism of the Cistercian Order specifically include the care of the neglected and marginalised of society? Yet, there was also concern that the tranquillity needed for the contemplative life might be compromised in some way by the new proposal. Dom Burder believed in the rightness of the project and recalled the Benedictine ideals of educating people in the faith and of hospitality to the poor. He pressed ahead with his plans.

His plans entailed using the original monastery buildings which had become redundant when the new monastery was built. From the ruins of the old emerged a new venture which came to be called 'St. Mary's Agricultural Colony'. Although the misgivings of some of the monks remained, the idea gained sufficient support generally to attract funding for the renovation work that would adapt the old buildings for their new purpose. Under the direction of Abbot Burder, a convert from the Anglican Church and filled with zeal for the Catholic cause, plans were enthusiastically set in hand so that by 1855 notice was given in the area of the intention to set up the Agricultural Colony to which juvenile offenders would be referred. Financial backing came through widespread appeals, despite some reluctance expressed by the local inhabitants who eyed the new project with some scepticism and perhaps some trepidation.

The boys who were destined to come to The Colony were from prisons or penal institutions and reformatories of various kinds, mainly in the north of England and notably from the dioceses of Salford, Birmingham and Liverpoool. In the opinion of most people they were the offal of society, but at The Colony they could find a welcome, a home and a new chance in life. It was for these Catholic youngsters a chance of a new beginning, their

Second Spring. The Colony eventually opened its doors to the first group of them in 1856 and although the project was to have its share of woes and bring considerable heartache to Abbot Burder and the local community, it served a useful purpose for the limited time that it flourished. Although nothing remains of St. Mary's Colony today, except a small area of land marked with a wooden memorial cross indicating the burial place of 42 of its erstwhile residents, a partial record of its brief history is extant in the Monastery archives.

Several of the young men who were sent to the Colony between 1856 and 1881 were referred from the Catholic Reformatory Association in Liverpool and Abbot Burder travelled to Liverpool to speak with the members of the Committee there. At first there was not unanimous agreement about the details of the scheme. Bishop Goss had serious reservations about sending boys to The Colony. What irked him most was in fact the amount of money required in fees, and he warned – rightly as it turned out - that costs would only escalate in the future. The other stated reason for hesitating was the doubts he had about the idea of sending rough town boys, whose lives had revolved around the streets, the docks, and the seaport of Liverpool, into a life in the country. He believed the transition would be traumatic.

At a meeting of his Diocesan Chapter on April 15th, 1863, it was clear that the costs were the real sticking point and after lengthy discussions the go ahead was reluctantly given, bearing in mind the Bishop's support for the Reformatory Committee, to pursue the idea further, subject to an agreement that a share of the costs would be paid by the Monastery. A collection in all the parishes of the diocese was proposed and a general note of caution was sent by the Chapter to the effect that the increasing number of reformatory projects all requiring finance, all with their particular demands on resources, must be curbed. It was a warning shot across the bows of Father Nugent and the Reformatory Committee.

There are a few indications of what life was really like at St. Mary's Agricultural Colony in Leicestershire. Boys of various ages were given basic residential accommodation and enrolled in a programme of formation, spirituality and education. While working on the farm, they were given the necessary clothing and all members of the Colony were given a uniform and a badge to wear which bore the initials 'AC' (Agricultural Colony). A sense of identity and belonging were imposed from the start. The alienation and lack of discipline these boys had experienced in their lives was corrected by this approach which treated them with dignity but with a firm hand. They were now part of a new family but the rules must be strictly adhered to. On arrival at The Colony they were given a registration number, a health check, a bath, and then were issued with their rough woollen uniform, which was distinct from a prisoner's outfit but retained something of the same purpose. They were then ready for the new life in the Colony.

Wherever these youngsters might go a cloud of rejection hung over them, and the stigma of being 'criminals' and 'offenders' stayed with them through life. Opposition to them also contained an element of religious prejudice. It is clear from the records of that time that some of the activities of the boys of the Colony did not endear them to everyone. On June 6th. 1858, the Rector at All Saints Church in Loughborough, gave a sermon in church in which he expressed his displeasure at the practice of "parading the young criminals" as he referred to them, "dressed out in some form of uniform different from a felon's uniform, through the neighbouring towns, with bands of music and colours flying, to be subsequently regaled with plum pudding and roast beef." The Rector complained that there was an injustice in criminals getting a better deal than hard-working respectable citizens and noted that the cost of keeping men in English prisons amounted to more than the ordinary man's income for the year.

The real cause of indignation was based more on

religious rivalry than anything else. The objection was to the conspicuous way these Catholic lads were marching in procession through the area and the Rector believed it was not for the sake of the delinquents but "to bring into prominent notice the operations of the Roman Catholic Church". These unwelcome excursions were thought to show what he regarded as "a singular lack of sound wisdom and discretion" on the part of that Church and, by implication, on the part of the Abbot himself.

Such a project, even if it had its critics, was very much what Father Nugent wanted in his plan for young offenders. The combination of a safe home, a house away from the evil influences of the streets, avoidance of prison or the workhouse and the chance of a Catholic education enabling them to come back into the community, all of these things were of the essence for Father Nugent and the Reformatory Association. He believed passionately in a rule of life as part of a road to responsible citizenship; duty to God and the elevating power of work were to be the watchwords imprinted on his heart and on his epitaph. Where most people saw only the pitfalls of bringing juvenile delinquents into an environment they had not chosen and imposing on them a way of life, a culture alien to them, Father Nugent appeared to think the other way, looking not for the pitfalls but only at the advantages.

The judgement of history weighs rather heavily against such a project. Today the risk assessment would not permit it. Yet at that time it was sincerely believed by many that the benefits justified both the risks and the costs. Given the dire situation in which these young boys had struggled to exist it is likely that many, on reflection, had much to be thankful for in the Colony. Others benefited too, the local landowners had extra hands to work on the farm and the Abbot, if not all the monks in his community, held the view that they were engaging, and seen to be engaging, in a work of mercy that served and enriched the wider community. Abbot Burder's rose-tinted view of the matter, and his evident optimism, was backed up by realism and enthusiastic effort. No enterprise aimed at reform was going to be plain sailing. Which brings us back to the Reformatory Ship on the Mersey.....

The Clarence Ship project took a while to get afloat. It was some eight or nine years after The Colony in Leicestershire had started that the Training Ship plans were fully operational. Even then, in the early stages there were teething troubles with 'The Clarence', signs perhaps of deeper, troubled waters ahead. In some instances there were very serious faults too and inadequacies that not only put youngsters on The Clarence Ship at risk but also led to tragic loss of life. Yet the good elements in both types of project, the Agricultural Farm School and the Training Ship, may now be seen as part of a sincere and concerted reformatory effort and should not be judged too harshly. Whilst these projects developed, back in the towns like Liverpool, girls were being referred to Institutions run by Religious Orders, such as The Good Shepherd Sisters and the Sisters of Charity. Whilst taking an active interest in The Clarence project Father Nugent was not unaware of the need to support the work of the Sisters.

The Sisters took their role very seriously and with utter commitment. History owes them a debt of gratitude for so many things. In most of the Homes, laundries were located to provide a useful service to the local community, and an occupation for the girls - far preferable to languishing in prison or in a house of ill-repute. The principles operating in the Girl's Homes were the same as those for the boys – work to occupy them, an ordered and strict life characterised by daily routine and prayer. A uniform or pinafore, regulation shoes and linen hat were worn. The Reformatory Movement was quintessentially Victorian in its ethos and its aims and this approach to orphanage care and reform work in the Catholic Church, as in other Churches, was typical of its time.

On the River Mersey, the 'The Clarence' Training Ship came to provide yet another key element in the development of Bishop Goss's vision for the Children's

Charter he had so energetically set out to establish. Before the statutory provision of schools, religious groups like the Society of Friends, The Salvation Army and the Baptist Church had offered basic education for the very poorest and the advent of Reformatory Schools had highlighted the extent of the need. Such schools were already functioning on the Continent, especially in Germany and France. At home there was scepticism about where funding would come from. Inevitably this had to be drawn from voluntary and charitable sources until Parliament passed the Reformatory Schools Act in 1854, which led to a more centrally funded method. In this period of experimentation in reform and child rescue work it was largely a matter of the combined voluntary and statutory bodies, the Town Council grants, private grants and spontaneous or annual subscriptions which helped to produce much needed funds, whilst this effort was urged on with enthusiasm by the officials at court, who were overwhelmed with referrals.

Nugent had learnt to tap in to all available resources in his endless quest for funding. Ever since his Blackburn days when he raised money for the Irish Fund his skill in this had become legendry. The boys who had gone aboard 'The Clarence' in 1864 were aged between 11 and 15, and the average length of stay on the ship would be about three to four years. It would be costly. The expectation after that time was that they would either go to sea, earning their living with the Merchant Navy, or be found some other employment at sea or ashore. The Reformatory Association believed it was an investment for the longer term.

The Superintendent of the newly equipped 'Clarence' was Naval Captain Edward Algar who had already played a prominent advisory role in the negotiations to acquire 'The Clarence'. He literally ran a tight ship; the boys and staff were disciplined and well-drilled. Reports for the end of 1865 indicate that 180 boys were accommodated that year and a schoolmaster, Mr. McGovern, was appointed to supervise the lessons in basic subjects like Geography, Maths and English, whilst manual skills of carpentry, tailoring, seamanship and shoemaking were also taught. It was important to Bishop Goss, Father Nugent and members of the Catholic Reformatory Association, that the spiritual welfare of the boys was not neglected and this was mainly looked after by the Bishop of Shrewsbury in whose diocese the ship lay at anchor. He acted as Chaplain to the ship, following the pattern already in place for the Akbar which was regularly visited by the Anglican Bishop of Chester under whose authority it lay.

Nugent was a frequent visitor on the 'The Clarence' and he and his colleagues began to assert their independence in the matter, working to lift restrictions placed on Catholic instruction which had applied in earlier times. Catholics should be free to look after their own. There is clear evidence that in regard to the Clarence Ship Nugent followed his usual policy and brought on board influential and wealthy benefactors, allies in support of the project, to bolster publicity and morale. In the case of 'The Clarence' he enjoyed the invaluable support and financial help of Samuel Smith, a local MP and philanthropist, who had warmed to the project and gave it his full personal backing.

The year 1866 was a good one for the Clarence project. During that year the ship fulfilled its purpose and forty-three boys graduated and were sent to sea as the first batch of equipped sailors with the basic skills of their trade. Nine of these eventually returned home to Liverpool with excellent reports from their employers. Others found a permanent life at sea, a few returned in ignominy or were never heard of again. Financial support for the ship continued to come from Liverpool Corporation in the form of one shilling a week for each boy sent to 'The Clarence'. Morale was boosted by the visits of high profile dignitaries like the Duke of Edinburgh and the President of the Board of Trade. Father Nugent always saw the benefit of this type of visit as an exercise in breaking down the barriers of

Class and status which he believed was a vital part of reform and renewal.

As might be expected, things were not to remain entirely ship-shape on 'The Clarence'. Running repairs had to be made, at extra cost, to the moorings which were often in danger of breaking loose. More serious problems were soon to follow. 1870 was to be a dark year for the project. It saw the deaths of nine shipmates from Consumption. A health inspector (the bane of Nugent's life) revealed an acute need for improved ventilation on board the ship and a change of diet was also recommended. Porridge, potatoes and Ship's biscuit palled after a while! At times there was too little meat or fruit for the boys whose busy day on board required a more balanced diet. The correct diet had hardly been a priority for the members of the crisis-wracked Reformatory Committee but now continual monitoring and the need for better safety standards put a further strain on their resources.

The number of boys on the ship was growing, reaching 220 by 1871, and to add to their problems, one night a large Steamer without lights, which had slipped its moorings, drifted silently across the Sloyne in the dark and collided with the 'The Clarence'. There were no injuries and the damage was paid for by the owners of the Steamer, but already the Reformatory Association, under pressure from Bishop Goss, was looking for alternative places to send some of the boys with less aptitude for training and less suitability for a life at sea. There was need for greater scope for the different types and ages of child. Father Nugent and his colleagues worked hard for the establishment of a Farm School at Birkdale, then a rural area between Liverpool and Southport, and a house was opened there on March 9th 1872. Twenty-six of the boys from the 'The Clarence' were rehoused there.

Before these Clarence troubles had unfolded, the good will of the Community at Mount St. Bernard in agreeing to take 200 boys from Liverpool, and some from other urban areas in the north, was being sorely tried. Members of the Community, who had, in the spirit of Christ, tried to set aside anxieties and objections to the plan for The Colony, were later to rue the day their Abbot took the decision on their behalf. A sum of £2000 was paid to the Monastery for the boys but the cost of looking after the youngsters would prove to be more than twice that figure. Bishop Goss, having expressed his great reservations about the transaction was beginning to see his forebodings realised. The Colony building, which was close to the new Monastery and which had been opened, appropriately perhaps, on Ash Wednesday, the 6th February 1856, had proved to require £4000 to restore it for its new purpose, - a figure that was likely to rise still further. But many people, rich and poor, gave generously to the project and among the donations recorded in the list of subscribers is that of Father John Henry Newman, who donated the sum of five pounds.

As Secretary of the Reformatory Association, Nugent would certainly have had direct involvement in the arrangements to send boys to The Colony at Mount St. Bernard. He was keen to find ways of literally 'farming out' any of the boys who could be provided for in this way. Perhaps no one really foresaw the real costs or dangers inherent in the project, with the possible exception of the wise and wily Bishop Goss, but the willingness to give it the best effort is to the credit of those who took it on despite the potential difficulties. As ever, Father Nugent's unshakeable belief in the effectiveness of reform bound him to the project. Of course he would, as often before, leave others to carry the can at times!

The Managers of the Colony were members of a Third Order community of the Cistercians, a status conferred on them by the Abbot, and they were known as the 'Oblates of La Trappe'. After an initial time of responsibility for the new venture they relinquished control to the Rosminian Order, but tensions and difficulties continued to haunt the new venture. Disagreements about the running and the purpose of The Colony, and grievances voiced by the local residents who were being inconvenienced and harassed by the boys, who attacked local property and caused disturbances, eventually came to the point where civic and parliamentary figures approached Church authorities in England who approached Rome and Pope Pius IX. In due course he ordered an Apostolic Visitation to take place to restore order. Scandal in the Catholic Church was at issue here and the Pope was perhaps still eyeing tentatively the Catholic community in England.

Abbot Burder finally resigned his care of the Colony in the December of 1858. In spite of the mixed fortunes experienced up to this point, it would have been a big consolation to Abbot Burder that an inspection around this time or shortly afterwards, gave a strong commendation which said that for such a large school with such a specialised purpose: "there is much to justify the hope that it may yet become the best and most successful school of its kind as it is the largest Catholic establishment of its kind in England".

Following Dom Bernard Burder with a worthy successor to run the school was hard. He had established it as his own project, mainly with his own driving force, and, of course, gave it into the power of God in prayer. It must surely have cost him a few sleepless nights. Nearly 300 boys had been housed there, including a large contingent from Liverpool and other north west towns.

In 1859 The new Abbot at Mount St. Bernard, Bartholomew Anderson, faced multiple difficulties, not least with internal differences and misconduct among the management group itself. Responsibility for the overall care of the school went through a series of different hands as the Abbey deferred to the diocese of Clifton and then to the diocese of Salford. The motivation and driving force for its continuation in the years that followed came from the top, from Cardinal Nicholas Wiseman in Westminster, who a few years earlier had been bombarded by Abbot Burder by a long and complex exchange of letters that must have kept their respective secretaries busy and bemused. This correspondence had been largely an 'apologia' for the project on the part of Bernard Burder, and requests for support.

By 1862, whilst 'The Clarence' was in full swing in Liverpool, the reports of the Colony as a reformatory School were not so encouraging and there were indications of failure. There were clearly faults in a system that allowed at least 50% of the boys to relapse into ways of crime after their discharge from the school. In April of 1858 a serious outbreak of rebellious misconduct had taken place that gained some adverse publicity. Some of the older boys attacked the staff, and a local police constable, P.C. Challoner, from Shepshed, was called in. He tried to arrest the troublemakers while they were in bed in the dormitory and conduct some of them off to the cells. He was forced to summon special officers from Coalville to assist him and their efforts were met by further indignity as the refractory youths, nerves possibly steadied by alcohol for battle, emptied a torrent of urine upon the unfortunate constables below. The disturbance affected not only the quiet of the Abbey Community but the local people too and eventually came to the attention of the Secretary of State, Sir George Gray, who threatened to withdraw the Government Certificate from the school. Other incidents of rebellion and vandalism came from local areas, including one attack on a local pub, The Forest Rock, which had its windows smashed by a gang of the youths. When the Bishop of Salford, William Turner, took over responsibility for the Colony in the summer of 1863, giving the Abbey a boost in income of an annual rental payment of £200, he secured the first appointment of a master to take charge and try to turn around the situation. Father Thomas Quick was appointed.

Father Quick's undoubted gifts evidently did not include running an establishment like The Colony. His well-meaning efforts were deemed woefully insufficient for the task, especially when further behavioural problems arose the next year, in 1864. The local M.P., Mr. Packe, said of Thomas Quick that he was: "a respectable man and clergyman who wished to manage these unruly lads by mildness and kindness but he was no more capable of managing such an institution than he was of being Governor of Newgate". In all fairness, there would have been few people in the country ready or able to take it on and make a successful go of it. Often, a time of failure and weakness prompts a draconian response, and Salford Diocese appointed a disciplinarian of much sterner stuff to take charge of the Agricultural Colony.

The appointment of Thomas Carroll, a Dublin man, and a layman, brought to the Colony an independent kind of zeal and he ruled the place with an iron hand. By 1870 the Inspector's reports were glowing again. The tough approach had worked, but at a great cost. The place was deemed to be a model of its kind for the whole country, but the price paid for the iron-fisted tactics was that some young men were left brutalised even more than they had been before they entered The Colony. A disturbance had broken out whilst Mr. Carroll was absent and a telegram was sent that led to his return to Liecestershire from London, where he had been attending the National Reformatory Exhibition at which Father Nugent was also present. On his return he set about putting down a rebellion by a rigorous inquisition of the offenders, dealing out to the ring-leaders a severe punishment of beatings using the cat and the birch. The approach was perhaps a model of Victorian discipline but did those whose offences had been 'their misfortune not their fault' (to quote Nugent) really need such heavy-handedness? Perhaps some of the recipients of this harsh discipline may have thought, as they nursed their wounds, that they would have been better off in prison, or at sea, after all?

Notwithstanding the failures of reformatory policy at this time it should be recognised that trades useful to the youngsters, such as tailoring and shoe-making, were passed on to them. Those who wished to make a new start and enjoy their chance of a second spring derived obvious benefits of training in the Reformatory system and, despite the great cost, financial and human, entailed in running them, places like The Colony, the Farm schools and the Clarence Ship brought great advantages to many youngsters. Religious Orders were often preferred by the Catholic Bishops to manage these national institutions and after Thomas Carroll's successful but fierce reign the work was undertaken by The Brothers of Christian Instruction and later by the Institute of Charity, The Rosminians. The high praise that the Colony won in the 1860s waned in the 1870s. Further instances occurred in 1878 and 1880 of boys absconding and the writing was on the wall for the bold venture. The inevitable closure came in 1881.

Over time it became clear to members of the Reformatory Association that Liverpool street children who, from as young as four or five had learnt the precarious art of survival that went with their dreadful plight, and whose experiences around the docks and the river were "indelibly stamped on their minds" to quote Bishop Goss, took very badly to being sent to schools in the country. Even exiles feel the hurt of further exile. Father Nugent was aware of this; he looked for places nearer home, in surroundings more familiar to these unfortunate souls. This was part of the reason for the pride and joy he took in 'The Clarence' Training Ship. Sad to relate, the life story of 'The Clarence' turned out to be as fraught with difficulties and disasters as the Colony. Nugent experienced great personal disappointment here too and it was obvious there was not an ideal solution, only dogged perseverance, learning through trial and error, falling and getting up again. He had become good at that.

A series of fires led ultimately to the demise of 'The Clarence'. Fire on board ship was quite common and always potentially dangerous, in peacetime or in War. In 1876 the Training Ship 'Warspite' on the Thames, was set on fire by its disenchanted inmates. The General Inspector of Training Ships believed that copycat incidents would follow. His prediction came horribly true and 'The Clarence' was at the centre of one such disaster. In 1880 a boy on board 'The Clarence' started a blaze. Evidence later suggested that he and his accomplices had with cold calculation gathered flammable material over a period of time with the intention of burning the ship down. This fire was put out before extensive damage could be caused. Boys were sent to other Reform centres, including St. Mary's Colony, as an emergency measure. However, in 1884 a far worse incident occurred which led to the total destruction of the 'The Clarence' Training Ship.

The record shows that it was on the afternoon of January 17th 1884 that the fire was started. The 210 boys on board were taken to safety. The ferryboat 'Oxton' was standing by to carry out rescue but an over-officious superintendent prevented it coming alongside 'The Clarence' in time to save it from being burnt to within a foot of the waterline. It sank with its moorings and the only relief was that the moorings, repaired and strengthened by the Reformatory Committee with donations received, held firm and prevented the blazing wreck from drifting across the river to other ships. Such care had saved lives. Understandable consternation among the relatives of the boys over the incident led to recriminations and protests. As so often when tragedy strikes, panic added to the chaos. A large group of relatives would have stormed the evacuation ship 'The Gypsy Queen' that was assigned to help bring the boys off, had the boat not been too far from the landing stage for them to reach it. Efforts were quickly made to secure the redundant building of the Port Sanitary Hospital at Bebbington, on the Wirral, where the evacuees were housed. The necessary certificate was rushed through from the Corporation and in the meantime, a full Enquiry into the fire on 'The Clarence' resulted in six boys being sentenced to five years penal servitude.

Shocked and understandably saddened by the disaster

Father Nugent still refused to give up. He soon set about working with others to find a replacement ship. 'The Clarence' project was one of his most determined enterprises, especially when he had seen the benefits it brought to many young people. With a group of eight volunteers and the support of the Reformatory Association, he acquired from the Admiralty a ship called the 'Royal William', originally a 120-gun ship, but never commissioned by the Navy. The Admiralty, knowing of the previous debacle, which had been a very public affair, wanted insurance monies paid directly to them as the original owners of the vessel. Months of protracted negotiations followed, and it was three years before the 'Royal William' came into service, in 1887, under a new and very efficient boss, Captain E. P. Stratham. A king's ransome of a sum - £6000 - had come from the insurance payout for 'The Clarence' and Father Nugent, not good on relative values of money, naively thought this would pay for the refit of the new ship. The long delay had led to further deterioration of the 'Royal William' so that it was well under the sum needed for the refit and Liverpool MPs got involved in trying to persuade the Admiralty to tone down their demands, but to no avail. A total of £13,000 was required in the end (perhaps over half a million pounds today) to ensure the new project. The lion's share of the costs were to fall to the Reformatory Association.

Yet more obstacles and frustration loomed. The Port Sanitary Hospital housing the boys from 'The Clarence' was suddenly requisitioned by the Local Authority because of the threat of a Cholera outbreak in the area. They were given twenty-four hours notice to quit and find temporary homes until the ship was ready. Patience however was eventually rewarded as the new 'Clarence' took on its young cargo once again and money for improvements in the years that followed was found by subscriptions and collections. A gymnasium, hospital, reading room, carpenters' shop and stores were gradually added to The Clarence mark II in seven years that ensued.

Father Nugent's experience with 'The Clarence' ships gave him plenty of material for his speeches and orations in the course of his charity work, though by the mid 1890s his restless thoughts had turned in other directions again, still with a general eye to rescue work. He was not to enjoy much peace of mind over 'The Clarence'. Money was a constant factor, a continual drag on resources and energy. The Inspector's Report of 1896 criticised the ship strongly, highlighting a high level of absconding, "listlessness and lethargy" among some of the boys, though this improved markedly with changes in the ventilation system. The days of this imaginative project were numbered. Once again, fire was to seal its fate. In the early hours of July 26th 1899, fire was discovered in the hold. The recovery vessel 'Firefly' took off 235 boys and led them to safety; the 'Mersey' ferry steamer was in attendance but with inadequate equipment to fight the blaze. Stiff breezes along the river fanned the flames on the ill-fated Training Ship as onlookers helplessly watched the demise of 'The Clarence'. The boys who had come off the ship were to be seen blowing kisses of ironic affection as they saw their former home disappear in flames. Wearing the only clothing they had left to them they were taken off to find yet another temporary home at St. Anne's school, Rock Ferry, until their transfer to a more permanent home at the St. Vincent de Paul Hostel in Liverpool's Shaw Street.

No overview of Father Nugent's work would be complete without a proper account of his venture into Training Ships. The idea of a battle ship turned into a rehabilitation vessel in peacetime was both symbolic of the movement from war to peace, and at the same time a noble attempt to address the problem of juvenile offenders. There was often a quiet desperation among charity workers in their efforts to keep good-for-nothing children out of prison, out of the workhouse and off the streets. 'The Clarence' was, in a roundabout way, a success whilst it lasted and its story marks one of the highlights of Father Nugent's career and the work of the Catholic Reformatory Movement.

Other developments had meanwhile been taking place, not least Father Nugent's pioneering work with Child Emigration and the adventurous attempts to place orphaned children in a totally new environment where life for them could begin again. He had been central in the work of setting up a Reformatory for Girls at May Place, in Liverpool, in 1876 in an effort to ensure that girls did not miss out in the provision of opportunities, care and shelter – above all that they had the same chances of reform and training as the boys. The Sisters of Charity played a key role in this Reformatory.

Street Trading 1900

Chapter 9

The Old Country and
The New World

On August 18th, 1870, on a warm, auspicious summer's day, Father James Nugent had stepped onto the Princes Landing Stage at Liverpool docks bound for Montreal, Canada. With him were 24 children, boys and girls in equal number – a deliberate statement in itself - who were to be the first ones to go out from the Homes in Liverpool to start another life in the New World. Emigration in itself was nothing new but the decision to take children from Catholic Orphanages as part of an organised attempt to find homes and families for them abroad was a new departure for the Catholic reformatory movement. There was no one more eligible than Father Nugent to pioneer the project, since he had followed the children's progress from the start and shown himself to be a leading advocate of the scheme since its inception. The socio-economic conditions that prevailed in Liverpool since the late 1840s when mass immigration had led to immense shortage of housing, overcrowding, and lack of work that entailed multiple social problems, Nugent had witnessed and understood. He had stated clearly that Liverpool was not prepared for the influx from Ireland. These circumstances formed part of the reason for emigration.

He undertook an extensive nine month lecture tour whilst he was away. He had family in Minnesota where his brother, Joseph, had gone to live and the trip would give him the opportunity to visit the family. He had been supported in his plans for the emigration of children by a number of prominent figures in Liverpool, notably a Dr. Hayward who had pointed out to the local authorities that 2000 orphan children cost them £26,000 a year to maintain

(£13 per child) and that there was a saving, by his calculations, of £5,000 to be made by the emigration of children to Canada. The clear financial equation helped to secure support for the first tentative stages of the plan to be put in place and it was understood that more parties of children would follow in due course, once Father Nugent had been able to find suitable places for them. Emigrant children were not a new phenomenon, it had been known to take place since the 17th. Century, but the Poor Law Act of 1834 had allowed the Poor Law Guardians the freedom to send children, under their authority, to places abroad and so the way was already paved for the Catholic Reformatory Association to proceed. They recognised the advantage of sending selected children from the Industrial Schools who had at least the rudiments of an education and could conduct themselves well.

It was to be a busy tour of Canada and America that would last nine months in all, until the following May. It was during this fruitful time in America that Father Nugent promoted his views about prison reform and training of delinquent youths which had occupied so much of his time over the last fifteen years. Away from the fetid and confining atmosphere of the prison walls where he had spent the last seven years of his ministry, he would be able to recoup his equilibrium, get the benefit of the sea air and have a much needed break, at the same time furthering the work of the Reformatory Association and the emigration plans. The sea had always held a fascination for him since he first looked out on it from his home in Liverpool. Now he had the chance to explore what lay beyond it. It was to be one of many trips to America for him, mostly on lecture tours concerned with reform work, and later with the Temperance Movement.

On board he prepared notes for his talks, having done his homework in order to give his American audience the facts behind his plea for help. In one of his Lectures he told them: "It is estimated that there are at the present time (1870) 350,000 children under 16 who are more or less a burden on the parochial rates. I am sure you will agree that poverty is not a crime but a misfortune. These are poor children and in most large towns there are Parish Industrial Schools for this class. We have one in Liverpool in which there are 1,200 -1,500 children. I brought out 24 of these children with me a few weeks ago, all orphans, 12 boys and 12 girls. They are all well instructed in their religion and their book learning. The girls were all in excellent situations within two days in Montreal, four of the youngest being adopted into the most respectable families where they will be treated as their own children. The youngest boy was 11, the oldest 15. They had all been accustomed to labour, nine of them had trades, they all know how to read and write well and they have all made their Communion".

This description of the children Nugent took with him reveals how anxious he was to show that the principles of the emigration policy which had been agreed were adhered to fully. The parties of children eligible for emigration should be of varying age, boys and girls, literate, instructed in their Catholic faith, attending Mass and the Sacraments. Different situations were to be found for them but always with good and respectable families, families who would treat them well as if they were their own, as indeed they were in a real way. The agreed national policy back in England would allow for children to be properly prepared before they left and in later years a 'Receiving Home' was set up, where possible, in the country of emigration so they would acclimatise and not be left stranded whilst a place was found for them. Southwark Diocese had such a place – New Orpington Lodge in New Brunswick.

By 1902 the organisation of the emigration policy had developed considerably in light of experience and many of the early snags and problems, which undoubtedly caused distress to some children, were avoided. Four Catholic diocesan Emigration Societies amalgamated in 1903 to form one Society, The Catholic Emigration Society established on 24th April that year. Father Hudson who became very well known for the Children's Homes in Coleshill, Birmingham, was its secretary. Here, the happy association of the Sisters of Charity of St. Paul The Apostle with that project, is one of the highlights of the story of Religious Orders' involvement in Catholic Child Care over the years. The Sisters, based at Selly Oak, Birmingham, were put in charge of St. George's Receiving Home, formerly Orpington Lodge, in Ottowa

Canada was favoured as a place for emigration since there were Catholic communities there who would be favourable to the children's religious upbringing and sensitive to the requirements about attending Mass. The farming areas were often favoured, but those not old enough to earn their keep in this way were adopted into other types of family, especially those without too many children already, so as not to be a financial burden and so that they would receive the individual attention they needed from their adoptive parents. The outcome was that Father Nugent and his colleagues had succeeded in turning street children into Home children – as they became known in Canada, with new lives, a new start and new prospects.

Most of the young emigrants settled in Ontario and the region of the western coast and the St. Lawrence River. Though favourable, on the whole, to the children's spiritual welfare, the region's harsh climate made life on the land a challenging one for many of them and whatever advantages they experienced they were no doubt tinged with a sadness and longing for home. The policy in the Westminster Diocese, under the administration of Father Seddon, was to ask local clergy to keep a watching brief over the children when they arrived in their new country, but Father Nugent had instead asked local leading citizens to do this. He felt that it should not just be seen as a Church initiative but rather something in which everyone had a responsibility. He advocated the use of an Agent who could act as a 'go-between' when the children arrived, to smooth the way and report any difficulties. If people were shown to be acting unjustly or neglecting the children they could be subject to a fine. This certainly helped to regulate matters but it did not prevent abuses and individual difficulties.

Not everyone agreed with the idea of emigration, and especially at the beginning many pointed to the pitfalls and dangers of the scheme. Many said -and rightly, as it turned out – that young people would be exploited. There was justified cynicism about the ability of many American families to cope with this type of child, especially teen-agers, or understand the background from which they came. As usual Father Nugent rode the storm and pressed ahead with what he was convinced was right. There were problems but not insuperable ones. He was prepared to see it through and watch the scheme develop. The policy of Catholic child emigration continued into the early part of the 20th Century. Influential in its development was the Bans Report in which one of the protagonists of the scheme, Father Emmanuel Bans, together with Arthur Chilton-Thomas, strongly recommended a coordinated approach among the English dioceses. Their Report of November 17th 1902 proved to be the criteria by which the scheme was measured from then on and Bishop Whiteside, in Liverpool, gave the idea of a single Emigration Society his support.

Ten years on from that watershed in his life when he first went to Canada and America to personally supervise the first 'intake' of children, Father Nugent was in the West of Ireland trying to put into effect a similar scheme for the impoverished population there. He was born and bred in Liverpool but James Nugent had Irish blood in him and his empathy with the Irish people has already been abundantly demonstrated. From very early days his father would have spoken to him of his native land and perhaps had taken him there with the family. On visits to the West of Ireland he had become aware of the great poverty in which many lived. He had long known the problems that had brought thousands to Liverpool's shores. Now the 'Old Country' became the focus of his concern as he set about arranging a policy of emigration, in light of the experience already gleaned in helping the children from the Liverpool Orphanages. He was determined to forge better links between some of Ireland's poor and those living in the New World.

During January and February of 1880 Father Nugent was in County Mayo for this purpose, liaising with local priests and acquaintances. He focussed on Connemara and several times sent reports to the Liverpool Relief Committee, and to the Irish Government, on the state of the poor there. Concentrating on the barren areas of the West, Connemara and Sligo, he highlighted the situation of the people who were the worst off and barely able to survive. Among other things, he advocated, in typical fashion, the construction of harbour walls and sea defences to protect the fishing industry which was crucial to the people's livelihood in that region. He called for the purchase and better distribution of seed potatoes, the staple diet of so many. Whilst in Ireland he wrote a letter in the Irish Press stating that: "The population in places is far too dense to be supported by the poor patches of boggy land interspersed with rocks and stones. There are large districts where the average holdings are three to five acres of the poorest land imaginable and every cabin on such holdings seems to swarm with children". He painted a desperate picture but it helped to alert the public to the situation that had developed.

Others began to get involved in the plans for emigration which became seen by many as a way of resolving the problem. This was to be not just the emigration of individuals but also of whole families in some instances. One of his greatest allies was the unlikely one of James Hack Tuke, a Quaker activist who spread the gospel of emigration with great zeal. Although of different persuasions, Tuke and Nugent had things in common – their Christian names and their enthusiasm for the cause of

Irish emigration. Many of the places Tuke focussed on where in Canada but he greatly assisted Father Nugent in the publicity, organisation and raising of funds for the scheme. Like Nugent he had been to Canada and America, had seen for himself potentially suitable places for families to go.

The Relief Committee and the Irish Government got behind the effort and Nugent also found wonderful allies in America where his friend Archbishop John Ireland of St. Paul's diocese, Minnesota, and Bishop James O'Connor of Omaha, Nebraska, welcomed what he was trying to do. With their help Nugent found in-roads into the territory where families from Ireland would receive a warm and understanding reception. Between them they devised a plan whereby 50 families could settle, whilst James Hack Tuke came to an equivalent arrangement in Ontario, Winnipeg and Dekota. As the first hopeful emigrants set off from the West of Ireland, money having been pledged but not raised, it became clear that Nugent may have acted too quickly – not unusual for him, for despite the money that came from wealthy sponsors and grants from the likes of the Duchesse of Marlborough Relief Fund, which gave £800, the money needed was far greater. An estimated £2000 was required to transport families from Galway to Boston on the main leg of the journey. To make matters worse, many of the pledges were not honoured and Nugent was faced with debts.

This played into the hands of his critics among the Irish Nationalists who opposed the scheme on the grounds that it was taking away the able-bodied, future citizens of Ireland. Nugent parried this with a robust reply in the 'The Freeman's Journal' saying: " To let people drag on in a miserable existence of poverty and every form of suffering when they can by such an effort be lifted up from the misery by which they are surrounded does not show much real patriotism". He believed that the Nationalists were ignoring the wishes of their own people, many of whom wanted to leave and find a new life.

In spite of these difficulties, Nugent's efforts enjoyed some success and in 1881 and 1882 he was rewarded by the knowledge that 309 people (individuals and families) had made their way out to Graceville, Minnesota from their home in Connemara. By means of a much publicised Appeal through the 'Daily Chronicle', a further £800 was raised for the project. All the same, Nugent did not have it all his own way and had to admit the reality of some of the Irish who had gone to America, even in his beloved Minnesota, queuing up at soup kitchens and begging in the streets. The success of the Emigration scheme was not an unequivocal one. Nevertheless, he had tried to make an important link between the old country of his ancestors and the new world where the chance of life was given again, and for some at least it was a chance they did not regret taking. Nugent also saw in this enterprise a kind of reconciliation taking place. The difficulties experienced by the impoverished migrants who had come to Liverpool would not be repeated for this new generation in the New World.

Father Nugent's activities on behalf of emigrants in Ireland are not generally well-known in Liverpool. His own family connections made a strong bond for him in Ireland, he had shown his desire to help very early on when still in Blackburn when he raised money for the Irish Famine Fund, and in some ways he felt he owed his own vocation as a priest to his Irish background. Over time, several members of the Nugent family gave their commitment to the Church in Ireland and in America, including two nieces and a nephew of James Nugent, so that for the Nugents a great deal was both derived from, and given back to, 'The Old Country.'

Chapter 10

Temperance, a Virtue

When Father Nugent was in America for nine months in 1870-1871, five years after the end of Civil War, he met, among many other leading figures, the Mayor of Indiana, in Terre Haute, who had once worked in Liverpool at a foundry on Vauxhall Road. There were many ex-patriots as well as Irish migrants in America with whom Nugent would have been able to exchange thoughts about their old home, and it was the Mayor of Indiana who urged him to become another Father Theobold Matthew, who a generation earlier had persuaded so many in America and Ireland to renounce drink. He was encouraged to go back and work the same miracle for the people of Liverpool. Father Nugent could see for himself how in so many parts of America the far-reaching effects and benefits of Father Matthew's great crusade were evident.

The seeds of the crusade that Nugent spearheaded in Liverpool in the 1870s had been sown by that earlier "mighty work" of the Franciscan priest Father Matthew. The Irish Leader, Daniel O'Connell, had praised him. What had been launched on April 10th.1838 in Ireland as a religious and moral renewal movement had flourished not only in that country but in America and India too. He had famously teamed up with an unlikely partner in the Quaker, William Martin, to take the campaigning ideals far and wide in a common cause to rid society of the root of many of its ills. Crime, immorality and destitution were seen as springing directly from the effects of excessive drinking among both men and women. Of the many crusades that were undertaken all those years ago it is this one that Nugent considered to be his "real work" and the one that resonates most strongly with our own times.

By the year 1843 several hundred thousand people had taken the pledge of total abstinence. Father Matthew brought his message to Glasgow and in July of that year his campaign reached the heart of Liverpool. Matthew found some ready disciples in the Temperance Movement already quite strongly established in the town and could draw on the support of many who approved of the further step of Total Abstinence. In the parish of St. Peter's Seel Street, for example, there was already a group of adherents, and Father Matthew was received by William Rathbone of Wavertree who was happy to be his host in Liverpool. As a reformer and benefactor, Rathbone shared many of the ideals that his guest stood for. William Rathbone was in attendance at the Mass in St. Patrick's Church that marked the official launch of the campaign in July 1843 and great crowds gathered there for the occasion. St. Anthony's, Scotland Road, was also the venue for thousands who gathered in support of the crusade. The success of the crusade was clear by October of that year when it was said that some 60,000 people had taken the pledge.

It was on a later visit to Liverpool in 1854 that Theobold Matthew called at the Nugent's home and the two priests met for the first time. James Nugent had still been a student in Rome when Father Matthew had made his earlier triumphant tour. He no doubt impressed upon Nugent, still a young man flushed with the success of the Catholic Institute and the reforms it was bringing in education, that the Tee-Total Campaign was about much more than condemning the use of "alcoholic liquorrr.." (Father Matthew's stress on the last syllable became well-known everywhere). It was about a deeper, widespread social reform, a religious and moral reawakening, leading on to better literacy, numeracy, education and citizenship. In the course of his work Matthew came to be acclaimed as a benefactor of considerable renown who had not been afraid to put his words into action and had collected money for the Irish Famine Fund in America and Britain. He helped to create more efficient ways of distributing food and resources during the worst days of the crisis.

Father Matthew found supporters on all sides of the religious and political scene.

Father Nugent had been known to espouse the Temperance Movement in Liverpool from his earliest days as a priest there, but it was not until a year after his return home from the United States tour that he founded 'The Total Abstinence League of the Cross' which he officially launched on 29th. February 1872. The time gap may have been partially due to the commitments of his prison ministry but also to the fact that he himself was not ready to give up drink completely and so could hardly preach Tee-Totalism to others! The experience of his prison chaplaincy gradually convinced him of the rightness of the Cause.

Of the many different projects and campaigns in which James Nugent became involved, the Temperance Movement – which only later became an all-out moral crusade for Teetotalism – was both the most successful and the most controversial. It was this campaign above all that put him in the spotlight of public attention and brought him wide recognition in the community. Oddly, it is also the aspect of his ministry that is the least documented in appraisals of Nugent's career, though he himself saw it as his most important work. As it was getting close to the root of the evil that assailed so many lives, this very moral and Victorian crusade fitted into a pattern of religious and moral reform that Nugent embraced wholeheartedly.

So it was that in the 1870s, when he was in the middle, years of his ministry, he embarked upon an ambitious and courageous, some might even say foolhardy mission, which would often land him in some very hot water. It would make his troubles with the Catholic Institute, or his spats with Micheal Whitty of the 'Daily Post', look very tame indeed. As a crusade based on humanitarian concern for the moral and physical welfare of men, women and children, Father Nugent made it plain from the start, and at every subsequent rally or meeting in crowded Temperance Halls and from the pulpit, that the crusade against drink stemmed directly from the Gospel parable of the 'Good Shepherd' and the mandate of Christ to "seek out and save that which is lost". He saw it, as Father Matthew had done a generation earlier, as part of a religious renewal movement for Catholics.

The Liverpool weekly satirical journal 'The Porcupine' often featured Nugent's Temperance work in its columns and, generally, gave it a favourable press. The journal was clearly not in favour of the campaign for Teetotalism and had trenchant criticisms of the methods and approach adopted by its more extreme exponents. The paper made an exception in Father Nugent's case as it considered him to have a more enlightened, common sense approach to the issue and saw that he led by example, without the language of condemnation. It did not go unnoticed though, that Father Nugent was in attendance at a meeting to greet the new Lord Mayor of Liverpool, a certain Councillor A. B. Walker of the famous Brewery family!

It is generally thought that Father Nugent was one of the very first in the field to set up an official North West branch of 'The Total Abstinence League of The Cross' as an organisation within the Catholic sector. The issues surrounding the Temperance Movement came to have a sharper focus in the cause of Teetotalism and differences of opinion often became much more defined and aggressive. The call for Total Abstinence caught the imagination and also attracted the wrath of many people. Inspiration came from the national body which Cardinal Henry Manning had begun in Westminster under the title of 'The League of The Cross' and which Nugent started at the same time in the north, but he knew it was never going to be a straightforward or pleasant campaign.

He may have been unprepared for the strength of reaction. The great number of pubs and licensed premises in the town, especially along the Waterloo Road (Dock Road), the trade in beer and spirits, the wine merchants in a busy sea port like Liverpool – a place full of thirsty and lusty sailors in need of a drink when they came ashore -

was hardly promising ground for such a mission! By the year 1875 it was recorded that the town of Liverpool accounted for 10% of all the drink-related crime in Britain. The call for restricted pub opening times and other sanctions on the sale of alcohol was destined to become a fight for survival on the part of those whose livelihood, enjoyment or profit, seemed to depend on it.

Deeper undercurrents of social unrest in Liverpool were at work too. There was a drinking culture in the town. Unsettled feelings in the world of work had a bearing on this as Liverpool gained a reputation for drink-related crime. Between 1871 and 1874 there was widespread discomfort in the Liverpool labour market. Discontented workmen took issue over their poor rate of pay and working conditions, especially the unwarranted length of the working day. By that time the manufacturing base of the town had declined and the former sources of employment in the Pottery Factories, in watch-making, food-processing and some aspects of Shipbuilding were no longer the labour intensive industries they had once been. The expansion of commerce and trade led to jobs being concentrated around the docks and service industries attached to the docks, the railways and the canals, with plentiful work available only when business was brisk. Whilst there was abundant work for bargemen, stevedores, carters and warehousemen many casual workers could be found waiting hopefully at the dockside and it was often the unskilled men who suffered most, succeeding or failing in their bid for jobs according to the trade coming through the port.

Housing in the area was poor, jerry-built by untrained builders, and parts of Liverpool began to take on an air of what Ramsay Muir described as "genteel poverty". A general state of depression left workers with little or no incentive to press for a better deal in any organised way, and since the huge influx of penniless immigrants in the late 1840s there had grown up a sense of helpless lethargy, a state of poor health and sanitation and a measure of religious tension and conflict. Militancy in the area of Union activity was, with a few exceptions, something rare up to this point. In these circumstances, especially in dockland, recourse to the pubs and the polarisation of the community into nationalist groupings was a natural drift.

Abstaining from drink was an idea alien to those who, from any class of society, took their leisure in pubs, found solace in the bottle, or made financial gains from the sale of it. Abuse of alcohol was an undeniable fact and was the immediate cause of a lot of crime, but there was also much hypocrisy about this and those who regarded themselves as legitimate users of alcohol resented interference from what seemed like religious do-gooders out to make them feel guilty and ruin their trade. No wonder matters like Sunday closing of pubs became a political as well as a religious hot potato in the elections of 1875. It seems that James Nugent was actively canvassing, on the eve of poll in St. Anne's Ward, Vauxhall, for the candidate who supported the call for Sunday closing, Laurence Connolly – of the Irish National Party. With hindsight – always a wonderful thing - Father Nugent may well have contemplated that he had strayed too far and too easily into this controversial area. Temperance might be considered a virtue to strive for whereas Teetotalism and total abstinence, was essentially an option, an ideal that relatively few could be expected to attain or aspire to.

The maxim of 'all things in moderation' was surely a tried and tested one, but always achieving the balance, the middle way, as advocated in Catholic tradition, was not easy in practice. James Nugent was one of those who believed that crime should be tackled at its root and that crises demanded crisis management. He believed, along with many others in the society of his day, that a radical approach was needed to sort out the underlying causes of the problem of crime and saw drink as being foremost among the reasons for the high number of inmates in prison.

Nugent believed that the cycle of depravity had to be checked, especially amongst the young. Juvenile offenders were often the offspring of drunken parents who had a criminal history but for the children of the parents who had fallen into this vortex of drink and crime there was, in Father Nugent's view, always hope. A start must be made in helping them and the guiding principle remained for him that for many youngsters "their circumstances were their misfortune not their fault." Those attempting to rescue the victims of drink-related crime in Liverpool would be well aware of the successful crusade in London under Archbishop Manning of Westminster. In the debate as to who was first in the field, it is a close call but the balance is in favour of Nugent as the initiator. Others helped to make it a prominent issue around the country, especially in towns, and it had caught the imagination nationally, though it had met with considerable resistance among English and Irish Catholics, not least the clergy. Some undoubtedly saw it as an imposition by an over-zealous missionary.

Henry Manning's background in the Anglican Church, from which he brought many ideals into Catholicism, helping to create a new status for Catholics in England, still caused him to be regarded by many as an 'outsider'. Similar sentiments were at work under the surface in Liverpool too. The street crusade approach of Christian Sects and Evangelical groups might have been welcomed and supported by some but it was strongly resented by others. A working-class Catholic ghetto was always ready to repel with violence what it saw as an alien or Protestant incursion onto its territory! Use of coal as a weapon was not uncommon even among small children when processions passed by in the street. This was the crux of the problem Father Nugent faced; how to avoid the campaign he had started from becoming a cause of social or sectarian division.

For Liverpool, and for the country in general, the early 1870s marked a time of great social upheaval. From his prison work Nugent may have gained some insight into the deeper political and sociological undercurrents that provided the more profound reasons for drunkenness and its correlative-depravity. He referred a number of times, in reports to the Select Committee of the Home Office, to the special problems of workers and unemployment issues in Liverpool, and the relation of excess drinking to crime statistics. It was not well received. Some Government officials simply lumped together in their minds the concept of Irishness, Catholicism and criminal tendency. Nugent was one of many Liverpool reformers who had to fight prejudice of this kind.

Although there had been relatively little militancy in the workforce there were a few high profile examples of it. Workers at the Wheetsheaf Factory in Seel Street successfully petitioned employers for a nine-hour working day, and the nine-hour day became the bench mark for many other factories and businesses around the country. The leading businessman, William Simpson, was supportive of workers efforts to secure a better deal for themselves, and negotiated settlements became common, with the threat of strike-action to back them up. A general Transport Strike at this time had far-reaching effects since there was a monopoly held by the Liverpool Road and Railway Omnibus Company and the Liverpool Tramway Company, which employed over 1000 people between them. The matter was resolved by a combination of pay increases and concessions by the two beleaguered Companies.

Places where women worked proved to be an even bigger focus of unrest and difficulty as it became more acknowledged that women's wages, and their need for more free time to look after their families, were crucial for the social cohesion of the community. More than in most British towns, it was the women in Liverpool who suffered the greatest exploitation and injustice. In some instances women worked a twelve hour day for the sum of nine pence. Their domestic role was not sufficiently recognised as the important contribution to social stability that it really was. Victorian girls and women still had stereotyped roles within the strict codes of family life that prevailed and when women rose up in protest the response was to discredit them as incompetent, to label them as troublemakers. This attitude contributed to the demise of organised union activity and the effectiveness of strike action. Meanwhile, in the docks strike action was spasmodic and the Union's presence there too small to make a great deal of difference.

This is probably why much of James Nugent's early work followed the pattern of other reformers and placed the emphasis on the training and skills of boys and men for work appropriate to a large seaport. It meant that the woman's place was seen as being in the home and her role seen as the up-bringing of children. Among the local Catholic clergy Nugent had already been pre-eminent for some time in forging ahead with better conditions for working class people among the Irish-Catholic community. However he was limited in what he could do, or wanted to do, for women's rights, and he was restricted by the political and social attitudes of the day. The gender issues of our own time were at that stage still a very long way off. Victorian Society was changing, but not in its improvement of human rights and working conditions or in its attitudes to the poor, and in the process of economic growth many town dwellers were getting left behind in the rat race. They were joined by hundreds of hurt refugees who found themselves rejected by the effects of the Industrial Revolution.

To a certain extent James Nugent was alert to this background. It could however be said that his crusading sprit and busy schedule did not always give him time to stop and think deeply enough. He saw crying needs all around him, not least the predicament of the prisoner unable to work or live an independent life, in a cycle of decline through alcohol and depression. He was alert to the power of influential people in the community and he had worked to recruit key people in the Temperance cause. He knew that 'converts' often made the strongest advocates and could serve to bring many wavering souls and wondering sheep back into the fold. As someone already gaining a reputation as a 'Good Shepherd' Father Nugent was not afraid to exploit this potential. When the campaign for Total Abstinence was at its height and the pledge was being advocated and taken in Temperance Halls around the area, John Denvir, one of Nugent's closest allies at this time, declared that he had taken the pledge three times in one day. His enthusiasm for the cause was a great strength to Nugent. Denvir had the interests of the Irish Catholics at heart, and, from a different angle than that of Nugent. He came to the fray with a very clear political agenda. Denvir helped Nugent to think through the deeper implications of his work.

When James Nugent began his version of Father Matthew's crusade and began the 'League of the Cross for Total Abstinence' in Liverpool, he raised a standard, a flag that served as a rallying point for reform. But as well as having a cause he needed a building and, as so often before, his project began humbly in an old school building in Edgar Street, in the parish of St. Joseph. As always he looked for strong leadership and good allies and found one in a redoubtable Catholic layman Mr. J.J. Fitzpatrick from the parish of St. Peter's, Seel Street. He took on the role of Secretary to the League. Once he had an organiser and a clearer focus for his work, things moved quickly and well. In all his missionary endeavours to this date, the presence of a suitable building had always been a crucial factor – The Ragged School in Spitalfields, The Middle School in Rodney Street, The Catholic Institute in Hope Street and the Boys' Night Refuge and Orphans' Asylums in Soho Street and later in St. Annes's Street, had all been visible landmarks, tangible focal points for his mission. He needed that.

A crucial element in Nugent's psyche was a deep need for a familiar point of reference, a control point, a house or place where family and community could be formed and where people could be gathered and mobilised. There his personal desires could be projected and promoted in his plans for the care of the poor. Establishing a central League Hall for example was an important objective but this would come later; it was already in his mind as he pressed continually for the setting up of a branch of the new 'Leaugue of the Cross' in every parish, using his Catholic newspapers to promote this and arranging adverts and posters on factory walls and bill boards. The regularity of a weekly meeting at the same time and place - a local school, a Men's Club - was part and parcel of the strategy of the campaign, and within the project itself there was always another project. Nugent was driven by a need to keep things going at full pelt, he hated half-heartedness and was fearful of failure, and so he proposed 'Persevering Meetings' which were interspersed with the regular ones; they were a kind of 'booster class'.

Until a central Hall could be found, various premises near Lime Street Station were often used for League of the Cross meetings. Later, when The Jubilee Hall was established in the wake of Father Nugent's Golden Jubilee of Priesthood, it became a focal point for the anti-drink campaign in the same way that the Catholic Institute had become the flagship for Catholic Education. Prior to finding that suitable, permanent place in which to focus his work, James Nugent often convened the meetings, on Saturday afternoons, in St. George's Hall, which became a regular venue. Evening meetings were held at Footit's Circus in the middle of town or at Quaglione's Circus in what is now William Brown Street, or Newsome's Circus near Whitechapel - basically wherever there was a hall large enough for a crowd, and a platform from which to address it.

'The Porcupine' reported on some of these gatherings, as for example on May 18th 1872, when Father Nugent was said to have proudly announced that to date the Pledge had been administered to more than 6,000 people. Perhaps their names were also registered in heaven! Almost every district, if not every parish, had its League of the Cross and Father Nugent, strongly reminiscent of his predecessor Father Matthew, would announce such figures as he travelled around incessantly, visiting parishes and speaking to groups of every kind. In time, he was able to purchase land on which to build his League Hall, at Rose Place, off St. Anne's Street, so that in 1875 the work became more centred, more coordinated.

Key to the success of the crusade was the introduction of free Music Concerts that Father Nugent helped to arranged, or 'stage manage' as Micheal Whitty might have disparagingly said, to raise money and draw support. To lure would-be pledge takers and deliberately tempt people away from the vacuum created by habitual drinking and debauchery, he offered culture and refinement, music and art; the finer things of life. He related the universal appeal of music to the hard-hitting call for sobriety. He spoke to people's nobler instincts and senses. Having seen just how many Irish immigrants, sailors and dock hands were drawn into the salons and cheap beer houses that were the first enticing refuge they found when they came ashore, Nugent made these his special target. He came to realise though that the pubs served important purposes other than offering beer and the prospect of oblivion through drink. Jack Langan's pub was well known for offering a service of reading aloud the Irish papers, such as 'The Nation', on Sundays, to give the Irish community news from home. To buy a Sunday paper would cost six pence, and many were illiterate in any case, so the practice of reading aloud was popular. There was a whole culture built around such places which served to unite and support the poorer Immigrant community. Nugent and his colleagues had to step carefully lest the advantages of this culture were lost in the purge on pubs. At first costly mistakes were made because of too much haste.

In a way the proposed Free Concerts (Free meant a collection rather than a ticket!) were part of a kind of concerted counter-movement to languishing in pubs. One contemporary account likened the battle for sobriety to turning around a mighty ship in full flow. Father Nugent expected all the staff from 'The Catholic Times' to be at all the Concerts and at the weekly rallies, though he never attempted to force The Pledge on anyone. The Pledge was essentially a voluntary matter; that was vitally important. Yet the routine procedure for the rallies was something everyone was asked to support. Often there would be a procession from an agreed rendez-vue to the place of the Meeting, increasing the sense of purpose and solidarity, and raising the level of interest so as to encourage fervour in taking the Pledge. The presence and performance of the band on such occasions was, as you would expect, 'de rigeur' and sashes and medals were worn at public occasions or at Masses, both by the Veterans and the younger members.

The early influence on Nugent of the remarkable Franciscan priest from Cork, Theo Matthew was, as we have seen, a crucial one that cannot be too strongly emphasised. His efforts in Ireland, nearly forty years earlier, had inspired many to take the pledge and lead a moderate, religious and responsible life. The battle cry he used, "Here goes in the name of God!" may not seem to modern ears the most compelling of slogans but it conveyed the notion of a battle, a war against immorality and evil, which caught the contemporary imagination and swept people along on a wave of enthusiasm. Father Nugent's own slogan that became his trademark in the "Save The Boy" Campaign owed much to the influence of his hero Father Matthew's crusading spirit and his skilful use of publicity and propaganda. The fact that Father Matthew had brought his message to the centre of Liverpool convinced Nugent, years later, that there was support for such a cause. Knowing about the enthusiastic welcome given by leading figures of the town, including William Rathbone and the Stipendiary Edward Rushton, and the general response from Liverpool residents, particularly in the Irish quarters around St. Patrick's

Church in Toxteth and St. Anthony's, led Nugent to believe his efforts would also be well-received.

Father Nugent, always aware of the importance of fund-raising, must surely have been impressed by the fact that Father Matthew had regularly raised over £600 a month from wide-ranging appeals for essential relief work for the poor in Ireland, and that on the back of his Tee-Total campaign had achieved so much in the improvement of opportunities for his compatriots. The seventeen or eighteen years intervening before Nugent brought Temperance work into the full-blown Movement of 'League of The Cross for Total Abstinence' were not idle years. Experience in the prison service supplied him with the hard facts and statistics he would later use in conveying the merits of, and the urgent need for, 'The League'. From the time he set out his stall as a young priest on the staff at St. Nicholas's Church, advocating temperance, spelling out the dangers and evils of excessive drinking with impassioned speeches at places like Jim Ward's Boxing Salon in Williamson square, he had gradually developed what he regarded as his "real work". Easter Monday 1853, which had seen him making an appeal to the parishioners at Holy Cross Church in Great Crosshall Street, was always to be seen as a starting point on this road. Many times from then on his powers of oratory were being called upon to bolster efforts already being made or inspire new ones.

It was characteristic that the mission had begun inauspiciously in a tumbledown building that led on to a more organised and presentable centre for his work. From the humble origins of the meeting in the old St. Thomas and St. William School building, Edgar Street in the town centre parish of St. Joseph, to the Jubilee Hall that came later, there was a shift in thinking across the town and among many organisations, families and groups. Campaigners, many of them inspired as youngsters by Father Matthew, joined in the weekly meetings that Nugent and his friend John Denvir convened. Denvir, the first to step forward at the first meeting to take the pledge in a very public show of support to the Irish community, was the catalyst Father Nugent needed. The essence of the Movement, as Father Nugent well knew, lay in the number of branches set up around the region - ideally a branch of the Movement in every parish, with which local parishioners could easily identify. In 1888 there were 17 branches of the 'League' in the Liverpool diocese as a whole, 10 of them in Liverpool, including the main branch at the 'League Hall', named 'The Father Matthew Branch'. Despite the opposition it attracted from the obvious antagonists, Nugent pressed ahead, seeing it as a parish-based movement of the people for the people and as such virtually unstoppable.

There is no doubt that James Nugent himself considered the League to be the most important work of his life. He was still only 53 when he began it. The danger was that he would become so single-minded about it that he paid scant attention to its unpopularity from other quarters and claimed too much for it as a panacea for all social ills. The middle-class communities, and many of the clergy, did not embrace it with the enthusiasm he had hoped for. Unpopularity never once deterred him, and when he had set his hand to the plough, he seemed to have the determination of fifty men and never looked back. Yet there was a price to pay in a measure of isolation he experienced from the main stream of parochial and clerical life.

Nugent's notebooks of this time contain many references to meetings of the League of The Cross, well advertised in the press, set for Saturday afternoons at 3.00pm. at venues like St. George's Hall or on the corner of Stanley Road (before the days of football such gatherings were possible), and the feeling conveyed is one of a popular, working-class Movement. In September 1872 when the Weekly Concerts began, free of charge but with collecting baskets at the ready for the Middle-Class and incomed people, and with sponsorship sought from local firms, everyone was invited to take the pledge publicly. It was not long before Father James Nugent had been voted the most popular man in Liverpool and had become, by this stage, one of the most celebrated figures in the community.

The regularity of events and the insistent theme, gave the project its impetus. It had a contagious effect. People felt they were doing something to help, and at the same time felt better about themselves. Part of Father Nugent's own 'indefatigable' effort was to fire with enthusiasm as many people as he could so that they were convinced not by him but by the rightness of the cause. John Denvir helped to provide the oxygen of publicity and this side of the work was boosted greatly later on by the arrival of Gabriel Ellis who worked as Nugent's public relations officer. His loyalty to Nugent may have also carried an element of awe. Many felt unable to deny Father Nugent. He could feel deeply the hurt of failure and lack of support from those who would not go the extra mile with him, so allies often comprised a mixture of those who were drawn to him by his magnetism, by love for his holiness and sincerity, by his strength of purpose and by fear of his considerable wrath if they crossed him.

Once again the Gospel-based mission at the heart of this crusade is vital for understanding Father Nugent's work. It connects with that view already referred to, held by many engaged in social welfare and reform, that an unconditional, all-out effort to help and serve the poor, and to give unstintingly, was not only a means but an end in itself. It was as Beatrice Webb expressed it "one of the main channels through which the individual entered into communion with the supreme spirit of love at work in the universe". Our understanding of Nugent's involvement in the anti-drink campaign is incomplete if we do not grasp this fact that for him it was a work of Evangelisation.

It must be added that whilst The Temperance Hall was used on Monday Nights for the purpose its name suggests, Father Nugent took the opportunity of being on the platform to address other themes. It was at one such Rally that Nugent was reported in the Press as having used the occasion to take political advantage of the situation. The Liverpool Review on October 17th 1885, reported on his talk of the previous Monday in which he made some direct comments in relation to the forthcoming Parliamentary Elections. It recorded his words as follows: "If a good Catholic presents himself, Catholics are to vote for him". This in itself was deemed innocuous enough but his further statement was more controversial. He suggested that if the Candidate was not a Catholic but had "got the right colour" as he put it, then everybody was "at liberty to support him". The Liverpool Review, being a pro-Liberal newspaper, looked on this as interfering in party politics and as trying to exert undue influence on people's vote. He always denied party-political interference. In spite of this denial there were very obvious forays into politics, even if he was at pains to state that he remained focussed on the principle theme of his campaign.

Regular Saturday Evening Concerts were started in the early 1880s at the Picton Hall (then known as the Rotunda Lecture Hall), a venue that seated 1300 people. The Concerts became well-known and attracted crowds from outside town who were well entertained. Later a performance of Handel's 'Messiah' was given in the Concert Room of St. George's Hall each year for fourteen years. The quality and consistency of these Concerts helped to establish Nugent's reputation and for his part it provided a steady income for his charity work. He kept a close association with the Concerts until serious illness befell him again in 1896. Exhaustion and pneumonia was dignosed and his bishop sent him off to convalesce in the warmer climate of The Canary Islands. It is no surprise that his month or two there extended into yet another tour of America.

How can we try to summarise this long and fruitful episode in James Nugent's life? The editor of 'The Porcupine', once again defending him, wrote of Father

Nugent: "He seems at length resolved to brave the monster (of Drunkenness) in his den." The reference is to the fact that although Father Nugent had long been recognised for his stance on Temperance, for a long time he did not come out openly in favour of Total Abstinence. The American experience helped to trigger this move. Religious leaders in Britain, especially Cardinal Manning, were now making statements about Tee-Totalism as the only effective means of stopping the evils of drink among the poorer classes of Catholics.

'The Porcupine', by no means a Pro-Catholic publication, though it appeared to have a sneaking admiration for Father Nugent – (a warm-hearted, impul-sive man in the Irish tradition was how it saw him) usually led a tirade against Tee-total campaigners for their 'bigotry' and against Catholics for their papist views or triumphalist approach. This made many people cautious. Nugent was seen, in contrast to this, as a man with a perception of the deeper causes of crime in the complex social situation of people's lives, and at the same time a traditional Catholic understanding of personal failing and sinfulness at the root of evil, largely free of denominational bias. His motives seemed different from those of most other people

An interesting aspect of this whole crusade is that the people who crowded in to the meetings included the down-and-outs from the streets. They were not the parents who had neglected or abandoned their children in drunken stupors and, obviously, they were not the people sentenced to prison convicted of sundry drink-related offences, but a contingent of the really poor. Nugent and his companions were preaching mainly to the converted or at least to the sympathetic and interested men, women and young people of the area, but they were also giving a sense of inclusion to those very much on the margin. There were people who only dared to slink warily in the shadows at the back of the Hall, some just for warmth, others out of curiosity, but they were there and listening. There were undoubtedly those who, if nothing else, enjoyed the music and the prospect of a free Concert. Free entrance ensured that it was not just the middle-classes who attended and that it was not just from these that the support came.

The Temperance League had become, by the late 1870s, something more than a symbol of a pledge not to drink. It had come to represent a renaissance of Catholic intent, the moral high ground and a focus of religious fervour and commitment. Some might detect Nugent's underlying intention to make a strong Catholic statement to the rest of the religious bodies. Furthermore, the power of Father Nugent's influence, building on Father Matthew's foundation, is clear, but the effectiveness of the campaign was only partial and he had to come to terms with that. To save that which was lost had to be viewed in the cold light of statistics and there were many who remained untouched by any amount of zealous campaigning.

As the call to Temperance continued to ring through the land and throughout the 1880s, Father Nugent was given a boost by the appointment, in March 1881, of Gabriel Ellis to the post of advertising manager for "The Catholic Times". Ellis described his first memorable encounter with the great man at one of the Monday Night Concerts at the League Hall. It was the evening of Monday March 1st. "There was over a foot of snow and a more north-pole-ish outlook cannot be imagined. In spite of the inclemency of the weather, or possibly because of it, that great establishment (the League Hall) was packed to the doors by the poorest and most unkempt looking mass of humanity imaginable. Many of the women, girls and boys, were barefooted.....It was here that I first saw Father Nugent at what he described as his real work. He sat in a seat in the centre of the front row nearest the platform, a frail looking, wistfully sad figure, huddled in a great overcoat, with never a sign of life until the interval. Then there seemed to be three movements in one: first a leap out of the overcoat, secondly a flying bound towards the platform, and then the raising of an imperious hand to stem the applause, as if to say "let me speak first".

Ellis was upbeat about the success of the Movement in Liverpool. He expressed the view that many individuals had been saved from evil ways or diverted from a life of crime. He provides no figures to bear this out but his testimony seems to be an objective one. Whatever the effects of the whole enterprise, a great deal of good was done, awareness heightened, morale strengthened. Apart from this a good deal must have been learnt since the speakers Nugent brought to his Concerts and Rallies were of a high standard, entertaining and informative. The League became another important platform in the preaching of the gospel, in teaching the faith. At a time when the Sunday Masses were losing their congregations, it appears that the poorest of the poor attended the rallies at Temperance Halls in their droves.

If not all clergy supported the methods of 'The League of the Cross' many supported the ideals behind it. Father Nugent enjoyed warm and whole-hearted support from a Father Edward Powell at St. Alexander's parish, Bootle, and from Father Ignatius Harris who was a well-known speaker and a good friend of the League. Among the bishops, Cardinal Manning obviously upheld the full intent of the campaign whilst Bishop Vaughan of Salford would not countenance the Total Abstinence Movement yet firmly believed in and preached Temperance. The Total Abstinence lobby was much more of an overt, formal organisation than Temperance, with medals and sashes, a confraternity with its defining rules and regulations. It had a membership, a body to belong to and be proud of. Each year in the South of England a great annual rally was held in the Crystal Palace. In the North the equivalent annual gathering was in Bidston. Whatever the South could produce the North could match and Cardinal Manning acknowledged Nugent's contribution to the success of the Movement in the North of England.

Father Nugent's own attendance, over the years, at these Concerts and Meetings was unfailing and he continued to be unstinting with his time and energy on behalf of the

League, even though he held his main post as Senior Catholic Prison Chaplain at Walton until the early part of 1885. His arduous labours in many directions took their toll of his health and in 1886 he had to take time away. It was to the Continent he went for a long recuperation and light lecture tour combined. On his visit to Rome in 1886 he was granted an audience with the Pope who encouraged and blessed his mission of Temperance. News of this was duly reported at the main branch of the League and recorded in its report of July 25th 1886.

The branches of the League grew more and more into a useful network of charitable schemes. One instance of this was the custom Nugent had at Christmastime of giving hampers to widows: special treats of geese, coal, and clothing. Around this was a sort of credit union concept whereby the recipients of these annual treats and bonuses could show, by means of their bank books, that they had saved some money during the year. It was an encouragement to thrift and it is recorded that over 800 women(including those referred to as the 'basket women'), had been helped directly in this way by what was called 'The Widows' Christmas Trust'. No doubt a good deal of money otherwise going on drink, was saved for use on the family. So the work of the League came to symbolise what we might today term a wrap-around provision of pastoral care.

No mention is made in all of this of abstaining from smoking. Presumably this would have been far more difficult to endorse and was, in any case, an accessory of fashion that was widespread through every class of Victorian Society. Tobacco Companies were riding high in Liverpool and elsewhere and the import of tobacco from the docks was a virtually unstoppable trade. Awareness of the use of chemical drugs as a criminal matter did not yet feature.

But the Temperance work went from strength to strength, into the 1890s, symbolised by the culminating development of the setting up of Jubilee Hall in 1896, situated in Burlington Street in a former Non-Conformist Chapel. This became the replacement for the old League Hall in St Anne's Street. Nugent was pleased to be able to re-house the movement in the new building and to give the movement a boost with some of the proceeds of his Priestly Golden Jubilee, and as a mark of fifty years dedicated service to the community.

Before long, the climate that made the League of the Cross popular began to change with the legislation of the day, and by the turn of the century the emphasis on renunciation by voluntary movements became less necessary. Government regulations and healthier attitudes brought about a change that eventually led to the decline and closure of the League. James Nugent's nephew, Father Hayes of Nottingham diocese, continued the Movement for a while in memory of his uncle but he could not sustain it for more than a few years. Society had moved on, for good or ill, and the time for the Campaign had passed. In all the confused and varied opinions about the value of the project we might be wise to end with Father Nugent's own description of it as "an organisation which takes by the hand the poor drunkard, who was deaf and dumb, blind and palsied by drink, and enobles him to help himself...... to deliver men from the curse and slavery of drink and bring them, through the sacraments, to God Himself."

We have a better understanding today of the complex combination of social and psychological factors that affect people's lives and the relationship this sometimes has to the use or abuse of drink and drugs. Do we however see the connection that there is between a crisis of belief, a loss of the sense of God, the need for security in Him, that produces a deeper kind of thirst, a thirst which only faith can assuage?

Chapter 11

In The House of Providence

Life was proving as eventful as ever for Father Nugent. By the time of the destruction of the first 'Clarence' Training Ship, he was 62 years of age. He had been working in the prison for twenty years and the years had taken their toll on him. The shear breadth and variety of projects he had already been involved with would have wrecked a much younger man.

What he had tried to do for poor boys in Liverpool he also wanted for the girls and young women. We have already noted the unwarranted criticism that Father Nugent did not work as hard for the care of girls as he did for boys. In fact his close and long-standing association with the Good Shepherd Sisters at Ford had inspired him to seek a home there for girls referred by the Courts on leaving prison. He valued the work of the Sisters and sought to widen the influence of Religious Orders in the reform and training work he had begun for boys and girls of all ages.

In the laundries and kitchens of the Good Shepherd Home at Ford, wayward and disaffected young women could pick up useful skills and recover some of the self-esteem they had so painfully lost. From the point of view of the nuns in the Convent, it was now practically possible to run the Home and their own house whilst providing a service for the local people, without having to face crippling wage bills. A neat solution all round! The success of the Girls' Home at Ford went on into the latter part of the 1890s and over 2000 female residents were housed there over the years.

Police would often escort young women to the door of the Home in Ford when they found them destitute and begging on the streets or engaged in prostitution, some of them trying pathetically to care for their babies, having been abandoned by their partners. A huge operation to purge the brothels led to even greater dereliction for women on the streets. Over 300 brothels were closed by force of law in one particular purge. The Home at Ford became a refuge for many of the disgraced women and their babies. The problem was, the Home provided by the heroic Sisters of the Good Shepherd, so true to their name and their mission, was a long way out from the centre of town and its resources were already over-stretched. It was always Father Nugent's instinct to go for what was close at hand and he began to search for possible ways of enlisting the help of other Sisters for a new scheme in the city.

Mother Magdalen (Fanny Taylor), formerly an Anglican and a nurse who had served in the Crimea with Florence Nightingale, had used her experience and her sense of God's call to found the Order of The Poor Servants of the Mother of God in 1870 for the care of the sick and needy. The Sisters had a special concern for vulnerable women and girls in the cities. The Order was essentially focussed on nursing as its main charism, and ran hospitals, including the famous Providence Hospital, as it became known, in the town of St. Helens, Lancashire. Always on the look out with what seemed like twenty pairs of eyes, Father Nugent had espied a building in Bevington Bush, north of Scotland Road on the corner of Paul Street, not far from his old family home. It had previously been a Public Baths and Wash House and was now derelict. He had a penchant for derelict buildings. He enjoyed the challenge of restoring them and had done so since the time of the first Ragged School in Spitalfields forty years earlier. To this project in Bevington Bush he decided to direct Mother Magdalen's expertise and the heroic efforts of her dedicated Sisters.

Until the large premises could be renovated as a Women's Hostel, he worked with the Poor Servants to secure temporary accommodation in Lime Kiln Lane. After about six months in the temporary building it became possible to move to the new house at Bevington Bush in the autumn of 1891. The vacated premises in Lime Kiln Lane then became a Night Shelter for Homeless Women, open from six in the evening to nine in the morning, where a basic supper, bed and breakfast could be had. Even the temporary became a long-term provision in Father Nugent's hands. By 1905, the year of Father Nugent's death, the hostel was still going and 19,338 needy women had passed through the Lime Kiln Lane Shelter.

The Bevington Bush Hostel, which would come to bear the name of St. Saviour's Refuge, proved to be a very expensive project. Building costs and workmen's wages had soared. Fund-raising efforts brought in over £6000, allowing a refurbishment that made it possible to house up to fifty women. There was a steam laundry and the facilities for training women in basic skills of sewing and knitting. Rehabilitation, as always, was the main purpose in all of this and had he lived Father Nugent would have had the satisfaction of knowing that by the end of 1905, 2,213 homeless and destitute women had been successfully trained there by the Sisters of The Poor Servants and their helpers.

Caring for the Carers was also a priority for Father Nugent. He bought up a property at 309 Edge Lane, Liverpool, as a rest home for retired and infirm Sisters along with some of the residents from St. Saviour's. From this sprang up the Convent and Home later known as 'Rosemont' and here too the ubiquitous laundry was added as the numbers housed there increased and the purpose of the place changed. The Convent later moved to premises in Mossley Hill. New projects gave rise to new needs among the carers themselves; they had to be sustained, supported and spiritually nourished. They had their own community needs and personal needs since they were flesh and blood, not automatons. When the sisters themselves were tired who would look after them? Hence the need for the Sisters' Rest Home.

Even as the Paul Street Refuge was still being planned new thoughts, always with the same charitable intention, were forming in Father James Nugent's restless mind. It seems that the plight of young women and their families, unmarried mothers, prostitutes and vagrants, had, by now, become the chief focus of his ministry and concern. There is the story, apocryphal no doubt, of his housekeeper at the Presbytery in Blundellsands running in fright from the front door shouting that there was priest to see him. A Priest! She had only been used to seeing prostitutes and ragged orphans at his door.

Stories like this say much about the general image Nugent had gained towards the end of his career. He had become totally identified with the poorest and neediest people and although it set him apart among the clergy it was an image he was proud to have. He had become totally synonymous with care of the most abject poor.

November 1891 saw Father Nugent announcing with enthusiasm the realisation of his new Refuge project. For some years he had been discerning and studying what he came to identify as the need for a refuge for fallen women whose situation had been rendered more problematic by recent Government policy on brothels and 'disorderly houses'. At this time Nugent was resident at 2 Lorne Road in Waterloo and had for a time taken charge of the new mission and parish of St. Josephs' in Blundellsands. He remained there only long enough to build the church. He had become aware, no doubt by scouring the daily papers, of the current scandal which was receiving considerable publicity and was the cause of strong emotions. Police purges had cleared a large number of brothels and many women were thrown out on the streets without any means of support. They had in fact been deprived of the only security they knew.

It was necessary always to sell an idea to those who could make it happen. Otherwise it would remain an idea on James Nugent's desk. He had to campaign for the hearts and minds of benefactors before he could bring the service he wanted to the people who needed it. He had to give them the rationale and convince a sceptical public – not least his bishop. However by this time it seems the bishop was content to let Father Nugent get on with it! Opposition was futile!

The much publicised police crack-down led to the persecution of 818 people in the space of one year on a charge of keeping and running illicit houses. The attempt to purge the town of a perceived evil led not only to the displacement of many women, but in many cases their babies and children too. Without publicly condemning the purge of the brothels, Father Nugent, with his customary diplomacy, suggested the possibility of pastoral care for such people rather than the judgment of immorality. He believed, given appropriate help, a new direction in life was possible for them.

The Home for Women at Ford outside Liverpool was still available but was over-crowded. He did not want to over stretch the Sisters good will and the police practice of referring prostitutes there directly off the streets was adding an impossible strain. The accommodation in Magdalen Houses (a term attributable to the Mary in the Gospel) and the various Women's Night Shelters which he had long advocated, were inadequate to cope with the growing needs. Nugent believed in a two-fold approach of prevention and reform. He wanted new premises much nearer to the heart of town to provide for the women and to make a point against marginalising in society. Here was the inspiration behind his Home for Women in Paul Street, Bevington Bush. He saw it as a Half-Way House, a Reception Home for the women who had been dumped by the police (or more accurately by government policy). He also envisaged other vulnerable and poor women being housed there temporarily in order to get back onto the right track and be steered away from the dangers and temptations of the street. Rehabilitation was the watchword of his plans, just as it had been during his time as prison chaplain at Walton Gaol. He deliberately sought a place in an area "where poverty and misery abound and in the midst of what might be termed the submerged classes". But in practice he had chosen a location that polite society inhabited and he was not entirely popular for it among the people who lived and worked there. Paul Street was a respectable area. The former Baths and Washhouse building owned by the Liverpool Corporation, needed extensive repair and the eventual cost of refurbishment and adaptation would prove to be in the region of a staggering £7,500. The cost of purchasing the building from the Corporation was £1500. An essential part of the new use of the building was the laundry, (appropriately in view of its former purpose,) because Father Nugent saw the potential of it as a source of income and a means of service to the local community.

In the rather patronising tone that sometimes characterised his pronouncements, he expressed the wish that the new Home would fulfil the purpose of offering an anti-dote to the women's former situation: "Active occupation is one of the best means of dealing with this class of women, and the training in laundry work will enable them not only to contribute to their own support but also to acquire the means by which they may hereafter gain their own livelihood".

After a probationary period in the Bevington Bush Home the women would go to other Institutions around the country on a more permanent basis. Again, no one was to be turned away on grounds of religious faith, class or age but if Catholic Institutions willing to take them were available they were to be housed there. No one was taken in to the new Home in Liverpool if they could be shown to be able to sustain themselves adequately - it was meant for the poorest, those who genuinely had no means of their own, rather than those who simply pleaded poverty as a cover to get money. Obviously Nugent had learnt that distinction by long experience.

The acting treasurer for the new project was a prominent Catholic benefactor, Henry Jump, (his name is commemorated in a stained glass window in St. Peter and Pauls's Church, Crosby) who had lent his assistance to Nugent in earlier projects and was keen to promote Catholic Charities that benefitted the whole community. Nugent publicised details of how donations and subscriptions for the Home in Paul Street could be paid: to the Union Bank in Liverpool or to the project headquarters at 11 Drury Lane. It is clear that Nugent had come a long way from any suggestion of kitchen draw accounting that had once been a criticism made against him. He now had financial advisers and a proper accounting system behind the business plans - a far cry from the Ragged School days.

By far the most important aspect of the whole venture was the fact that he had secured the services of the Sisters of the Poor Servants of the Mother of God to take charge of it. He watched with satisfaction as the Sisters set up their first Charitable Home at Lime Kiln Lane and transferred this to the new premises at Paul Street, giving the new premises the name of St. Saviour's Refuge. Such were the beginnings of a wonderful work of outreach to the poor in the community of Liverpool. The admiration and gratitude to the Sisters for their work over the years was expressed by Archbishop Downey of Liverpool when over thirty years later in 1934, he opened the extension to the Lourdes Hospital saying: "We are grateful to the Poor Servants of the Mother of God for their splendid, humanitarian work in the Archdiocese. They attend to the needs of the sick, the poor, the destitute, the fallen, and the orphaned". They did much more than that; they fulfilled so well the original mission of the Order as set out by the Foundress, Mother Magdalen Taylor, not simply to dispense charity but to dispense the love of God, spreading hope among the poor as a sign of their solidarity with all mankind.

The recollections of the Sisters on arriving in Liverpool

are recorded in an account of the St. Saviour's Refuge Mission. It is recalled there how Father Nugent personally took it on himself to cook supper for the Sisters on their arrival. It was a Friday and so fish was on the menu. After leaving the Sisters to eat their meal he returned later to discuss plans for the work ahead.

The special charism of the Sisters, reflected Father Nugent's underlying mission: it was as a sign of God's love in the world that they came to the aid of the poor and not merely as part of a humanitarian effort. This concept was probably as unfamiliar and strange to some people of the day as it is to so many in our own time. The success of St. Saviour's Women's Refuge was such that in May 1894, four years on from its foundation, Father Nugent could report with a deep sense of fulfilment that "1466 women had been provided for" within its walls during that period, and he noted that many of them were the "incorrigible women" of the type he had described in his prison work.

Fund raising went on a pace and a sum of £5000 had been raised towards the total requirement of £7,500, for the Paul Street Refuge. Nugent resolved with all the means in his power to get the rest of it. He appealed, in a typical, emotionally charged manner, for this final sum, stating that he had "adopted a practical and satisfactory plan for dealing with a large class of women whose condition seemed hopeless, who otherwise would have been a mortal plague and a permanent, heavy burthen(sic) on society". He went on, "I turn to all classes to aid me in placing this Institution out of debt. I have touched but the fringe of one of the great problems of the day". In our own times, the 'world's oldest profession' continues to frustrate, fascinate and defy the social thinkers and no one offers much more of an answer in Britain than the tolerance zone idea that Nugent applied, though he looked for reform of life and the saving remedy of an honest occupation. He may be accused of addressing symptoms not root causes but deep in his own plans was a belief that prevention was better than cure and that people could be helped to change, with the grace of God and the strong hand of kindness. He believed in the reformation of character after true repentance of spirit and nothing shook him from that belief throughout his long priestly career.

We may by now have ceased being surprised to learn that James Nugent, whilst working towards the completion of the financing of the Paul Street Refuge, had spotted the gap in the net of social care and was busy making plans, or at least forming ideas, for a Maternity Home where women from the streets, and women of what he called "a higher class" who were pregnant or had recently given birth, could come with their baby to seek shelter and sanctuary. Again we need to accept the mentality of the Victorian Society that shaped Nugent as we consider his plans for what he called a 'Refuge For Penitent Women'. These thoughts were the beginning of a new Home that eventually became known as "The House of Providence" which he established in the Dingle area of South Liverpool. The realisation of this scheme lay some years ahead in 1897, because, as already stated, the money needed for the Paul Street mission was still outstanding.

The official preview of the opening of St. Saviour's Refuge in 1891 had been typically stage-managed by Nugent for maximum propaganda. He invited the great and the good, the influential friends and benefactors of Liverpool, Catholic and Non-Catholic alike, to view the premises for themselves. The long and illustrious list of names of those invited was a sign of the sheer breadth of influence he had in the community. There was the Catholic Bishop of Liverpool, The Mayor of the City, Mr. Holt, (a Protestant and great ambassador for the town), Lord and Lady Howard of Glossop, who had become devoted admirers and generous patrons of Father Nugent's work, the Clergy of several denominations, prominent Business families such as the Rathbones, the Hemelrycks, the Broadbents and the Lightbounds, eminent figures in the community such as the Stipendiary Mr. Stewart and a number of Judges, Lawyers and Solicitors. It was the patronage of leading families and citizens like these, together with 'the pennies of the poor' that made a powerful impact and enabled even ambitious projects to get off on the ground. Doubtless, there were those in the neighbourhood and in the city who would have shouted the equivalent of "not in my backyard!" and not so politely either, since not everyone was overjoyed that a House for destitute or Fallen Women be situated in the heart of the city. They would have preferred to push the distasteful problem, and the stigma attached to it out of sight. Nugent knew exactly what he was about! Rehabilitation into Society required an acceptance not only on the part of the former outcasts themselves but also on the part of Society around them. Nugent was anxious to demonstrate that God had a "House of Providence" for the most destitute and sinful in His great purpose.

Chapter 12

Father Berry's Homes

The long and successful life of the Catholic Children's Protection Society began officially on 16th.April 1881 under the authority of Bishop Bernard O'Reilly, inspired by the efforts of Father Nugent. Both men benefited from their experience of setting up the Catholic Reformatory Association 17 years earlier in 1864. The primary purpose of the new Society was different from the Association since it was intended for the protection of the interests and the religion of poor Catholic children in danger of losing their right to Catholic instruction. This danger applied just as much to the Home Children abroad as to those in Liverpool. In all Father Nugent's work the religious and sacramental upbringing of the children was central to his purpose.

As well as setting up an organisation at home it had been essential to form a tangible link with Canada and America where children were now being sent in considerable numbers from different parts of Britain. There was not at that time any official Reception Home nor any agreed policy for allocating children to their homes of adoption. The appeal for funding to launch the new Society in Liverpool was met with a characteristically generous response from the Catholic parishes in the town. All Souls gave £17, St. Patrick's £64, Our Lady of Mount Carmel £67, St. Edward's £38, St. John's £62, St. Sylvester's £21, St. Bridget's £16, St. Joseph's £67, and - by far the biggest amount - Holy Cross, which donated £100. The response came from a wider area too and the total initial collection realised £2000.

With this money it became possible to plan for the sending out of selected children to new homes in Canada, especially in Ontario, and to coordinate Catholic policy of Emigration. From 1882, girls from the Home in Mason Street and boys from Beacon Lane, under the care of the Sisters of Charity, formed part of the first organised party. 16 children were received in Lindsay, Ontario, by the Reverend Stafford who arranged for their onward journey to the adoptive families. Later, other groups followed. Within the first year of the Society's existence some 82 youngsters had been looked after in this way.

We have seen that the Committee of the Liverpool Catholic Reformatory Association asked Father Nugent in 1870 to go out to Canada to find suitable accommodation for the orphaned children and seek help from among the Religious Orders in Canada. Meanwhile, at home the Sisters of Charity continued to play a key role in the welfare of the children. A house at 99 Shaw Street was rented, which Nugent described in a business like way as "a good house giving such facilities as the nature of the work required", and put into the capable hands of a matron, Mrs. Lacy, together with an appointed Bursar and a financial manager, Paul Cullen, who had an office in James Street. The nature of the work in the Shaw Street Home most definitely did not entail replacing the role of potential 'parents' or families who might care for the children in their own homes.

The Society's policy on adoption or fostering was to look first for good possibilities near the children's own place of birth and to help natural parents take care of their own children where possible. Meanwhile from Canada, Father Stafford sent back photographs of the children happily settling into their new surroundings and letters from the host families or from the children themselves began to arrive. In some cases, the adoptive parents were writing to ask for more details about the children they had taken on, such as their parentage, their birth and baptism details.

It seems that some of the children were fortunate enough to attend the Select School in the Loretto Convent at Lindsay, a fact that would have pleased Father Nugent.

The educational provision in Canada remained high on the agenda of the Society. On 10th May 1883, 50 children were sent by the Society under the care of Mrs Hudson to Canada and on 6th September that same year 36 young hopefuls set off on the SS Polynesia with Mrs. Lacy from the Shaw Street Home. The Society drew heavily on the willing support of these 'Matrons' of the Homes and Nugent was a great believer in having someone of a strong mental and physical capacity in charge of them.

Mrs Lacy was bound for Canada again on 2nd may 1884 with 85 children under her ample wing. She had managed to place all of them in homes before she returned to England. Religious Orders in Hamilton and in Kingston had helped to provide what was needed. The intrepid Mrs. Lacy paid more visits to Canada, taking out further groups of children and visiting those already established there, until her much lamented death in the May of 1894. Her role in this scheme was clearly a very crucial one. Meanwhile, the on-going success of the emigration and adoption scheme inevitably depended on more funding. Bishop Bernard O'Reilly allocated more than half of the parish 'Lenten Alms' collections for 1883 to the project and parishes again responded well to the Appeals. On the Canadian side too bishops encouraged generous donations from the area where the children were housed. Favourable reports continued to come in from the Reverend Stafford and from the Government Emigration Agent in Quebec and by the time Bishop Whiteside succeeded Bishop O'Reilly as patron of the Liverpool Catholic Children's Protection Society in 1894, it had an excellent record to its credit.

Yet the successes had also to be balanced against the failures. At times information was inadequate and the wrong type of family was selected for adoption. There can be no disguising the fact that some children had a very unhappy time of it and were out of place in their new environment. The brief and insufficient comment on this aspect of Nugent's work in the book 'Liverpool - The First

1000 Years' expresses the view that some of the children thrived and prospered but not all. Some were placed with families who used them as cheap labour - or worse, and it was considered that "Nugent's kind intentions turned to ash in a different kind of hell for some of Liverpool's neglected children". If this judgement of history is thought accurate it is a sad conclusion, but it does not do justice to the overall good achieved or to the intention to do the best for Liverpool's forgotten and unfortunate youngsters.

The other needs on the home front did not decline at all and as James Nugent's work took more out of him with the advancing years, the concern grew about a possible successor. Canon Bennett had intended to write about Father Berry in the second part of his book on Monsignor Nugent but it was never published in book form. It is as much out of respect for Canon Bennett's intention and efforts as out of a desire to maintain the integrity of this story of Catholic Child Care that I now include this summary of John Berry's work and the Homes that bore his name.

Bennett wrote about Father Berry in a separate series of articles in 'The Cathedral Record' in 1948 and it is clear that if any worthy successor was in Nugent's mind it was certainly John Berry. However it is very important for an understanding of Nugent's work and legacy that John Berry's contribution is seen not merely as a continuation of his predecessor's achievements. John Berry was probably thought of as a possible successor by Nugent himself but Nugent had already created a standard, a 'benchmark' in child care that made it an act impossible to follow. His reputation was so high no-one could hope to emulate it, but his enthusiasm had also left heavy debts and it would cost Father Berry dear, not only financially but also in his own personal health, to take up the torch for the Protection Society.

For twenty years or so after relinquishing the job, Father Berry would live in relative seclusion away from Liverpool, spent up in every sense, after his strenuous efforts to open and maintain a string of Homes and projects for boys in the City. He died on 8th September 1921 and is buried in the private cemetery at Mount St. Bernard Abbey. His sister, with whom he had lived, is buried in an adjacent grave there. In some ways it is a fitting resting place, even though his precise connection with the Abbey is not clear. His retirement home in Measham was not far away, but the happy coincidence lies in the fact that the Abbey, through the Agricultural Colony, had been an important part of the story of the Catholic Reformatory Movement which John Berry helped to develop. He had brought to his task an intellect and a gift for languages and did some teaching when he had worked with the boys in the Homes at Liverpool.

So what of John Berry's background? Born in Aughton, near Ormskirk, on 29th May 1859, John Berry was, like Father Nugent, a man who displayed proudly his Lancashire credentials. His Catholic faith and practical approach endeared him to those under his care. In 1873 he had begun his studies at St Edward's College and after ordination served as a curate at St Patrick's in Liverpool, his ordination being at English Martyrs' Church in Preston in 1884. It was in the mid-1880's that he came to the notice of Father Nugent, who recognised his talents and the fact that his interests were similar to his own in the welfare of children. A sign of the trust he put in him was that he would entrust the care of the 'Catholic Times' to him.

Father Berry's special concern was for street-trading boys, especially boys who were without any support of family or lodgings, on the streets day and night. Later he was to make his name synonymous with the care of these children under the protection of the Homes he founded.

The current legislation did not give these lads a chance, so it was his intention to provide the opportunities they were denied. The problem of street-trading boys and young working men who had no real homes, continued to be a feature of late nineteenth century Liverpool and every other major town in Britain. Father Berry shared James

Nugent's concern that their tendency to crime and delinquency, and the moral dangers they faced, was something that needed urgent attention. Often in spite of their own best efforts the boys were vulnerable in all sorts of ways and needed both shelter and guidance.

It was in 1887, when he was appointed as Rector of the Oratory of St Philip's in Catherine Street and, at the same time, Director of the Catholic Institute, that John Berry began to demonstrate his ability and concern for social betterment of vulnerable youngsters. His rapport with young people seems to have been magnetic, like Nugent's, but in some ways more effective for the organisation he brought to his work. His attempt at a Rallying Cry – "Give the lad a Chance" – did not have the same impact as "Save The Boy". It was intended to emphasise the fact that it was older boys of working age that he was dealing with. Even if his slogan, similar to that of Canon Thomas Lester, has not gone down in history as the greatest sound-bite, it had considerable success at the time. The sentiment behind it was the same as Nugent's had been.

The long saga of Father Berry's Homes is closely associated with the activities of the St. Vincent de Paul Society in Liverpool. The Society leased some property at 105 Shaw Street on 1 November 1891 as a Working Boys' Home and Night Shelter under the presidency of Mr.Peter Hemelryk, a local Justice of the Peace. The dual purpose of the new Home – for working boys as well as destitute ones – had a common objective of keeping them safe and off the streets, where they were constantly a prey to unscrupulous characters and owners of doubtful lodging houses. Under Hemelryk's presidency, Mr Chilton Thomas, a barrister, was appointed as manager, a task he fulfilled with distinction for Father Berry's Homes until his death in July 1906. Arthur Chilton Thomas had a profound influence on the shaping and running of the Society and therefore on the Homes, the official title of which became 'Father Berry's Homes For Catholic Friendless Youths'.

From the time when John Berry calculated there were 1,100 Catholic boys living rough on the streets (an attention to detailed statistics being another similarity with James Nugent), he began opening other Shelters for Boys, with the establishment of St Philip's House in 1892 following the lease of property at 1 Marble Street, off Williamson Square. He opened it on Boxing Day of that year. Two months later on 17 February 1893 the first Home, St. Vincent's, came under the authority of the Diocese and Bishop O'Reilly, since the St. Vincent de Paul members found it beyond their means to maintain. Bishop O'Reilly promptly placed it under the care of John Berry. His first task was to extend the provision for homeless boys with a new Night Shelter made out of a disused stable at the back of the building. The active support of his bishop, Bernard O'Reilly was matched, if not exceeded by Bishop Thomas Whiteside, O'Reilly's successor in 1894. In the year 1895, the former much-loved bishop's name was honoured when a further Home for Young Street Boys was opened as St Bernard's Training Home, in Bute Street. This was intended as a sort of transition home to train and prepare boys off the streets for their residency at St. Vincent's.

The need for such intermediate care was quickly recognised by John Berry when he saw that those who had been destitute and roaming the streets from an early age were often incapable of looking after or disciplining themselves for life in an Institution. It is not unlikely that some of them were almost wild children who had grown used to uncivilised life, a dehumanised existence among the dregs and destitutes of the streets they inhabited. They would be incompatible with boys at St. Vincent's House and the stigma of delinquency and crime added to their plight of homelessness. John Berry saw the injustice of this as his slogan "Give the Lad a Chance" indicated. A chance at least, and the hand of friendship, was extended by the Homes to hundreds of youngsters.

It must not be forgotten that the first chance had been provided by the work of the St. Vincent de Paul Society, part of the rescue and charitable role it had long played in the noble history of Catholic concern for local needs. The 'President's Scheme' as it was at first called, because of the St. Vincent de Paul Society's President's own involvement in the St. Vincent's House project, drew the attention of the local Press, which, with a strongly Catholic slant called on the wealthier Protestant community of Liverpool to put their hands deep in their pockets and support this venture. Clearly some tension lay around the community over Catholic versus Protestant interest since the paper, not pulling any punches, included the plea to set denominational differences aside in the interests of the homeless boys. There was still considerable feeling about the legacy of Irish-Catholic immigrants whose offspring now formed the next impoverished generation in the city.

Bishop O'Reilly's decision to become personally involved in the St. Vincent's House project gave vital impetus to the efforts of local St. Vincent de Paul Conferences – of which there were twelve in the town. It helped them to secure the necessary backing and finance for the project. It was estimated that £400 annually for three years was needed to secure the new Home. In promoting the scheme volunteers would make it clear that the boys being housed were in effect being rescued from the dangers of vice and crime and that the existing laws made no provision for such boys – whether employed or not. They were forced to seek accommodation in all kinds of unsavoury places.

The new scheme would bring in those who were leaving orphanages because of their age, coming from Catholic Industrial Schools or reformatories, with a measure of training and formation gained in those Institutions. Some boys might earn 3 to 5 shillings a week and could be given the new accommodation for a small fee, in exchange for which they obtained safe shelter and regained their self-respect. They were also encouraged to save, by means of a

Savings' Bank scheme. The scheme obviously met with God's blessing as it succeeded quickly in its aim and boys were taught to mange their money better. The building, once run as a small school by The Christian Brothers in the 1880's and then under the ownership of the St. Vincent de Paul Society, now developed fully into a Home for Boys.

St. Vincent's was superintended by an ex-army sergeant, Garnett Barry and his wife, with Chilton Thomas as its Manager. The latter was a Welshman, as might be surmised. He was a Stoneyhurst College student where he had excelled in drama and debating, going on to study law, and later being called to the Bar in 1886. His work as a barrister in the Northern Circuit was short-lived as his overriding concern for the charitable care of homeless children took over his life as it did with so many others. His death at the relatively early age of 43, in July of 1906, was greatly lamented by all who had come to associate this fine man with the cause of Catholic Childcare in Liverpool.

Contrary to early indications of success, the President of the St. Vincent de Paul Society called a crisis meeting on 11th February 1893. He himself had been an 'absentee landlord' for the first 15 months of the scheme and had not given it as much personal attention as was expected. What he had succeeded in doing was to guard the finances but not the day-to-day practicalities that faced the SVP members. A quite bitter feeling grew up between himself and the Members who had not worked together in the opening months and so the President's wish to shed the financial liability of St. Vincent's came as a shock that caused ripples of resentment. Described as a 'punctilious' man of high principle, dubbed by some as a 'martinet', controversy raged for a while around his Presidency, but a resolution of the matter was reached and the outcome of the 11th February Meeting was that the Diocesan Bishop be asked to take on St. Vincent's house.

Bishop O'Reilly felt, despite the obvious difficulties of the project, it would not be right to let the boys of St. Vincent's down and it was at this point that he called in

Father John Berry, on the 17th February 1893, to take charge of the House. It may be counted as one of those key dates in the story, a turning point for Catholic Child Care. It was however not long before the size of the task undertaken was recognised as too big for any one person.

Father Berry's first annual report from St. Philip's House in 1893 included mention of the plight of the boys in his care; how on cold winter nights when 'business' was slack and life dull "the poor lad finds himself homeless and helpless, then on application to this House particulars of his case are taken, his immediate wants are cared for, a comfortable bed is given to him and next morning, if possible, started again in life with stock money or a set of blacking brushes." St. Philip's House could take up to 60 boys; and "for the modest sum of sixpence the boy is provided with a supper consisting of coffee or tea, bread with butter or jam, a like meal for breakfast, a hot bath and a bed". A supplement of two pence would entitle him to a hot meal in the middle of the day.

Father Berry's approach mirrored that of Father Nugent – expecting the boys to put in some work if not able or willing to pay for their keep. The work usually consisted of chopping wood into chips, with a target number of chips being required. If they were working during the day as shoeblacks, as many boys did around Lime Street Station and Exchange area, they could hire a uniform (shirt, trousers and cap) for four pence a day. In an effort to keep the fees down the Home was inevitably running into difficulties and St. Vincent's House gave rise to financial burdens for Father Berry. Unlike his predecessor he was very concerned about balancing the books and carefully budgeting for his expenses. Chilton Thomas, as general manager of the home at St. Vincent's was an able and conscientious helper but resources were slender.

In a letter to Bishop O'Reilly on April 12th 1893 Father Berry referred to his acute difficulties: "I am declining to pay all overdue bills until I have seen the treasurer's books for which I have applied hitherto unsuccessfully......... I send you this information that you may still further correct the impression that the House was in a safe financial position when you took over the Home". He wrote his letter on notepaper headed: "Father Berry's Homes" – a title that would soon become generally well-known.

In these early months he also recognised the plight and the needs of young girls, below the age of fifteen, who worked out a living on the streets, as papergirls or match-sellers. The moral dangers they faced were grave. Provision for them however was not yet possible. He wanted a good place as a Training School (Industrial School) for boys and for girls. His hopes and ideals were not matched with resources. Meanwhile Father Nugent was trying to support Father Berry's efforts: "He has made arrangements which will materially assist me to carry out the idea as soon as circumstances allow," he wrote in his report. What this assistance was was made clear soon afterwards when he was given, by Father Nugent, charge of the "Catholic Times" newspaper which in itself was a prestigoius means of spreading information and a good source of income. At this same time, however, a valuable ally was lost with the death of Bernard O'Reilly in 1894. He had been bishop of Liverpool since 1873 .

Mgr Carr was the Vicar Capitular, in charge of diocesan affairs during the interim or "interregnum", and he strongly encouraged Father Berry to open up a Night Shelter at the back of St. Vincent's house, in a dilapidated stable building off Haigh Street. It was to be a halfway-house, caring for the most destitute children, until they could enter St. Vincent's or St. Philip's. Their only payment was a small task such as chopping wood, during their overnight stay, where they were given food and a bed. St. James's was the poorest of poor homes, taking its name not from Father Nugent but from Monsignor John James Carr whose idea it was.

In the November of 1894 the lease ran out on the Marble Street property and St. Philip's House was moved to 31 Everton Crescent at a cost of £1,942, which meant a shortfall of £600. John Berry struggled on with the scheme of providing a 'penny supper, penny-bed, and penny-breakfast' policy as best he could . The answer to his aspirations for a Training Home came about in the form of St. Bernard's Home in Bute Street on 1st October 1895. St Bernard's Training School was to convert wild and disorderly street orphans into solid citizens – or at least into the right material for citizenship. He said in his report "we believe this House will be of the greatest use". He imposed a tough and disciplined regime on the boys, as in a Reformatory, but none was held there against their will as in a prison.

But the dark clouds of financial problems were looming. "The year (1895/96), has not been one of financial success" he reported. "I am more than £400 in debt not to speak of a mortgage of £600 on the Home in Everton Crescent. This responsibility weighs heavily on my mind." However he seemed determined to "drag on" and to put his trust in the "practical financial sympathy of the charitable public" who he believed would help him "to weather the storm". Bazaars were held, appeals and fund-raising activities organised, to keep the projects alive.

Diocesan policy towards the various Homes was ambivalent and Father Berry, along with Chilton Thomas, felt unsure about the level of support from Canon Green the Diocesan Treasurer. The public donations had amounted to £10,000 over five years but at the close of that period the threat of closure, so long overshadowing St. Philips House, came to a head on 20th May 1897. The Penny a Bed policy had been well meant but financially disastrous. Not only did St. Philip's house fold but also St. James's Night Shelter behind St. Vincent's, that same fateful day. In the winter of 1896/97 the night Shelter had provided 4,271 meals and 2,188 beds for destitute boys of all creeds and backgrounds. The record is as impressive as that of Father Nugent's, the same recording of each night's provision carefully written down. Even a makeshift soup kitchen in the city had now been discontinued. Another blow still, was the closure of St. Bernard's Training Centre – Father Berry's proudest achievement and the project he held most dear – on 30th October 1897, leaving only the original St. Vincent's House foundation in existence for Working Boys.

On a sad day for the valiant Father Berry, he tended his resignation and that of his Committee, 30th October 1897. Chiltern Thomas, as Secretary, received the letter of resignation. It conveyed Father Berry's sense of disillusionment, his efforts were described as "a gallant failure", and yet this must be offset by the proud acknowledgement he made of so much good work and Christian charitable effort expended by so many – including Monsignor John Carr and the members of the Homes' Committee, Chilton Thomas in particular, and stalwart helpers such as Messrs. Sweeney, O'Dowd and Gregson. A personal debt of £840 for Father Berry and a change of title to "Homes for Catholic Friendless Youths" (late Father Berry's Homes) seemed to seal the courageous but doomed career of this brave priest who had been seen as the nearest successor to Nugent.

Poignantly, he said in his resignation speech: "Of those who have never helped me I beg that they would spare me the contribution of their criticism .... of those from whom I have received assistance, and who, because they have helped me, will, I am confident not judge me harshly – of them I would ask they believe me when I express my gratitude for the help they so generously gave – whatever credit I may lose I have at least not lost my credit for honesty." He took some consolation from the fact that any financial losses at the time of closure had been made good by his own money and so there was no burden on others. His biggest regret however, naturally, was his inability personally to provide any further care for the boys who were in so much need and whom he had loved and served so well.

The SVP President, Peter Hemelryk, raised £450 towards the indemnity fund for John Berry to sweeten the bitter pill of penury, but it could not lessen his sense of failure. The departure of Father Berry from this courageous project on behalf of the poor probably disappointed Nugent, but both men knew each other well enough to recognise that, as was always the case, the work that had been done had been a gift of God, a vital contribution to the faith of many, and as such never a failed or useless enterprise. Nor did Father Berry withdraw altogether in 1897. He continued his work at St. Philip Neri parish and at the Catholic Institute for a further two years or so. His health, however, had been broken by the strenuous experiences of the Homes and in 1900 he retired and left Liverpool altogether. James Nugent's potential successor at the helm of the Liverpool Catholic Children's Protection Society accepted early retirement under orders from his doctor. He was nearly 42 when he reluctantly left Liverpool.

From that point life was lived in retirement in the comparative quiet of the countryside in Derbyshire. One source of information recorded by John Bennett is that he resided at Atherstone in Warwickshire. Evidence is clear that for most of his remaining 20 years he resided at a house called "The Firs" in Gallows Lane just outside the village of Measham, Derbyshire. His sister lived there too and there is a strong possibility the house was built with family money. They lived there, within the parish of Our Lady, Measham, and for a time helped to run a Sunday school for local children in a room of the house – the last vestige of the work of education to which he had given the energy of his life.

There was a sense of an era ending and a new one forming, partly built upon the legacy of the past. John Berry's active connection with his home diocese of Liverpool continued for a few years as he kept on his editorship of the Catholic Times, trying to raise money and writing articles under the pseudomyn of 'Papyrus'. Appeals for more money were a constant theme in 'The Catholic Times' and 'The Catholic Fireside'. The editorship of the latter publication was given into the hands of an Old

Boy of Father Nugent's Homes, Mr. Essington-Fay, who later succeeded to the role of Secretary of Father Berry's Homes in 1919, until the death of Archbishop Whiteside in 1924. The Archbishop was fully supportive of the Homes.

There was a continuity there that would have pleased Nugent. When Nugent first began publishing his 'Rescue Notes' to keep former friends and Old Boys in touch, wherever in the world they were dispersed, he was ensuring that the network of information and Catholic identity was preserved. For two years after his death, until 1907, his great friend Father Edmund Walsh, in St Thomas's Waterloo, carried on the publication of the 'Notes' but it could not be sustained further than that. It was an example of how the founder's death took away the momentum and the attraction of something synonymous with himself.

Refuge & Shelter for Fallen Women Paul St

Chapter 13

Golden Days and Last Days

Every life is entitled to a purple patch and Father Nugent had many of them. But now he was approaching the Golden days of his priestly career. It seems that the approach of his Golden Jubilee in August 1896 was a time of relative satisfaction and rejoicing amidst the "mighty work", as Canon Bennett has referred to it. Part of the celebration of the 50 years was a time of reflection on retreat at Holywell, North Wales, from where he wrote to his priest friend Father Byrne about his gratitude for priestly life over those long years, and in a mood of mellow contentment, though not of complacency, he gave thanks to God. Father Byrne read part of the letter at the solemn High Mass – which naturally took place in St. Nicholas' Church, Copperas Hill (by now known as the Pro-Cathedral) on Fr. Nugent's ordination anniversary, 30th August 1896.

We are already familiar with the letter but it is helpful to repeat it here as it captures the tone of these special days in his life. He recalled that he had been committed to:

> "addressing myself to the wants of the times, power of organisation, influence with young men and the working classes, a breadth of action, seeking to do good to all, not working within narrow lines but feeling the obligation of creating a better feeling among all classes by enforcing the duty of good citizenship what was running to waste or becoming a social plague, utilizing the natural power, ability and action of neglected children and fallen humanity, and lifting men and women up from the degradation of ignorance and vice."

Raising up fallen humanity, picking the detritus of human society off the streets and restoring people's self-esteem, these had been central elements in his fifty year-long mission. Few could claim to be as "hands-on" as he had been during that time. Nor did he rest on his laurels. Within a year of his Golden Jubilee he would be busy overseeing the opening of a new Home for Girls under the care of The Sisters of Nazareth, in Liverpool Road at Great Crosby, near to where his own parents had gone to live some years before. The new Home also took in disadvantaged young girls who experienced physical or mental difficulties of one kind or another. June 1897 saw the official opening of Nazareth House Orphanage, representing considerable efforts on the part of Bishop Thomas Whiteside, who, with Nugent, had been concerned to refurbish and staff the Home adequately. The building in Great Crosby had been found in a deplorable state of disrepair and the now familiar and protracted process of negotiation, fund-raising and repair work was needed to bring the large building into use.

As so often before, the task looked hopeless, but Nugent was never in doubt that the effort would be worthwhile. He had too much experience of rescue work to take any other view, and he encouraged all concerned to work together to bring the new Home into being. At his side in this was Father Pinnington with the considerable weight of his abilities and strength of purpose. A £5,000 bill was involved in the work on Nazareth House. Awareness of the need and of the project was broadcast in a variety of ways including notices in "Rescue Notes" which had become an important publication organ for Nugent and his colleagues in the whole work for Children's Homes. Bishop Whiteside found willing hands in the Sisters of Nazareth who were open to any task and relied on God's providence, and the project was an example of the strong cooperation between Nugent and Whiteside in the cause they both held very dear, – the care of underprivileged children.

Father Nugent was happy to get his hands on any funding he could legitimately lay claim to for charitable purposes, but he turned down categorically any suggestion that he write his Prison Memoirs for money. Home Office restrictions ruled it out any way, and quite apart from the legal restrictions Nugent had come to recognise the dignity of the prisoners in his care as sacred, and believed confidentiality must be safeguarded.

Meanwhile, letters of congratulations and good wishes for his Golden Jubilee had flooded in from every quarter, from the high and the lowly, from Catholic and Protestant, rich and poor. On the occasion of the Golden Jubilee this reflected, after all, the breadth of Nugent's pastoral care and the sheer variety of people he had influenced or helped. Contacts in the United States had established him as a firm friend and revered pastor, and letters or telegrams duly arrived from New York (Archbishop Corrigan,) St. Paul Minnesota (Archbishop Ireland) San Francisco (Archbishop Riordan) from many other prelates and dignitaries of the Church and State and a special Papal Blessing of the Holy Father, Pope Leo XIII, via Propaganda Fide in Rome.

In Liverpool there was general and enthusiastic support for Lord Derby's suggestion of a memorial to mark the Monsignor's Jubilee and pay tribute to his great achievements – an oil portrait and a subscription to the Monsignor's charitable works. The artist, James Jebusa Shannon was then 34 years of age and American born. In due course he would be knighted for his services to Art but was already, in 1896, an artist of some renown – and thought to be the right person to do justice to Nugent, who would be painted wearing his full Monsignorial processional robes. How Shannon succeeded in getting Nugent to remain still long enough to paint his portrait is a matter of some conjecture, but the final result was deemed very satisfactory by everyone concerned.

Nugent himself liked the portrait and considered it to be a good likeness but privately was probably more interested in the £2,000 that remained after payment of the painter's commission fee. To be precise, there was £1,926 remaining and of this he set aside £1,300 for the establishment of the Home, that came to be known as the House of Providence, in West Dingle, South Liverpool, for the shelter and rehabilitation of single abandoned mothers and their babies. Some may have thought it would be his last project. It was opened in 1897.

The presentation of the portrait took place on 5th May 1897 in St. George's Hall before a packed audience including William Rathbone, MP. As pre-arranged, Father Nugent handed it to the City Council for it to be placed in the Walker Art Gallery where it is housed today. Victorians liked their portraits; tangible and visible expressions of the individual at a given time in life, in the same way that modern society is in love with the camera and the digital images of today's photography or of the film-maker's art.

The Earl of Derby, Lord Mayor of Liverpool, had proposed the portrait memorial in a glowing tribute saying, "it is desirable to promote a testimonial to the Right Reverend Monsignor Nugent, in consideration of his philanthropic services to the city of Liverpool during the last fifty years". There followed a summary of all Nugent's achievements. Significant tributes were also paid by those unavoidably absent from the Lord Mayor's meeting. Thomas Ismay head of the White Star Line, who lived in the Waterloo area in a house overlooking the sea, was away at the time, but wrote a letter full of admiration for his friend Father Nugent and the work he had done, noting the "esteem and respect of all classes" which the Monsignor had won over the years.

In addition to the Nazareth House project at Crosby, the year 1897 saw another important event that claimed his careful attention. June 16th. 1897 saw the fiftieth anniversary of the death of ten Liverpool priests known as 'The Martyr Priests' who had died in the typhus epidemic of 1847. Requiem Mass in remembrance of them was sung by Bishop Thomas Whiteside at St. Patrick's, the Church associated with their memory. He was assisted by many of the priests including Monsignor Carr. In a sermon given by James Nugent the theme was that of the Good Shepherd who gave his life for his sheep. The sermon gives us valuable statistics of the fever and the effects of its devastation on the local community. Nugent recounted how the fever "swept over the north, south and central parts of the town, causing dreadful havoc and suffering among the poor where miseries resulting from the pest were aggravated by want." He recalled how, in the midst of the panic created by this terrible scourge, the devotion and calmness of the priests commanded universal admiration. Day and night they were with the people. "Into the dwellings of the poor, in attic and cellar, in the courts and alleys, where to breathe the fetid and pestilential air was death, they went fearlessly to give the Sacraments. They were at the bedside of the dying, and where the dead were left unburied more than one of that heroic band lifted the dead body all covered in typhus spots , and placed it in a coffin...."

According to Nugent, the first who fell ill was the Reverend Peter Nightingale of St. Anthony's, who died on the 2nd. of March 1847 and who Nugent had known well as a fellow student at Ushaw College and later as a companion in the priesthood, remembering him as "a bright, energetic, bold man - a true priest, a true friend and beloved by all around him".

Not long after the golden tributes, and this more sombre recollection of the fever days and the priests who had sacrificed their lives on the altar of duty, the dark clouds of conflict were gathering as the prospect of the Boer War loomed. The issue of the war in Africa divided Britain and was the first great British conflict on foreign soil since the Crimean War of 1854. It seems that Nugent, though opposing war in principle, supported this particular conflict. This was probably to do with the fact that he was chaplain to the Fifth Irish Volunteers and could not be seen to be opposing them. It had less to do with a bellicose attitude on his part. He had preached a gospel of peace by his words and his actions.

When 6,000 troops assembled at Wavertree on 20th June 1897, the time of Queen Victoria's Diamond Jubilee, Nugent preached a sermon encouraging the soldiers of his regiment in their forthcoming campaign. Colleagues from other denominations joined him that day. His support was largely that borne of loyalty to the men he served as spiritual guide. During the war that followed, as drafts of the Fifth Irish Volunteers were sent out to Africa, they would muster outside St. Patrick's Church for a farewell blessing. Nugent was there to encourage their efforts and commend them to God. He accurately predicted, on one occasion, as the troops gathered at St. Patrick's, that none would be lost in battle and all would return safely from the fray.

Although there were very few times when Nugent sat back to enjoy the acclaim, it must be fully acknowledged, at this point in his career, that he was looking to hand over much of his work to another. As we have seen, Father John Berry was looked on as a natural successor to Nugent. A younger man, with the same sort of credentials and similar priorities in regard to social welfare, especially of children, Father Berry's particular interest was in housing and training homeless working boys of the streets. The rehabilitation movement was therefore safe in his hands. He had already been following in the footsteps of Nugent by his appointment to St. Philip Neri in Catherine Street and as head of the Catholic Institute, for which job he was eminently well suited. Events would prove to be less satisfactory than the initial hopes had promised but it should be reported that the story of Father John Berry's efforts in the care of "Home" children remains one of the important contributions to Catholic Social Welfare at the turn of the 19th century.

It was the end of the century but not the end of James Nugent's ambitions and ideas. The Golden days of his

Priesthood, fifty years service in Liverpool, fifty-fourth year of ordination, a lifetime of arduous labour in the Lord's vineyard, had left his enthusiasm undiminished. It had never been his way to sit and rest on his laurels even though no-one would have criticised him for doing so. Instead he was looking round for new needs to address and found them in the plight of young women and their babies.

In a sermon at St. Thomas's Waterloo, where his friend Father Edmund Walsh was parish priest, he had based his ideas for a Women's Refuge on the Mary Magdalen story in the gospel. To him the social needs of the city had always been transparent, but what was even more significant was his utter inability to accept the stigma attached to moral misbehaviour and sexual sin. As always he looked first at the heart, at the potential for recovery and a new life, and this guided him in his thinking towards mothers of illegitimate babies or single mothers thrown out on the street to fend for themselves. He chose not to discriminate between circumstances as he regarded the spiritual welfare of the mother and the physical welfare of the child to be paramount.

The idea of opening yet another Home – a Maternity Home and safe haven for expectant mothers without any means of support - may have seemed like one ambition too many to some of Nugent's friends. He was anxious to continue the work, meeting each new need as it arose. It was a remarkable achievement that he did open such a Home, in the Dingle area of South Liverpool in 1903. Earlier, at the opening of the near-by House of Providence, he had gathered together likely supporters to expound to them the important reasons for this new Home. As ever, his powers of persuasion must have worked and the money was found.

The new project "The House of Good Counsel" was to be short-lived but demonstrated Nugent's determined spirit in his failing years to protect the Unborn Child. The House of Good Cousel emerged as a direct follow-up to the House of Providence, specifically to encourage women to have their babies and not abort them.

The time for tributes and for toil were coming to an end. There would be, however, a further and even more tangible expression of gratitude to James Nugent from the city of his birth. In the spring of 1903 when he returned from one of his many trips to America more accolades awaited him. It was to be his penultimate trip to the USA and a decline in health had been noticed already by his friends. Although his return in the springtime of 1903 was greeted with great acclaim, he had been travelling extensively in America and had to rest from time to time. He had the advantage of being with friends and family, staying with his brother, Joseph, in Minnesota. No doubt exhaustion played a part, as it had done several times before, amidst the relentless round of travelling and lecturing.

On 16th June a banquet was held in the Adelphi Hotel in Liverpool after his return home in 1903. A large and distinguished company gathered for the occasion, 120 guests were listed but many more were in attendance, including the Bishops of Liverpool and Shrewsbury, top civic dignitaries and many other church and community leaders. Once again the range and size of the gathering demonstrated the wide embrace of his ministry and the breadth of respect in which he was held. The Catholic Bishop of Liverpool's flowing words of tribute were responded to by a number of leading Liverpool personages; heads of the big companies like Tate and Lyle and the former Lord Mayor, Councillor Cohen, who was the head of Lewis's and a close friend of Nugent. It was Cohen who mentioned the idea of a statue and the plans to have it erected in a suitable and prominent place in the city centre.

The sculptor, Frederick William Pomeroy, was appointed for the work, but Nugent would not live to see it unveiled. This eventually took place on 8th December 1906 in St. John's Gardens where it has stood to the present time. The bronze figure of Nugent looks confidently out over the city and towards the sea. The right hand is raised in blessing, the left hand is held in a protective embrace on the shoulder of a ragged child, skilfully portraying the role he had played as priest and philanthropist, evangeliser of God and shepherd of lost sheep.

At the Adelphi Dinner in 1903 at what was obviously an emotional and historic moment in his long career, Nugent had the privilege of responding to the accolades that had been made. He heard his bishop, Thomas Whiteside, propose the health of "The Guest of the Evening" with great warmth. Whiteside said that the history of the Monsignor's work was written in the history of the city, that he had worked and lived amid the seamiest aspects of human society and seen the most degraded forms of human nature, but that his recognition even there of the "innate nobility of the human soul that its Creator had stamped upon it" rendered him capable of hope and optimism. The speech was greeted with great applause. Equally warm was the response to Nugent's reply, his "acceptance speech," on that day.

He rose to his feet in the glow of appreciation that was evident all around him and proceeded to affirm his indebtedness to Liverpool and his love for the city and its people. He said he had tried "in some small measure to better the people". He went on to remind people that "life was a gift from God, and, whatever their positions, each one in his walk of life had certain and heavy responsibilities". He recalled that he "had seen the city grow and had grown with it" anything he had done for the city was done as part of a "Divine responsibility". The city had made him, and had itself been the context and motivation of his life's work. That life had two more years to run and in that time there was still a work of service to be done.

Final accolades were still to come and fulsome praise would be given him. The tributes to Monsignor James Nugent at the time of his death in June 1905 are all a matter of public record. Local Liverpool newspapers would carry lengthy appreciations and cover several columns of print and there were countless other tributes from far and wide, from the Liverpool community and the Church abroad, together with an extraordinary record of praise and an expression of genuine sadness following his death. Flags on public buildings throughout the city would be at half-mast and in the print room memorial cards prepared in huge numbers for distribution on the streets. Besides the well reported panegyric of Father Edmund Walsh, long and trusted friend from St. Thomas's Waterloo, and the praise of his faithful doctor who tended him Dr Roughan, many representatives of the Catholic, Protestant and Free Church communities would pay handsome compliments and respectful honour to a much cherished colleague and friend, who had championed the cause of Christian Unity by his enlightened efforts to walk hand in hand with people of all religions. Before all this there was a final work of transition to be done to ensure the continuity of things. There would be the hand of Providence at work in the ministrations of Liverpool's Catholic Bishop Whiteside who recognised the significance of Father Nugent's work.

Chapter 14

The Children's Bishop

Before the turn of the century, 1899, Monsignor Nugent was still alert at the age of seventy-nine, to new needs and anxious to oversee the succession of Father Jean Renaud as parish priest at the Oratory and Director of the C.I. He was still personally watching over the 'baby' he had reared since 1853. Considering its teething troubles half a century earlier, Nugent's faith in it had been justified.

It was a time of transition, and something in the way of a caretaker was needed until the new Bishop, Thomas Whiteside, who had been appointed Bishop of Liverpool in succession to Bernard O'Reilly in 1894, was to enter into the front room of the Diocese like a new broom sweeping everything clean. He would make a significant move in arranging for the Christian Brothers to come to Liverpool and take charge of the Catholic Institute. This new start would give fresh impetus for its growth. Meanwhile a new committee had been formed to supervise the work of the Boys' Homes, under the chairmanship of Francis Reynolds, members of whose family were all wealthy Cotton Merchants. He became a vitally important financial backer of the project, in fact the family was largely responsible for keeping it in existence at this time.

A new location had been found for the Headquarters of the Liverpool Catholic Children's Protection Society and in 1898 the staff moved office to 53 Everton Road, whilst the former building at 99 Shaw Street reopened under the new title of Newman House as a hostel for boys able to support themselves in work. It also served as a club for Old Boys of the Children's Homes. The house was named after John Henry Newman and Cardinal Newman's influence remained very strong not only for Father Nugent but among English Catholics generally, after his death.

The network of "Old Boys" from the Homes had grown over the years and this prompted a new publication, "St. Vincent's Record" which was produced on a monthly basis to enable a network of both former and current residents to stay in touch with news and events. From the day Nugent took over The Northern Press, communication and information had been a vital ingredient in the whole enterprise of rescue and reform.

Nugent's pioneering role in the Emigration of Children to Canada took a new development in 1900 when children were sent directly there from the Homes rather than as an 'ad hoc' arrangement. The work of St. Vincent's House was put on a completely different footing and tied in with a business partnership that gave new confidence to all involved. A new Committee, made up of clerical and lay members, together with better links to the local civic authorities, provided a boost to the whole scheme. The care of poor boys had been sustained, at least for the foreseeable future, and there seemed to be a sense of optimism, of looking ahead. Yet, a bizarre process of naming and renaming the project meant that the title 'Father Berry's Homes' was restored, and so his name, happily for Father Berry, was once again given prominence, and so it remained for several years into the new century. Even today Father Berry's Homes are remembered by those whose relatives were once given refuge there.

The involvement of the large and well-connected businesses of the Reynolds and Gibson's Families,- prominent Catholic families,- restored the reputation and confidence that was needed in the project. It was a matter of pride to have one's name on the subscription list of such a worthy cause. The new start and management had come too late for Father Berry, but at least his name was still remembered.

The Magistrates' Courts at this time were making clear distinctions between proven delinquents and vagrants not guilty of crimes. This separation of "sheep from goats" meant added pressure on an Institution like St. Bernard's Home which Father Berry had founded. The new Committee reopened the original Saint Bernard's and in the course of the first year, 1898, 127 boys were admitted. About half this number went on to gain respectable jobs but the other half didn't enjoy such success, leaving St. Bernard's at various intervals because they were unable to accept the regime. It was a hard regime but not all work. The ubiquitous Boys' Band and other musical opportunities so integral to all these Homes, provided a welcome outlet for talented and energetic boys. The new Committee of Father Berry's Homes was not immune to the problems which their founder had struggled with. The Institutions had to do the work that the local authorities and Central Government were not doing, that is, tackling crime at its root, in the streets which Father Berry had described as "the forming ground of crime".

The Children's Homes were offering a respite rather than a cure. The root of the problem lay in the social structures and legal provisions of the day which were inadequate to address the real causes of crime. Crime was dealt with by flogging, or by imposing harsh fines or by imprisonment. Charities such as St. Bernard's Home, and efforts to produce a Night School provision at the Catholic Institute, represented practically the only constructive type of response to the increasing problem of street vagrancy and street crime.

Attempts to redress this imbalance were taken forward by the passing of the Liverpool Corporation Act of 1898 which restricted Street Traders' activities and put tougher conditions on permission for children to trade. It became illegal to do so if the child was considered unfit for work or lacking clothes or education. Father Nugent was one of many who had long campaigned for street trading to be made illegal. As street traders were driven more into illegal and potentially more vulnerable situations, so the need for a proper place of care became more acute. Accommodation for both boys and girls was sorely needed and the Committee, helped by the Liverpool Corporation, set about re-opening St. Philip's Home in Everton Crescent to provide shelter. The Corporation gave a grant of £25. The finance gave the Corporation a stake in the enterprise and so, to an extent, some control over it. It meant, importantly, that there was no particular provision for the Religious welfare of the children in care. Ironically no street trader boys were sent to St. Philip's so its intended purpose, and the concerns about religious instruction, did not materialise.

The year 1899 proved to be a crisis point for the Committee of St. Vincent's Home when the offloading of "The Clarence" ship added to their problems. The accommodation problem was solved by the renting of premises adjacent to 105 Shaw Street and the help of the staff from St. Francis Xavier's who lent items needed for feeding and clothing 250 extra bodies. These adjacent properties were in the ownership of the Liverpool School Board and the Board demanded the end of the rental arrangement in January 1900 since they wanted space for disabled children there. Thus Shaw Street became the focus of constant activity and transition for the various people in need of care, including the patients of the Women's Hospital, which was located in Shaw Street before it moved to Catherine Street opposite St. Philip's Oratory.

The Catholic Female Orphanage in Faulkner Street – which earlier in James Nugent's time was called 'The Catholic Orphanage Asylum, had to relocate too, amidst all the changes and pressures of this time. Nugent's own brief account of the history of the Asylum states that there was originally accommodation for 65 girls, when the Sisters of Mercy took charge of it. They had handed over to the Notre Dame Sisters in 1851. Improvements to the basic conditions of the orphanage were imposed after the

1866 Industrial Schools Act which required of the sisters a number of new work rooms for basic skills such as sewing and an extension to the dormitory. Eventually, a total of 100 girls could be housed there and the neat, soulless Victorian house, organised by strict but kindly nuns, survived another chapter of its existence.

Many of the girls from the Orphanage had emigrated. The comment made about Father Nugent's good intentions in Emigration landing some children in a worse plight, and his plans "turning to ashes in another kind of hell", had an element of truth in it. Perhaps the warning signs were already there when it was becoming apparent that some children were being sent abroad to relations or host families that were neither prepared nor suitable to be foster parents. Some re-arrangements had to be made to avoid this. In other cases it proved to be a sad fact that Canadian and American hosts were not always free of the tendency to abuse, neglect or mistreat their new charges. The Catholic Emigrating Society under Canon St. John of Southwark made efforts to prevent such disasters. The policy of having a House of Reception, like the one at New Orpington Lodge in Hintenburg, Ottawa, was designed to be a transition post until suitable, adoptive homes were found. Two stalwarts of Child Welfare work, Arthur Chilton Thomas and Father Bans of 'The Crusade of Rescue', visited Canada to better acquaint themselves with Child Emigration policy and the problems surrounding it.

1903 proved to be a very significant year in the history of Childcare in Britain for in that year the wisdom and experience of different organisations came together under the one umbrella of "The Catholic Emigration Association". Under the one banner now were united Father Berry's Homes, The Crusade of Rescue and the excellent Father Hudson's Children's Homes based in Birmingham. Canon St. John became President with Father Bans working at full stretch and Reception Houses for the boys at Hintenburg, and in Montreal for Girls, were arranged to meet the fairly continuous arrival of more groups. Money, the ever pressing need, was being gathered in a constant round of fundraising.

Time was running out for the man who had spearheaded all this activity for so long. Father Nugent's death in June 1905 would mark the end of a remarkable era in Catholic Childcare. It would not mean the end. He had ensured that by the things he had put in place. In fact the effort and financial backing was on a very strong footing at the time of his death and later that year, in October, a well-organised, large-scale bazaar held in St. George's Hall raised £4,500. It would have pleased the "Little Corporal" as the Press had dubbed him, that the battle of fundraising was still going strong.

In the same year of his death, Father Nugent had undertaken yet one further visit to his beloved America. Whether or not he knew this year might be his last, Nugent made plans to accompany his friend Abbot Gasquet around America in furtherance of Catholic interests and as an opportunity to visit Home Children and his own family. It was a fateful journey too many. Not only was he ill there but he also fell badly on the ship coming home. It was the beginning of a final decline in his health. He had several medical appointments – for poor eye-sight and painful joints, but his days were now ending.

The era was ending with the death of others too. A House for abandoned babies, Our Lady's Home, at 93 Shaw Street, was taken over in 1906 by Father Berry's Homes and when the death of Chilton Thomas occurred on 21 July that year – a moment of great sadness that represented the passing of one of the key figures in Liverpool Catholic history – the Babies' Home was renamed after him as a mark of the esteem in which he was held. Glowing tributes were paid to this extraordinary man who had steered the Homes through a time of crisis and established them on a better financial footing. Sadly, he went too soon; he was only 43 years of age when he died. Certain people already deeply involved in Child Care work were now able to come more to the foreground.

The baton was passed on to someone who had already assumed a prominent position in Liverpool Diocese: Father William Pinnington. He would acquire considerable status in the sphere of Child Care, though his first appointment to the position in Liverpool was not to be for long. Father Pinnington had been Secretary of the Catholic Children's Aid Committee and now, on 4th February 1907, at an Annual general Meeting of the Father Berry's Homes Committee in the Town Hall, he was announced as the new Director of the Homes. However, the name of Father Berry continued to be used on all the publicity, and perhaps due to the disapproval of Austin Oates who edited the magazine, it was not until 1908 that Father Pinnington's name appeared in the publication 'Homeless'. Pinnington soon followed in the footsteps of his predecessors by taking groups of children to Canada. Becoming a Canon of the Chapter of the diocese the following year he began to make it clear that, allegedly, due to other commitments he could not continue in post as Director of the Homes, though he would work to support the enterprise in whatever way he could.

In fact it was his difficulty in working with the publicity secretary, Austin Oates, that was the real problem. His place was taken in 1911 by Father Thomas George who found it easier than his predecessor had done to work with Austin Oates. The fact that the 'chemistry' had not worked previously had been a well-known 'running sore' in the organisation. Oates had the task of organising not only the publicity but much of the fund-raising for the Homes by means of the magazine 'Homeless'. Among the many high profile events he organised was a recital of poetry at St. George's Hall given by Father Bernard Vaughan, a Jesuit, and famous public speaker and orator. Such events were in line with the Nugent tradition and Austin Oates was given recognition with a Knighthood of St. Gregory, but Canon Pinnington had found Oates' methods unacceptable.

Because of the prestigious financial position he held perhaps Oates was too powerful a colleague to work with comfortably.

Before Father Thomas George could do much more than establish workshops and training facilities for the youngsters in care: – laundry, shoe-making and tailoring (all the usual and traditional skills associated with the Catholic Children's Homes) he found himself appointed Rector of the Beda College in Rome. He went off to pastures new together with a new title of "Monsignor". It was in this same year that the title of Archbishop of Liverpool was established and Thomas Whiteside made history as the first to hold that title in 1911, becoming Archbishop and Metropolitan. It was a further consolidation of the Catholic position in Liverpool. One of his first tasks was to pay tribute to Austin Oates who died unexpectedly that same year, and to maintain the link with Father Nugent by appointing to the post of Homes' Manager Mr. Essington-Fay – an old boy from Father Nugent's time at St. George's School.

A short time later, in the momentous year of 1914 the Great War brought the suspension of nearly all organised work and there was a difficult hiatus in Childcare efforts for the duration. Many Institutions were commandeered for War-related purposes and everyone's efforts were channelled towards the same cause. It was estimated that about 200 "old boys" of the Homes were engaged in active service during the war. After the war there would be a hard time of recouping and bolstering the existing provision and the process began of amalgamating the various strands of Catholic Childcare provision between 1918 and 1924, by which date a new Archbishop, Thomas Keating had taken over the Archdiocese of Liverpool.

On the 1st March 1924 the process of regrouping reached its zenith with the official combining of three main organisations into one: The Liverpool Catholic Children's Protection Society; the Catholic Children's Aid Society; Father Berry's Homes. The three were known from that time on as 'The Liverpool Catholic Children's Protection Society'. The single title for all the strands of work made co-ordination easier, even though each one had retained its specific remit. The way was now clear for Monsignor William Pinnington to resume his post as administrator and he worked tirelessly in the tradition of Father Nugent, his mentor, to ensure the proper referral of destitute children to various Institutions suitable to their needs. Crisis management was beginning to be replaced with forward planning.

In a sense the seeds of this better time for Catholic Child Care had been planted by Father Nugent seventy-five years before. With the good offices of the Catholic Children's Aid Committee (founded in 1899,) advice and support was beginning to materialise in relation to all matters of Catholic Child Welfare from a central office in Trueman Street. This successful venture meant that more children were presented for assistance and so there came about the need for larger orphanages outside the city. Nazareth House Convent in Crosby had already been established in 1897, and also, Residential Home for Boys at Nazareth House, Ditton, near Widnes. Another opened up for the Girls, at Nazareth House in Lancaster. The Order in charge, The Poor Sisters of Nazareth, was one of the key strands in the field of Child Care at this time. The history of social welfare would be much poorer without their contribution.

The increasing business of residential Childcare required a concerted fundraising. Archbishop Whiteside began the 'Good Shepherd Fund', as it became known, in 1902, calling on the children in school to raise money during Lent, something already established in the Archdiocese of Westminster. An indication of the rising success of the Fund is seen in the figure for 1902: £270, which increased to £10,055 by 1945, despite the War, and in recent times sums of £70,000 to £80,000.

The improved position that prevailed after 1924 was therefore largely due to the planning Nugent and

Whiteside had done in those important years at the turn of the century. In the post- 1920 period many changes took place and the work of Catholic Childcare took giant steps forward. Under the single umbrella of LCCPS between 1924 and 1932 and a new Committee comprising most of the members of the previous three committees, work progressed steadily. William Pinnington was Administrator and John Bennett was secretary of the Liverpool arm of the new organisation.

An appraisal of Canon William Pinnington's contribution is important for he was directly in line with Father Nugent's original purpose and ideals. He was from Scarisbrick, Lancashire, where he was born on 19th. June 1856. He went to the English College in Lisbon for his theological studies, and was ordained in 1880 just before Christmas. His ability and authority were amply recognised, even before ordination, by the fact that the President of the College, Mgr. Baines, virtually treated him as his assistant and as Prefect of Discipline in the College. The English College Lisbon never had a more loyal and enthusiastic ambassador than he. Bishop O'Reilly, at that time (1881) holding the reigns as Bishop of Liverpool would not contemplate any request for him to be retained in Lisbon. Despite pleas from the President there, Father Pinnington returned to the diocese in August 1881. Two years of uncertainty, back and forth to the College in Lisbon, followed, but it was clear that as far as Bernard O'Reilly was concerned his future lay in Liverpool. His first assignment was not in fact to Liverpool but to Garstang in Lancashire as curate to Mgr. Gradwell. His reputation was soon established both as a sympathetic and able priest and as a competent medical man who could even reset broken collarbones!

The year 1886 had seen him at St. Alphonsus, Liverpool where he began the task of building schools and generally showing a flair for educational matters in which he became quite expert, especially on legal aspects. He was sought after on local education committees and became a firm favourite as a chairman who could effect progress at meetings. Naturally, in due course, he came to the notice of Father Nugent and shared many of the great man's concerns about the Catholic education of the young. He became a member of The West Derby Board of Guardians which controlled admission to schools and argued effectively for poor Catholics to be referred to the Catholic Poor Schools and receive whatever education was available to them. He was not afraid to argue fiercely on behalf of the poor in front of the Board members.

Advocacy of poor Catholic children and their families was a growing business and it was this that had led Bishop Whiteside to set up the Catholic Children's Aid Society in Trueman Street in 1899, William Pinnington being the obvious choice as secretary. Its chairman was Father Joseph Clarkson. The ten years which followed were ones of meteoric rise for William Pinnington but his resignation from the top position as head of The Children's Homes in 1909 was as sudden and dramatic as Father Berry's had been in 1897, though for different reasons. As already stated the principal reason was that he had felt compromised by the actions of Austin Oats, publicity manager, who had embarrassed more than a few people with over-persistent, and too frequent requests for money without reference to his Director.

William Pinnington, like his predecessor, James Nugent, combined humility with powers of persuasion. The Lisbonian Magazine June issue 1932 records a fine tribute to his work in Catholic Childcare. It cites two examples of the character and determination he brought to this work. First was an account of how a group of children from Ireland were subject to an act of proselytising when a group allocated them to a Protestant home for Children in England. William Pinnington, in poor health at the time, waited on the Liverpool Landing Stage for the ship carrying the children. He went on board and rounded up the children in the very presence of the group that had brought them and escorted them to a Catholic Home. The second story concerns two young boys who had been in a Catholic Home but by the action of a non-Catholic relative had been transferred to a non-Catholic Institution. After strenuous efforts to locate the two boys Father Pinnington set off to find and retrieve them. They were interviewed privately to come to a decision about which home they really wanted to go to. Fr. Pinnington meanwhile paced up and down, saying the rosary. One boy was asked why they finally decided in favour of the Catholic one; his answer was – "because the grub's better!"

The effects of the War in bringing most activities, except those related to the War, to a sudden end, might have meant a permanent closure of the important work for Catholic Child Care and the Children's Homes. But a large legacy of £20,000 brought the project back to life. One significant turn of events during the war years was the death in November 1915 of Monsignor Carr, Vicar General of the diocese and formerly one of Father Nugent's greatest friends. William Pinnington succeeded him as Vicar General. The new umbrella organisation, the Liverpool Catholic Children's Protection Society was placed under Pinnington's administration with John Osmond Bennett, later Canon Bennett, appointed as Secretary on 1st March 1924.

As we have said, much of the expansion and development that took place in Catholic Childcare between 1894 and 1921 was inspired and nurtured at its roots by Archbishop Thomas Whiteside. He was the Catholic bishop of Liverpool from 1894 to 1911 and then became Archbishop until his death in 1921. It was a significant period of change and development that he had to oversee. Undoubtedly his closest aid was William Pinnington who was in effect the chief executive of all that transpired in this area of the diocese's apostolate. The work was based on a deep-seated recognition that rescue work was complex and varied and that each boy or girl had to be understood in their own right and given the care appropriate to them, not treated as one amorphous group. William Pinnington became so identified with the Bishop's charity work that he was often known to be the author of his letters, even if the Bishop signed them.This reflected a far closer relationship than Father Nugent had enjoyed with his superiors. The coverage of Children's homes of different kinds began to expand to St. Helens, Preston and other parts of the diocese, spreading out from the original Liverpool base.

Lent 1903 yielded much needed funds from the efforts of school children for "The Good Shepherd Fund" and set the pattern that has continued and grown to the present day. Figures for 1909, in the annual report of the Liverpool Catholic Children's Protection Society reveal that 3,636 children were cared for that year in diocesan Homes. 904 of these fell into the category of Poor Law cases, financed by the local authority; 1,550 of them supported by voluntary contributions; 1,083 Industrial School cases; 393 Reformatory School children and 106 from other schools of special need such as St. Vincent's School For The Blind in West Derby.

Thomas Whiteside came to relish this side of his work. Even though he was regarded by many as austere, almost aloof, he displayed a surprising rapport with the children in Care and his time spent with them, and his natural empathy, gained him the title: "The Children's Bishop". The care of Christ's more unfortunate lambs was to be the special hallmark of his ministry as shepherd of the diocese.

He had been a student of St. Edward's College, Ushaw College and the Venerabile in Rome. After his ordination in 1885 he was appointed as a member of staff at the newly-established St. Joseph's College, Upholland becoming Vice-Rector within two years and then Rector in succession to Dr. Billsborrow, who became the Bishop of Salford. His time as Rector is remembered for the way he never yielded to sentiment or frivolity. Iron discipline in work and behaviour was the order of the day. No fire burnt in his cold room at college in winter and the same frugality prevailed when be became bishop. The appointment to the See of Liverpool came as a shock and cause of anguish to him in 1894 when Bishop O'Reilly went to his reward.   On his appointment he was just thirty-seven years old.

Stories of Bishop Whiteside abound. Legend has it that at his first public engagement in the diocese – a meeting of the Catholic Reformatory Association, he arrived without being known or noticed.   Time went on and he asked someone in the room when the meeting would begin as time was moving on.   "We are waiting for the bishop" was the reply – "not a good start – I hope he's not always going to keep us all waiting like this."   Then to everyone's embarrassment, and his own, he revealed his identity.   In a similar incident, visiting the Birkdale Reformatory School for Prize-giving Day with Monsignor Carr, the Vicar General, the Governor of the School, Captain Shee, met them at the door and said to Monsignor Carr "I thought you were bringing the bishop with you?"   He took a lot of persuading that the young looking stranger was in fact the new bishop.

Always fond of his Alma Mater, Upholland, he decided during the 1914-1918 War period to take successive groups of children from the Homes for a holiday there.   The College was virtually empty, as students had been called up. The story goes that it was the turn of St. Lucy's School, Holly Road, a special school for Girls suffering from sight defects, to visit the College.   One girl had to stay back for a day or two due to illness and the bishop arranged to meet her in person at Exchange Station in Liverpool to make the trip to the College.   He was her personal escort on the journey, and evidently as happy as the child herself.   The railway station at Upholland was 2 miles from the College and they alighted there, first stopping to buy sweets, and then setting off together on the two mile walk.   There are many stories of this type of personal intervention on behalf of young children, stories which today would make people hold up their hands in horror but which then were seen for what they were, genuine examples of a Good Shepherd going out of his way to care for his lost and needy sheep.

True to this name he would spend a day every three months at the Good Shepherd Convent, Blackbrook House, to hear confessions and say Mass, staying there for the night. His presence had a profound effect on the whole community. As with James Nugent, many years before in the dark prison cell, he had a charismatic way of soothing the fiercest temper or resolving the most delicate problem with his gentle words and patience. It was not just the little ones but the old and sick, terminally ill and destitute that he made his special concern. They found in him an extraordinary friend and comforter. A typical Christmas Day for him would include a Mass in a Children's Home, after he had celebrated the Midnight Mass in the Cathedral, and a third one at The Good Shepherd Convent, Ford. Christmas was for the children as far as he was concerned. He loved nothing more than to spend time among those he called his "wild flowers" in the Children's Homes.

Gaining access by the backdoor he would often surprise and delight the children by arriving unannounced, before even the watchful Sisters knew he was there. Other times his presence was only detected by the sound of screaming children as they ran down the drive to greet him. The children adored him; "He was not so much a great prelate as a great playmate" one of the nuns at St. Joseph's Home, Freshfield, said of him. He would dismiss the nuns from the room so as to be free to chat, joke and tell stories alone with the children, playing games like apples on a string (in one instance this took the form of bread and jam tied by string to the gas fittings above) and he enjoyed watching the children, hands behind their backs, trying to eat it. The high standards of decorum and tidiness usually associated with the Homes were not always observed when he was around, despite his reputation for fastidiousness and correctness in all things. The Sisters were said to be privately furious when the children, dressed in clean pinafores in the morning, returned completely dishevelled after some high spirited games with the Archbishop on a local building site.

Archbishop Whiteside was the complete anti-dote to the strict formality that characterised the ethos of much of the Children's Homes and Institutions. He was a paradox; cool and distant with people much of the time, but like a little excited boy in the company of small children. The only equivalent to him, many years later, was Cardinal Bernard Griffin, who at Coleshill, displayed a similar child-like approach in his work at Father Hudson's Homes. Dedication to promoting the Children's Charter and upholding their Rights at every opportunity was a priority of Archbishop Whiteside. In 1905, after the death of James Nugent, he declared, in the spirit of Nugent, that "the orphan children of this great city have special claim upon us. Over and above the natural helplessness of their condition, the dangers to which their faith and their virtue are exposed make it imperative on our charity to provide them with a sheltering home."

Whiteside employed all his talents of music and comedy, his interest in botany and, above all, his child-like sense of fun, to entertain the children. In the Homes he visited they would often come running when they heard the strains of the piano and "Mother of Mercy" his favourite hymn and signature tune. Not at all happy with modern hymns, he advocated only the traditional ones in the Westminster Hymnal, telling the poor Sister in charge of music to consign the nice new book to the fire. He never missed the children's parties and concerts – a copy of the programme from one of these at St. Saviour's Convent, Paul Street, was found in his pocket when he died. He suffered a stroke on 25th January 1921 and died three days later at the age of 64.

The Catholic children of Liverpool and all of the local church communities who knew him recognised that they had lost a great friend and champion. For he had chosen to 'keep a younger company' during his life and probably aspired, like the poet Francis Thompson, to spend his eternity "in the nurseries of heaven". In the lives of some of the greatest Catholic childcare pioneers, James Nugent, John Berry, Arthur Chilton Thomas, William Pinnington and Thomas Whiteside, the Catholics of Liverpool had been blessed with an awesome set of heroes who had sought to take the gospel of love seriously and literally in defence of the needs of Catholic children. They could not have achieved what they did without a host of dedicated helpers of all kinds, whom we have met in this book and who together made it possible for those young people in their charge to glimpse what it may be like to be in our Father's House, where the children are permitted to play.

Tenement Block 1936

Part Three (1924 – 2005)

Chapter 15

The Nugent Care Society
Yesterday &Today

"Every great Institution is the lengthened shadow of a single man. His character determines the character of his Organisation". (*American Philosopher, Ralph Waldo Emerson*)

The shadow of Father Nugent's influence must have been long, since the basic principles of his work remain today and the tone he set in the whole enterprise of child care and reform is still there in the Society he helped to found more than a hundred and twenty years ago. Many of the problems he addressed and the way he approached them still resonate with the concerns of our contemporary world.

The appropriate care of children is, arguably, the most important social issue of our day, together with the needs of the elderly and the sick. This in itself links us directly to Father Nugent's time, since he saw the welfare of children and the vulnerable as the salient and crying need in a society that was full of needs. When he provided shelter for the homeless on the streets, and enlisted the help of others in doing so, he was doing more than a humanitarian act or a corporal work of mercy, he was also giving back a birthright and making it clear that this was an enterprise in which the survival of society was at stake and in which the hand of God was present.

This book has been the story of how Father Nugent, and those who worked with him, responded to the critical mandate of the Gospel and made the care of the poor into a noble work. Nugent's life teaches us that charity is timeless and the poor will always be there, but that there is also another dimension to charity than mere philanthropy. Nugent reminded us that it is also a fundamental requirement of the Gospel, a call to hear again and put into action Christ's compelling words spoken to us in striking simplicity down the centuries: "In so far as you did this to the least of my brothers and sisters you did it to me".

We have no extant recording of Nugent's voice or any complete memoirs to draw upon. Unfortunately, as far as we know, he never wrote his own life-story and he naturally rejected a lucrative offer for the rights to sell the story of his remarkable years as a Prison Minister in Walton Gaol. Apart from any legal restrictions, he came to respect the right to confidentiality and the personal right to privacy for those in prison, even before this was a matter of general recognition. What we do have is his photograph, his portrait, his statue, his reputation, but above all his legacy of sixty years Christian mission which helps to ensure that the work he did lives on in the community. Through the services of the Society that now bears his name, The Nugent Care Society, we can see that his impact and his spirit are alive and strong. There were the Benevolent Societies in his day but now there are much greater and wider connections between organisations and agencies, statutory, voluntary, local, national and even international.

An outline of the history that has led to the present development of The Nugent Care Society now follows. It can be seen to draw upon the ideals and priorities of Father Nugent's own mission to the disadvantaged and underprivileged of his time. It is an important part of this whole story. Something of this development has been sketched by Kathleen Moriarty who was a member of The Society and to whom the Society is very much indebted. What follows can only be an outline of the main developments, a summary of the gains and losses which have led to a more stream-lined and efficient service of the people. It will read only like the dry bones of the matter, on which the flesh of loving and dedicated service has been placed by those involved.

1924 was a watershed year in the history of Catholic Child Care in Liverpool. It was in that year that three separate organisations - The Liverpool Catholic Children's Protection Society, The Catholic Children's Aid Society and Father Berry's Homes joined together as one under the guidance of Archbishop Frederick Keating. He appointed two men of calibre to take charge: Monsignor Pinnington (a true successor of Father Nugent and of Father Berry) and Father John Bennett who had a forty year association with Catholic Child Welfare. The Patronage of Sir James Reynolds and his family was a vital boost to the morale and finances of the new organisation which retained the title of Catholic Children's Protection Society. The focus was still on protection of children but it would shift in the years to come to an emphasis on the welfare of a wider variety of people of all ages and needs.

As three separate Committees learned to live as one, the work in this new chapter of the Society's history was based at 1a Trueman Street and at 99 Shaw Street - the first being an office that dealt with applications for help and the second the headquarters for organising appeals and finance. The new personnel in Liverpool were invited to meet their opposite numbers in Birmingham where the famous Father Hudson's Homes for Children were situated at Coleshill, so that experience could be gained and shared.

Progress meant a series of closures and new beginnings for the Children's Homes. St. Anthony's Home for Boys, at 97 Shaw Street, was closed in 1924 and two years later a Babies' Home, also in Shaw Street, transferred to 12 Holly Road, in the Fairfield area of Liverpool, under the care of the Sisters of Charity. That same year, 1926, saw the refurbishment and reorganisation of the Working Boys' Home, beloved of Father John Berry, at 105 Shaw Street, as the needs of that group were clearly acute after the war years had caused a slump in employment and a dislocation of family life.

1928 saw the death of Archbishop Keating who had done a lot to enhance the important work of child care for which his predecessors had been almost legendary. The new Archbishop was Richard Downey, a very different character, more aloof than Thomas Whiteside, whose intention was to relate the Church to the civic and academic life of the town. The moral and religious welfare of children was not in any way neglected as the Society continued to raise money, receive legacies and generally promote the rights of young and vulnerable people. Focus was brought onto the care of child victims of assault and abuse. Meanwhile Richard Downey made many gains for Catholic Status in Liverpool.

The Society was becoming less clericalised and more lay-led, and the Religious Orders, by which Nugent had placed such great store, gave place to lay staff, for example at The Babies' Home - an example of where expertise among the laity was growing and more opportunities being given to them. In the meantime, emigration of children continued a pace through a coordinated National Catholic Emigration Society. Tentative plans were being discussed by the Bishops at this time for emigration of children not only to Canada but also to the colonies of Western Australia. In Liverpool, John Bennett and his colleagues visited the ships before they sailed for Canada to ensure that all was satisfactory for the voyage and visited Canada and America too to monitor the accommodation and progress of the children personally, just as Father Nugent had done. There was a visit to the meeting of the National Catholic Welfare Organisations in Washington to learn about their methods. Following these sojourns abroad there was an expansion of the Society's work at home as, in 1936, Homes and schools opened at Pontville in Ormskirk, Gillibrand Hall in Chorley, Blackbrook House in St. Helens and St. Vincent's School in Beacon Lane, Liverpool, among others. Association with Beacon Lane meant there was a link with Father Nugent as the Boys'Orphanage there had been one of his firsts interests.

Money was fast running out for emigration work and greater attention was being given to Institutions at home as the possibilities for taking large groups abroad diminished. From Liverpool there had to be a certain amount of 'farming out' to other parts of the country - London, Birmingham and Manchester, for example, according to demands, and this was supervised by the St. Vincent de Paul Society in Liverpool whose work with vulnerable working boys had always been very prominent. St. Aidan's School, Farnworth - later in Scarborough - was the direct successor to 'The Clarence' Reformatory Ship and many boys were given a home there. Nugent too had seen the need for a variety of options in different parts of the country where children of different categories and age-groups could be provided for and given a new start, as for instance with The Colony at Mount St. Bernard.

It was a sign of the times that the need for legal advice and counselling services had increased and the Society responded to this by setting up firstly a Catholic Enquiry Office, in 1936, and then a Catholic Social Services Bureau in Trueman Street. It was in the midst of this new work that refugees began to arrive, ahead of the War in Europe, and needed to be cared for. This increased in 1938 as children and their families from Germany and Austria arrived in Liverpool and at other English ports. Just before the outbreak of World War II, a meeting of the Catholic Child Welfare Committee was held in Liverpool in November 1938 and a gathering of Child Care Committees was also convened there, chaired by Bishop Bernard Griffin, later Cardinal and Archbishop of Westminster, who had emerged as a leading light in the work of child care in the diocese of Birmingham.

The Second World War, like the First, brought evacuation and separation so that many of the Homes were disbanded and services discontinued. An indication of the effects of this was a drop of over £1000 in the Good Shepherd Collection on which the Society depended for its funds and which was drawn from the local schools during

Lent. The disruption of normal life everywhere had many implications. The May Blitz of 1941 caused extensive damage to Children's Homes in the centre of town, evacuation was stepped up and children were sent in to the country.

In the post-war period, when resources were weak but determination strong, The Society became a registered Adoption Agency to respond to the need for sharing out the costs of accommodation and also to cater for the many victims of families fragmented and traumatised by war. Child Guidance Clinics became commonplace around the country, one such opening in Maryland Place, Liverpool. The number of legal adoptions increased greatly but at the same time a little piece of history came to an end and a tangible link with Father Nugent's time was severed when The Working Boy's Home in Shaw Street was closed after 54 years of existence.

The 1948 Children's Act brought many of the Institutions of Child Care under the central authority of the Home Office, though Homes for people with special needs remained separate. The effects of the Education Act a few years earlier in 1944 had great implications for the whole provision in child care, akin to the sea change that compulsory primary education brought about in Father Nugent's life time.

The records of The Society make mention of the Centenary celebrations held for Father Nugent in 1950, in what was a special place for him, the Pro-Cathedral of St. Nicholas on Copperas Hill. This date presumably relates approximately to the occasion of his appointment as a priest in Liverpool Diocese which he took up on New Year's Day 1849. From the start, The Society has always been conscious of its links with Father Nugent who was its founder and its first inspiration.

A Family Group Home, opened in Aughton Park in that commemorative year of 1950, sent a clear signal that the youngest and most vulnerable in the community were worthy of the first attention and reflected The Society's intention to develop Nugent's original vision. This was a proclamation that there was a place in the family for everyone and that everyone was valued. The policy of providing the best possible start in life for the orphaned and disadvantaged child was indicative of a deep-seated philosophy that lay at the root of the whole enterprise.

In the same vein the establishment of a Home for single mothers and their babies in 1951 was a project that might have come straight from Nugent's heart. Perhaps something not so evident in his tradition, but nonetheless a significant development, was that during the 1950s there was a phasing out of the policy of segregation which had separated boys and girls in distinct Homes. This change meant that siblings could stay together and family bonding was easier to maintain, something Nugent had often advocated in the Workhouse almost a century earlier.

At Nazareth House in Ditton and in Crosby, for instance, there was admission for a mixture of both males and females to share the Home. Meanwhile the continuing emphasis on the development of the care of children was given further impetus by the introduction of a Child Welfare Clinic and Child Guidance Unit to look after both the physical and psychological needs of youngsters in care. What Nugent and his more forward-thinking colleagues glimpsed only in embryo form, now began to be widely accepted. In Nugent's day there was little or no real understanding of the psychological needs that lay beneath the surface of many children's lives. The indicators of mental health, and a more enlightened approach to this problem, were features of the 1950s and 1960s as behavioural psychology came to the fore. What was also evident at this time, in the post-war period, was the improvement of conditions generally in the homes of ordinary people with the result that there was a decrease in the number of full-time residential care homes for children.

Archbishop William Godfrey (1953 – 1956) and Archbishop John Carmel Heenan (1956 – 1963) steered the diocese and its work of Child Care into more settled times in the post-war era. The care of both young and old remained a top priority for them.

Father Nugent's biographer, Canon John Bennett, who was associated with the work of Catholic Child Care in Liverpool from as early as 1924 and who came to hear of Nugent through Nugent's successor, Monsignor Pinnington, was invited in 1954 to serve on the Central Advisory and Training Council which was a National Body dealing with Child Welfare. He was following in the footsteps of Nugent in taking an active part in the wider aspects of the Child Welfare service at national level. He was able to represent the interests of Liverpool Catholics more effectively through this Council. Canon Bennett continued at the helm until 1965 when his death, on 25th June that year, brought about the end of an era in Catholic Child Welfare in Liverpool. John Bennett left us not only a biography of Father Nugent but also a record of untarnished and selfless, priestly service, of which the diocese of Liverpool could be proud.

The year 1955 saw the end of an illustrious 104-year involvement of the Notre Dame Sisters in the care of Catholic Girls' Orphanages, which had been initiated by Father Nugent. The closure of Girl's Homes such as Leyfield Girls' Home on grounds of financial difficulties in 1956, was to be followed by the closure of other similar establishments for the same reason. Yet this gave way to smaller, more manageable units, such as the Home at 25 Fairfield crescent for no more than 10 boys. Meanwhile, the on-going problem of un-married mothers and their babies meant that there was still a need for provision, such as the Refuge at Holly Road in Liverpool and Mater Dei in Blundellsands.

The role played by the Sisters of The Little Ones and the Sisters of Charity was key to the development of such provision in these years, but the Society began to take a lead in the training of women as House Mothers who could take on some of the tasks the Sisters had performed. Formation and training remained, as it had done in Nugent's time, a vital part of the policy of these Homes and now the stage was set for much more lay involvement in a new approach to care work among a wide range of different age groups.

A new Archbishop, George Andrew Beck, came on the scene in 1964 and a new Administrator was appointed in the person of Father James Dunne. From the days of Bishop O'Reilly when the Society was founded, successive Archbishops maintained the tradition of being President of The Society, appointing able Administrators or Secretaries for the day to day work. Jimmy Dunne was to take the Society forward, in the spirit of Nugent, making it a well-established organisation that increased its provision for Children's Homes but also diversified its concerns well beyond Child Care issues. Children's Homes were established at St. Gabriel's, Walton, under the watchful eye of The Poor Servants of the Mother of God, one of Nugent's favourite Orders, and also at Crosby under the dedicated and loving care of the Sisters of Nazareth, Clumber Lodge in Freshfield in the care of the Good Shepherd Sisters, Newstead under the Sisters of Charity of St. Paul the Apostle and the Home at Druids Cross, Woolton which was looked after by the Sisters of St. Vincent de Paul. A pattern of Religious provision was emerging which would have pleased Father Nugent who had always put his absolute trust in the ability of the Religious Orders and who set a trend that was to continue way beyond his time.

Not only Homes for the residential care of orphans but also schools for the special requirements of boys and girls with delinquent tendencies (the Approved Schools) became a key part of the provision. This also was consistent with much of Father Nugent's original work of training and rehabilitation for life in society. The Bureau in Trueman Street, which had been in existence for some time, became the office Headquarters for the staff and the scope of the office was widened to include in its remit a Citizens Advice Bureau, a Training Unit for Family Care Workers and also an office for Court Advocacy work. At about this time staff of the Society could qualify for the Government's new Residential Child Care Certificate, which mirrored in its way the affiliation Nugent had recommended to the Industrial Schools' Certificate bringing advantages for both staff and children.

The emphasis at this time was on inclusion - the right of children with special needs to be part of main stream education and so have equal access to Catholic religious teaching and instruction, and preparation for the Sacraments. The original point of focus in the city spread to many areas outside Liverpool itself, including the Isle of Man, Ormskirk, Warrington, Leigh, St. Helens, Garston, Halewood and Chorley. But expansion means expense and the heavy financial burden which Nugent had always struggled with was an ever-present spectre in the growing work of the Society. Various aspects of the increasing work load in Adoption and Court Advocacy required new sources of funding.

The 1969 Children's Act brought stronger links between the Home Office and local Children's Charities and more recognition of the work being done on the ground. It recommended the appointment of Professional Advisors which the Society took on board the following year. It was at about this time that the 'Liverpool Catholic Children's Protection Society' changed its name to the 'Catholic Children's Society', shedding some of the Victorian encumbrances of its title and reflecting better the fact that the work was no longer just about protection but also active promotion of a wide variety of children's needs. The term 'Community Homes' came to be used to signify all types of residential child care centres. Meanwhile, the Society was now linking with statutory and voluntary bodies, Universities and Colleges, local apostolic and church-based groups. Obvious examples of this networking were seen in the St. Vincent de Paul Society, The Catholic Mens' Society, The Catholic Women's League and the Union of Catholic Mothers, among others.

By 1972 there were 218 youngsters being helped with learning difficulties with the assistance of a Training Officer. James Nugent would have rejoiced to see this development; new needs being recognised and met, traditional activities and personnel remaining as anchors in the whole process of change. The Society seemed to engender longevity. For instance when Marjorie Hughes retired as Children's Worker in 1973 she had served the Society for 49 years (almost equalling Nugent's own length of service).

In the years that followed one of the new needs to be realised, (not specifically part of Father Nugent's mission), was the care of the Elderly. It was the emerging social problem of the 1970s. In part, it was this development in The Society's work that led to it changing its title once again to 'Catholic Social Services' as the focus on children widened to other age groups and what was formerly thought of as charity work had clearly undergone a transformation into social work as a distinct concept. With the increase of social work the beaurocratic measures increased too and the next Children's Act in 1975 brought more stringent requirements not least the right of adopted children to obtain details of the records of birth. A far cry from the Victorian approach to children's rights! The Catholic Social Services endeavoured to meet new legislation and at the same time look more widely at the needs of Deaf People, Blind People and people with disabilities.

The tradition of having supportive Archbishops who lent not only their name but also their time and energy as Presidents of the Society - Whiteside, Keating, Downey, Godfrey, Heenan and Beck, now saw a new arrival on the scene in Archbishop Derek Worlock who had come from Portsmouth. One of the first photographs taken of him was in the Cathedral Crypt Shelter for the Homeless and so he proved himself willing to continue the cherished tradition that gave the official backing of the archdiocese and its resources to the care of the needy. The real work however was still at the coal face, done by the people on the ground in parishes and groups, and the establishment of the Twelve Apostles Scheme highlighted that it was the specific realm of lay people, in the way of Young Christian Workers and Family and Social Action, to promote a practical expression of the precept of charity in the community.

Not that this was the sole prerogative of the Laity. Notable clergy such as Bishop Augustine Harris, auxiliary bishop in Liverpool, and for a time Chairman of Catholic Social Services, had shown through his Prison Chaplaincy work a clear link with Nugent's pioneering efforts in addressing the day to day needs together; priests and laity. The service of vulnerable people such as prisoners and the noble but demanding enterprise of hospital ministry were examples of such collaboration. Such work was no longer the sole domain of individuals but called for team work.

Father James Dunne, who retired as Administrator in August 1978 after thirteen years, had seen through a work of both consolidation and innovation. Bishop Harris was appointed to new responsibilities as Bishop of Middlesbrough and this double change paved the way for new personnel and for the incoming Administrator, Anthony McCarthy, who took the work forward for the next three years. This was the first time there was not a priest in charge. A new tradition of an annual Mass in the Cathedral was established in 1980 and then, in December 1981, the first woman to be appointed as Director was Bridget Fann. She was able to give fresh impetus and new direction for the next twelve years. This period included an 'annus mirabilis' in 1985 with the opening of Lime House, at Lowton, linking up with the local Wigan Social Services and Wigan Health Authority to provide a fitting home for thirty elderly people. It was also the year that saw the opening of St. Thomas More Home (formerly the

Birkdale Farm School) and Crosby House, leading to the official opening a few years later of Margaret Roper House on an adjacent site.

In caring for the elderly and various groups of people with special needs, the work was changing significantly, not in its underlying purpose but in the scope of its remit; meeting new needs as they arose, needs not met by others. So the trend continued through the late 1980s and the 1990s. Clarence House School, which was so named to bring to mind the great project of reform and training inaugurated by Father Nugent himself, opened at Freshfield in 1986 for ninety resident pupils and the following year, on 2nd July, Bishop John Rawsthorne, Auxiliary Bishop of Liverpool, opened a further unit so that more pupils, including 25 day pupils, could be accommodated. Another Auxiliary Bishop of Liverpool, Anthony Hitchen, came to open 'Othona' Children's Home in Birkdale in 1990 and also opened two new units for those suffering from mental illness, at Hitchen Court in Garston, and Geel in Aigburth. Bishop Hitchen was to establish himself as a firm favourite with the Homes, bringing energetic enthusiasm and unstinting support to its work.

It might have been expected that by the turn of the century, almost a hundred years since Nugent's death, standards of health care would be such that the agency of Charities would be receding. Not so. At this time over 5000 referrals were being made to the Advice and Information Unit of the Agency. Restraints put on by the Social Fund and Government policy was partly responsible for this high incidence. The numbers of vagrant, refugee, or misplaced people was increasing. There was an anomaly in the fact that many people were "living off the parish" once again in a society that was ostensibly far more prosperous than before.

As the 1990s progressed, it became clear that things were moving towards another change of name. There were commitments at Kelton Grange Nursing Home, more accommodation at Clarence House and at Chain Lane, Blackbrook, where, on 1st April 1992, a children's Home was established and a Centre for Girls at St. Catherine's, Blackbrook House. Meanwhile another stalwart worker retired, Angela Plater, who even at the age of ninety was still to be seen at the Brownlow Hill office and involved in Court work. She lived to the age of 98 and was the only member of staff who would have been alive in Nugent's time, having been born in the year 1900. Nugent's name became directly connected for the first time with the title of the Organisation he had founded when 'The Nugent Care Society' was decided upon as the new designation in 1993.

The Duke of Norfolk agreed to become its patron and so the long tradition of influential support for The Society continued. Father Nugent's name was also given to the new School in Billinge near Wigan that housed 117 pupils aged 7-19, and which Archbishop Worlock opened as a Lower School building. It was around Christmas time 1993 that John Kennedy took his place in the illustrious succession of Administrators of the Society.

From the time of John Kennedy's appointment and the arrival of a new Archbishop in the person of Archbishop Patrick Kelly, who took on the role of Chairman with an active interest in all aspects of the work but especially the care of Deaf People, developments were many and varied. These concentrated on the care of homeless single people, links with Children's Homes in Canada, the appointment of field workers, a Volunteer Management Project, the setting up of a website to disseminate information far more efficiently, Child Care provision in the Isle of Man (in the year 2000), care of the Elderly at Holystead in Holy Road, Fairfield, and the move of location of the office from Brownlow Hill to premises in Edge Lane. Clearly a busy and fruitful time.

By good luck or by good management the Edge Lane headquarters was near to where Nugent had once founded a rest home for Sisters working in child care. The move, in the year 2000, from Brownlow Hill, site of the former

Victorian Workhouse, marked the end of a seventy- four year history of wonderful work there, and a new chapter in the life of The Nugent Care Society began.

The Society of the present day, under the direction of Kathleen Pitt, a former member of staff who was appointed as Chief Executive in March 2003, has set out its charter for the foreseeable future, with an eye to the lessons of its long history and another eye firmly fixed on new needs. The same principles of the Catholic Church's Social Teaching which have emerged over the decades remain in place. Father Nugent would probably have been bemused by expressions like "Strategic Aims" or "Management and Governance" which are part of all business today, and he may not have had much patience with Committee work, finance plans, objective setting and the like. These aspects of decision-making are all now part of modern life, but there is no doubt that the founder would recognise and approve of the underlying intentions of The Society which remain essentially the same as the ones he espoused.

The story of loss and gain continued in more recent times, with the handing over of the children's residential care project on the Isle of Man in July 2004 and the selling of Kelton Training Centre but with the rebuilding of other residential units at Crosby House and a community resource unit in St. Helens. The provision continues to be wide and generous as Nugent would have wanted it to be.

What the Master suffers is often also visited upon his disciples. In his time Nugent had to contend with criticism about his methods and about the adverse effects at times of what might today be called his 'expansion policy'. He met criticism and allegation with the same equanimity with which he met success and praise. The Nugent Care Society too, in recent times, has had to deal with painful allegations. It is not the purpose or remit of this book to address these. The positive outcome of learning from hurtful experiences is something we should all welcome and The Society has shown its desire to go forward, learning and benefiting from any mistakes, and, as Father Nugent always did, it looks forward not back.

In the very different social conditions of his day, and all through the vagaries of new policies and legislation down the years, there is a remarkable consistency in the work for the poor. We may define poverty differently according to the standards and expectations we have, but the age-old principle of caring for one another in Christ's name stands solidly behind the charitable work of the present day.

Organisations call for the eradication of poverty and Government has puts its considerable weight behind this cause, but if it is true that the poor we will always have with us (and it must be true as they are the Lord's words) an even greater challenge faces us: to see ourselves, all of us, as part of one world family without distinction or division. None of us are free of class and cultural divisions but that should not stop us consistently striving for greater equality.

Nugent's strong emphasis on the care of orphaned or abandoned children, the stray 'sheep' who roamed the inhospitable streets and whom the Victorians dubbed 'street arabs', was different from his practical yet humane approach to delinquency and crime among youths. He did not reject the value of tough measures and fitting punishment for crime where it was called for. Yet in both cases his love for all individuals was evident. Those who might be thought of as the equivalent to the asylum seekers and outcasts of today were his special concern and what he provided was put in place without the benefit of today's information technology which makes it possible to coordinate and relate more effectively. That linking and connecting which has been a hallmark of recent times in The Nugent Care Society, especially in regard to local parishes, is a logical progression of Nugent's ideals. It would have been Nugent's wish for the new technology and insights to be fully utilised so that as few individuals as possible slip through the net of care.

The practical nature of Christian outreach to the needy still holds good today, despite the new challenges. The recent development of a Child Protection Policy, new issues in Education, fresh ideas for Law and Order and prison reform, do not negate the need for a hands-on, practical evangelisation such as Nugent knew. He belonged to the Victorian era, but he was a man for all times. If the role of any Society or Institution is to promote good citizenship in this world and the next, then we need look no further for a role model than Father James Nugent.

As the great humanitarian issues of yesterday come back repeatedly to haunt us with still greater force, we face age-old problems in a modern guise on a global scale. A guiding light, from any era of history, is always needed and welcome. The example of people like James Nugent provide beacons that light up a pathway in the darkness and maybe it is this which led one writer to observe that, "in a veritable ocean of misery we find outstanding the strong and beautiful personality of Father Nugent."

Exploring that description has been the mainspring of this book. It has been a sincere, if inadequate attempt at a biography of one of the most elusive, fascinating, complex and underrated figures of the modern Church. The final part of this book will be a summary of all that went in to the making of the man, and the mission he undertook in the name of the God of Justice and Compassion.

...

Chapter 16

Father Nugent's Legacy and a Final Portait

"A priest's work and influence never end but with his life, and then his words and example ought to live and be a stimulating power".   (Canon John Bennett)

Throughout its long and eventful past, Liverpool has been a place of contrasting fortunes, as changing and volatile as the tides of the river on which it stands. The River Mersey has brought fame, trade and prosperity, but it has also been the conduit of tragedy and disaster too, as recounted so often in local legend and song. The geographical position by the sea and the status of a great seaport, that brought Liverpool renown and success, also brought great deprivation and poverty to its shores. Known as a Gateway to the Empire, as a 'Door to America' - grandiose titles that seem exaggerated to us now - the privileged location which gave rise to these descriptions has for many centuries made it welcoming to strangers but vulnerable to suffering. During its history the town has been like a mirror image of the river: proud, volatile, constantly in flux, a strong, unpredictable life force. The town's changing fortunes have produced strong people.

Discovering the "strong and beautiful personality" of Father Nugent in the drabness and darkness of past years, and the nature of the man behind the mission, understanding the motivations and the influences of his remarkable work, has been a difficult but worth-while quest. A personality cannot be conveyed in bronze, marble or in oil paintings. It can only be expressed in the living reality of an individual life. Tributes have been paid in different ways to countless other great men and women in the story of Britain's social and religious reform - people as diverse as William Wilberforce, William Roscoe, Florence Nightingale, Charles Dickens, Charles Darwin and many other heroes of the age, but this book sets out to redress an imbalance and to show why it was indeed fortunate for Liverpool that, over a hundred years ago on the banks of the Mersey, Father Nugent's lot was cast.

By the time of his death on 27th June, 1905, Father Nugent was a household name in Britain. He was a local legend, a celebrity in his native Liverpool and also well-known and highly regarded in Canada, America (his second home) and on the continent of Europe. His pioneering efforts in the field of Catholic Social Welfare were recognised in Westminster, where Cardinal Manning would dearly have liked him to work, and Rome where his work attracted the grateful attention of the Pope. Almost thirty years after his death a local paper 'The Liverpolitan', could still warmly record in these words the impact he had on people's lives: "His name was whispered with reverence at the hearthstones of the happy homes his counsels helped to create, he lived to see many of his dreams for the amelioration of mankind come true and when he passed away, all classes combined to raise the statue which perpetuates his memory."

This glowing tribute may sit uncomfortably with the observation made by Nugent's biographer Canon John Bennett, who in his book on Nugent written in 1949 said that few passers-by notice the statue today, and fewer still bother to stop and read the impressive words inscribed around the base, commemorating his life-long work of charity. Memories are often short-lived, even in respect of the greatest figures. Nugent perhaps stands a little below the statesmen and politicians whose contribution to the city is more readily acknowledged, but the statue made in his honour represents the first such memorial to a Catholic priest in this country and the public acclaim and subscriptions which gave rise to the monument were all the more impressive in what was a largely Protestant city.

Father Nugent's statue stands among the other legendry figures of Liverpool's philanthropy and history, heroes of war and peace time. It also stands parallel with the memorial to Major Lester, Nugent's great Anglican counterpart. If you visit St. John's Gardens today, with the giant classical bulk of St. George's Hall in the background, you will see a noble figure set on a pedestal (rather incongruous for someone who liked to be amongst the crowd), protecting a ragged child at his side which represents all the waifs and strays he shepherded in the streets during his campaign to "Save The Boy" and in his remarkable mission of rescue. The statue recalls a sad yet wonderful episode in the modern history of Liverpool. Visiting St. John's Gardens, full of flowers on a sunny day, in the summer of 2001, as the idea for this book was beginning to take shape, I became aware of two thoughts: why was Father Nugent's story so in danger of being forgotten, and why has it been so seldom celebrated?

How was I to interpret the long shadow cast at that moment by the sun against his figure, a shadow that stretched towards the town and the river, pointing towards the docks he had watched grow, and beyond them towards the Irish Sea and the Atlantic which he sailed so often he almost made it his own? Was it only a fleeting shadow or was it a striking reminder of the importance of Nugent for the city today which we may be in danger of underestimating? The American Philosopher and Unitarian, Ralph Waldo Emerson wrote : "Every institution is the lengthened shadow of a single man. His character determines the character of his organisation", and the British Poet and Educationalist Thomas Campbell said that "Coming events cast their shadows before". How far are the developments of today a product of Nugent's work, and how does his work cast its shadow of influence on the needs of today in a society which has so greatly changed?

It may be true that few passers-by today know about or notice his statue, but the impact of Father Nugent's presence is everywhere in the city. It is there in the opportunities, religious and cultural, that we now enjoy, in the provision of education, in child care, prisoner welfare, music, art and drama, and perhaps most directly it is there in the freedom to practise our religion and faith in a better climate of mutual acceptance and tolerance. Our present day culture owes a surprising debt of gratitude to Father Nugent and the true extent of it only becomes evident when we begin to examine his story in detail, a story that carries within it a prophetic element. We ignore at our peril the message his life proclaimed.

From ordinary beginnings James Nugent's life-story unfolded like a Victorian drama on the stage of the Liverpool streets. The stage is an apt metaphor because Nugent had drama in his soul, a strong sense of occasion, an ability to lift an audience. He knew how to use both pulpit and platform to good effect. His story is a rich and personal account of a man, sometimes isolated, pitted against a flood of evil, battling in an intense crusade for moral reform, a battle for people's hearts and souls that seemed at times to be the very dual between life and death. It is a story which bridges two centuries and two cultures, a city and two continents, the lives of four monarchs and seven popes. It is a life studded with an astonishing array of charitable projects and schemes into which he breathed his own unique life and which were often disjointed, even poorly thought through, but which were threaded into some kind of unity by a Christian faith and high ideals.

Lacordaire wrote of Nugent that he was "a man first and a Christian second". His obvious human failings were often writ as large as his virtues but it is unrealistic to separate too easily human nature and Christian mission. James Nugent was a human being and he made enemies, but his Christian intention was always clear and won the respect of all. His ministry was grounded in real lives, in the dilemmas of real people, in a practical Gospel. The work he did was rooted in the ugly, shameful world of crime and depravity, a world distorted by drink-related evils, and so it was essentially a human work but a Christian work too, preserved in the Institutions he founded.

Father Nugent is perhaps best remembered as a pioneer of Charity and of Catholic childcare, but it is not equally appreciated that he was one of the principal architects of a new Catholic identity which emerged in England in the 19th Century, an important player in the realisation of the Second Spring made famous by Cardinal Newman. In this Nugent stands only a little way behind men of the stature of Cardinals Newman, Manning and Hinsley in the Catholic roll-call of honour. They spearheaded the growth of a renewed Catholic community in our land. For them the promotion of a Catholic life, a Catholic Culture, was part and parcel of the Gospel. To understand James Nugent in this setting, as we celebrate the Centenary Year of his death, is part of the process of understanding what it is we now enjoy as a city, a city whose title of 'Capital of Culture' would have rejoiced Father Nugent's heart.

The Capital of Culture Award is due in part to the city's ability to adapt to changing needs and make a contribution to the wider human community. Among the attributes which have accompanied this are music and humour. These have been among Liverpool's strong suits. The power music has to communicate across the barriers of distance, age, language, nationality and culture, to endure down the centuries and link nations together, makes it an indispensable instrument of culture and a thread of unity. Music can sooth hurts, assuage anger, it can raise minds to nobler thoughts and make cold hearts warm. It is often linked to the spirit of place and time, identified with particular occasions and events.

The Sea Shanties, for instance, seem to capture the symbiosis between the land and the sea, evoking Liverpool's maritime history, echoes of great events, tragic or victorious, of sea-going episodes and adventures, evoking images of lone figures waving handkerchiefs in sad farewells at the dockside, conjuring up memories of Steam Packets and colourful sea-faring characters. The songs can still be heard around the bars and clubs of the city at night and can exercise a certain power over people with a heady mix of nostalgia and wistfulness. In more recent times The Beatles' music has endowed Liverpool with fame. Wherever you mention the city's name, wherever you go in the world, the Beatles' songs have assumed an ambassadorial role.

Nugent's life was deeply influenced by a love of music. He lived in the epoch of the great Classical Composers. He imbibed music from his early years and often used it in his ministry, notably in the performances of the parish Boys' Band and later when he inaugurated the popular Monday Evening People's Concerts as part of his campaign for Temperance and Total Abstinence.Any major event - the opening of a new home or a celebration of Solemn Mass was accompanied by music, choirs, or a band, and so became an essential part of Father Nugent's 'modus operandi'. He knew that music played a part in building up morale and in levelling the ground between people of different classes and backgrounds. Even the routine on board 'The Clarence' reformatory ship was alleviated by the music of the band. Nugent especially liked the Italian Opera and romantic composers, and from his college days he derived a love of Sacred Music in the Church's Liturgy.

The power of music, linked to the attractive prospect of a free show, was a way of bringing people together, forging links, creating bonds of friendship and focussing good will. In this way, Nugent, like many reformers, learnt to take aspects of local culture into his evangelising work. The timeless quality of much of the musical tradition we have grown up with ensures that we are linked with people who have gone before us who also heard, appreciated and enjoyed it. The classical, theatrical tradition of Shakespeare, or the immortal literature of the romantic novelists like Charles Dickens (whose social conscience and reforming zeal, if not his religious persuasion, found a kindred spirit in Nugent) were written in a form which was widely attractive, providing a link between life and fiction, as the television soap operas do today. In assessing Nugent's legacy we cannot help assessing his life and his world.

There is a strong link between the culture of Father Nugent's day and our own. His mission was rooted in the recognition of people's needs and their real lives. If they were going to become citizens of heaven they first had to learn to be citizens on earth and as such they were entitled to a broad education, the means to personal development, access to music art and entertainment, to the best chances of improving the quality of life, irrespective of wealth, poverty or social status. What we now welcome as a whole person approach was what he advocated.

James Nugent's many works of charity must be set in the context of Liverpool's modern history and its present culture, or else they will be forgotten with the passing generations. The name of Nugent is not really forgotten, except perhaps in the sense that names like Baird and Bell are 'forgotten' in the midst of the enjoyment of the benefits their inventions have brought. Had Nugent been able to utilise the television and the telephone in his ministry, or make use of the sophisticated E-mail communication technology of our day, who knows what further wonders he would have worked?

Almost all of the landmarks of James Nugent's world disappeared long before I was born, unceremoniously swept away by the incursions of The Second World War or by the relentless intrusions of the bulldozer. Sometimes to our enrichment sometimes to our impoverishment, the political and geographical landscape of our towns and cities has changed so radically, making the reconstruction of Father Nugent' s world, in any meaningful way, a difficult task. Nugent's birthplace in Hunter Street; the key church in his life, St. Nicholas, that stood on Copperas Hill, where he was baptised, where he was ordained priest and where his funeral was celebrated; the Ragged School in the decrepit and haunted Spitalfields, behind Whitechapel, where he created a place of safety for street urchins; the building that first housed the Catholic Institute in Hope Street and which was the fore-runner of the present St. Edward's College; the Boys' Refuge in St. Anne's Street and the Jubilee Temperance Hall - all of these constructs of his ministry are long since gone and forgotten.

Places that now have an archaic ring to them but which were favourite meeting places in his time, such as Footit's Circus and Quaglione's Circus and Jim Ward's Boxing Salon, where as a young priest Nugent spoke out defiantly to an inebriate crowd on the subject of sobriety and the virtues of taking the pledge, are now known only in folk-lore. 'The Clarence' Training Ship, a bold idea for reform and training of delinquent Catholic youths - a ship that never sailed anywhere, a floating prison, is gone from our consciousness, but it was a vital element in reform work at that time.

More recently we have seen the demolition of the Church of The Holy Cross in the centre of town. There in the original school building the young Father Nugent preached one of his first sermons. For him it was a defining moment of his early ministry, the wake up call that prompted him to act on behalf of uneducated Catholic children of the town. It was a time for building and expansion, whereas in our day, 150 years later, it is inevitably a time for scaling down. In the last few years we have witnessed the clearance of the site on which the Workhouse once stood and where Nugent spent a good deal of the middle years of his ministry visiting and teaching Catholic doctrine to its hapless inmates.

Even Walton Prison in Hornby Road - the Borough Gaol where he laboured night and day for over twenty years on behalf of the men and women he befriended there in the course of his chaplaincy from 1863 until 1885 (his "twenty years penal servitude") − has changed beyond all recognition from the Victorian Institution he would have known. Within those austere and forbidding walls he developed an extraordinary rapport with the criminal fraternity; it was the backbone of his whole career and a platform for many works of reform.

Although the landmarks have gone, the influences still remain. They are like the shadowy images that stay in the eyes after looking into the light. Emerson's reference to the 'lengthened shadow' might well be applied to Nugent as his familiar shadow was cast on the prison wall, over the floor of fever-ridden cellars, on the stage of the Temperance Hall or the 'Womens' Refuge'. Still discernible are the long-term effects of his pioneering, innovative work in the media and the tone he set for The Northern Press - leading to the publication of 'The Catholic Times' and 'Catholic Fireside' in which there was an unashamed appeal to the sentiments of family life and the virtues of the home. Whilst in the policies of adoption, education and emigration of children he set a trend that is vastly changed today, in a number of other ways his shadow falls on the Institutions of our day, through the ideals he held that still hold good. This man, and priest, standing tall not in physical stature but in the estimation of his friends and colleagues, touches our society and city which bear the marks of a man who bestrode the life of Liverpool "like a colossus".

The rather foolhardy attempt to reconstruct Father Nugent's story is perhaps justified by reference to the impact he has had in shaping our present religious identity, our Church, and, by extension, our priorities in areas such as Catholic Child Care. By attempting to trace the signs of his progress across Liverpool and beyond, I have only been concerned to show his true importance in context. He passionately sought a better deal for the poor of his city and the pursuit of this dream took him to the point where he lost some friends but influenced the lives of many. To understand his world and reconstruct it properly requires some stretching of the imagination, the creation of a kind of Victorian virtual reality in the mind, walking for a time in his shadow and in his light. This book has led me, figuratively speaking, through a labyrinth of little streets, courts and alleys, on strange and winding pathways that were the recesses and hidden places of Father Nugent's world.

The image of priests in their black cassocks, creeping into typhus-filled cellars to lie down beside dying fever victims in order to hear their whispered confessions, placing the holy oil of anointing and the sacred hosts of Communion on their top hats which formed a sort of altar for the sacrament on the dirt floor, administering the Last Rites to old and young alike as they lay dying, are scenes from a different era. At times I have had the distinctly uncomfortable feeling that I was not meant to go there, along those shadowy pathways that once formed Father Nugent's pastoral experience.

It is a good job that real lives are never fully contained in the text of a book. A biography cannot be held to account for unavailable information. Besides, the living reality of our heroes of the past is something to be celebrated, lived in a new way by those who have inherited the legacy of their example and who are the beneficiaries of their inspired deeds. A life cannot be celebrated fully in the written word. The image of Father Nugent, portrayed in painting, in a statue, or marble bust in an Art Gallery, present a mythical figure concealing the real man. Part of the aim of this biography has been to try to unravel the real man from the tangle of projects and schemes with which he filled his life and to find the hidden, inner motivations behind his often hectic life-style.

The time that Father Nugent spent in the arduous years of his prison rounds, the sad sights his eyes must have met daily, there and on the streets where hungry urchins roamed and scavenged, his pioneering work for Catholic Education and moral renewal, his contribution to the work for a Children's Charter, are associated for ever with him. They can only be properly evaluated and celebrated in relation to the standard of pastoral care people now strive to give to the needy people of our day. Like the boys in the St. Anne's Street Boy's Refuge whom he described, when challenged about his accountability, as the only real "balance sheet' necessary, Father Nugent's true worth is in the investment in people, in the practical outcome of his efforts on their behalf rather than in the minutiae of business acumen. Hopefully there is room for both organisation and individual charism in society today.

The Refugee, the Asylum Seeker, the displaced millions, the homeless drunks and addicts of our present world re-tell the story of Father Nugent on a global scale. If the Poor are always with us then the need to apply the Gospel to their needs is just as acute, if not more so, now. Example is still the greatest teacher. The Sacred Scriptures assure us: "virtue, held in remembrance, is a kind of immortality because it wins recognition from God and also from mankind.....in every age virtue makes its triumphal progress, crowned with victory in the contest for prizes that nothing can tarnish." *(Wisdom 4,2)*. A virtuous life then cannot be defined by memorials of stone or paintings in oil, which in time become tarnished or disfigured, but rather by an inner life of holiness which is imperishable.

Today's world looks for visible, measurable standards to mark success and often does not see the inner qualities. This book is an investigation into a virtuous life in an amoral and turbulent society. It is about the priestly career of someone who, in popular estimation, was truly a man of God, a "beatus vir", though there is no obvious clamour for his Canonisation. James Nugent was also flesh and blood, but a touch of Godly compassion drove him to become embroiled in the worst aspects of the human condition which "was seething all around him". He may not be deemed a candidate for official sainthood (which is perhaps a refreshing change anyway), but no one could gainsay the litany of praise inscribed on his memorial statue. Those who have studied Nugent's life have concurred that of all the titles given to him'The Good Shepherd' is still the most appropriate one.

James Nugent was a champion of impoverished Liverpool, of hard-pressed families, of juvenile criminals. He was a voice for the silent oppressed. A true mark of his achievement lay in the fact that he was a man for everyone, able to relate comfortably to the most abject and the most prestigious of people. His general appeal and acceptability won him a place in people's hearts, rich or poor, high or low, Catholic or Protestant, of any creed and background. In this lies a crucial aspect of his importance for today.

There is no lack of lavish tributes to Father Nugent. Impressive accolades attest to " the broad sympathies and gracious humanitarian aims which Liverpool has long since learned to associate with the name of Monsignor Nugent." As the name of Barnardo was in London, and Father Hudson in Birmingham, so was Nugent's in Liverpool. Such high praise and such a long and distinguished ministry present the biographer with a huge challenge because all of that adulation has to be sifted and assessed - a task made all the harder by being left dormant in the last fifty years.

The challenge is still best expressed in the words of James Nugent's great friend and ally, Archbishop Ireland of Minneapolis and St. Paul Diocese, Minnesota. "Someone in England" he said, "with mind to understand him, with heart to value him, with pen to picture him, will no doubt before long give us his biography". This has inspired more than just a pen-picture, and whether the expectations have been met for what he called "a blessed book - the very perfume of apostolic priestliness and of holiest Christian love of fellow-man" will have to be left to the judgement of the reader. No book can quite do justice to that, unless you happen to be someone who combines the literary genius of a Jane Austin with the artistry and skill of a Rembrant.

Catholic life in mid-nineteenth century Britain is itself an interesting subject for study. Nugent was at the heart of that life. Emerging from the dark shadow of oppression which had imprisoned them for so long, Catholics were in need of a vision and a leadership to restore morale. We have emphasised already that Father Nugent's mission of Catholic education and his crusade for religious and moral revival, took its inspiration from the "Second Spring" of Cardinal John Henry Newman and the events leading up to the Restoration of The Catholic Hierarchy in 1850. At a time when Catholics had no vote and few opportunities for an education, whether at home or abroad, Nugent was inspired by Cardinal Newman and others to press ahead with the effort to redress the imbalance and to fill the void in Catholic life.

The wish to emulate in Liverpool the Oratorian-style Community that Newman had inspired in London and Birmingham, was, for a variety of reasons, frustrated. In this we see one of the differences between Nugent and his more celebrated contemporary. Nugent did not have Newman's patience for one thing, nor did he have the time and measured approach to pursue all his plans with sustained thinking. He did not have the freedom, under episcopal authority and in parish ministry, to translate all his own ideals into practice. The considerable impact made on him by Cardinal Nicholas Wiseman's 'Crusade of Prayer' which aimed to increase and promote devotion in Catholic circles, along with the reforming zeal of Cardinal Manning's social welfare policy in London, working imaginatively with Archbishop Temple, gave Nugent the impetus and example he needed to make the rallying call to the Catholics of Liverpool. These influences are important for a proper understanding of Nugent.

Cardinal Manning, as a convert from Anglicanism, made a robust defence of Catholics in their plight in the Victorian Workhouses and prisons and this served as an encouragement to Nugent in his own efforts at Workhouse reform. The Cardinal spoke out vehemently about the way young Catholics in the Workhouses were forced to attend religious services and receive instruction that was different from that which their parents had taught them. He frequently spoke out against the Poor Law Guardians in their disregard for the new regulations which had made it clear that Catholics should have access to a Catholic priest. Public stances like these strengthened Nugent's arm in challenging the authorities to allow Catholics to enjoy their new-found rights provided by law. Catholics after so-called 'Emancipation' continued to feel constrained by the on-going failure of local authorities to adhere to the new concessions. In addition, in Liverpool, there was open sectarianism and fear to contend with. Allaying this fear and prejudice and at the same time asserting Catholic rights and freedom was at the heart of James Nugent's delicate task. His example in this has inspired others today.

As well as being a man on a mission, Nugent was a man in a hurry. This, as we have seen, was both his strength and his weakness. Packed with ideas to overflowing, his actions and decisions did not always keep pace with his ideals nor did he find that others all supported with equal enthusiasm his ideals. We have the impression of someone making a determined dash through the obstacles that officialdom placed in his path. In his innovative work for child care, it is no exaggeration to say, he was ahead of the field in England. At the time, his superiors were more cautious, more circumspect, and as a catalyst he was bound to be an irritant at times to those who had to take the wider view and make decisions to benefit everyone. The Church has always needed both catalysts and analysts.

In trying to evaluate Father James Nugent's work it must be remembered that his outreach to the poor came at a time when there was little or no statutory provision for the poorer classes, indeed when the class system itself prevented such provision. His ministry was recognised at all levels of the community, it was described as "large and liberal," it was a ministry in the course of which he won great respect, many friends and only a few notable enemies. His prodigality, his gifts and his kindness to the needy, to the ones whom society forgot, especially impoverished children and homeless outcasts, is part of the folk-lore of Liverpool.

There was a very deliberate decision on Father Nugent's part to stay with Liverpool people and apply himself totally to their needs. He could have accepted any number of assignments, in London, in Rome and certainly in America. But he threw in his lot with the people of the town of which he was both a product and a grateful beneficiary. He made a point of saying that in the Liverpool community he had known as a young man he learnt practical things, but there were deeper religious undercurrents that drove him in his missionary zeal. It is necessary to see that his work was rooted in a practical belief in the gospel message of Christ, the ultimate call of the gospel, 'The Last Judgment' in St. Matthew chapter 25: "I was hungry and you gave me food, thirsty and you gave me drink, a stranger and you made me welcome, lacking clothes and you clothed me, sick and you visited me, in prison and you came to see me."   *Matthew 25; 35-36)*

That call had also to be deeply rooted in specific tasks and in a specific place. In his book 'Liverpool, wondrous place' by Paul Du Noyer, there is a humorous and very typical illustration of what makes Liverpool the unique community it is. The author recalls the controversy over the proposed memorial statue to the Beatles in 1977 when some of the City Councillors opposed the suggestion, doubtful about the Beatles' contribution to Liverpool and sceptical about their worthiness of a place in its history. There were others who felt their contribution was immense and ought to be recognised. A solution put forward, half in jest, by Sir Paul McCartney's brother, Mike, was that there should be two memorials, one that people could throw rotten tomatoes at if they wanted to, and another one at which people could throw bunches of roses.

This solution reflects something essential in the culture and ethos of Liverpool: a light-heartedness that can take the sting out of a dispute and solve a dilemma, a unique blend of humour, tolerance and compromise; a place where there is a tradition of music and art unequalled anywhere, a solidarity that comes not from outside but from within and has been hard-earned, a fidelity to friends and gratitude to benefactors, a large measure of religious faith and a large measure of obvious self-indulgence. At the same time it is a place that is home to a people who can laugh, at themselves and others, and who, perhaps most importantly, have always desired to find practical ways forward in difficult times. These qualities are woven into the human fabric of the city. They are the attributes of a city which have helped to form its citizens, have helped to make it the successful candidate for the Capital of Culture Award, and which have blended into a new self-belief, under the banner of "The World In One City." Love it or hate it you cannot be indifferent to Liverpool. It works its magic on all who live, work and visit there, and has done so for centuries. It did so for Nugent.

Commentators on Liverpool have put forward their view of it in a variety of ways, some of them probably not repeatable in polite company, but also many that are highly complimentary. In 1907 Ramsay Muir wrote proudly of "A Citadel of Faith and a Citadel of Knowledge" as the building of the Universities and Cathedral was beginning, and he identified the river as the life-blood of the town at a time before the docks were built, when "the untainted tides of the Mersey raced past a cluster of mud hovels amid fields and untilled pastures." Fifty years later, George Chandler recorded how "Normans, Anglo Saxons, Irish, Welsh, Scots and Vikings united in common pride at being Liverpolitans." Today the two Cathedrals together symbolise the striving for unity and the strength of unity that Ramsay Muir was pointing to. The heritage is a rich one and all the richer for the cohesion of the churches acting together.

Approaching Liverpool from the river has been likened to approaching Venice from the Grand Canal, though even the greatest admirers of Liverpool would admit that the comparison probably ends there! Strategically, in history, the waterfront has been as important as that of its venetian counterpart and King John first recognised its potential for trade and the advantage of its proximity to Ireland when he granted it its Charter 800 years ago, in the year 1207. The pulse of Liverpool life has been racing ever since, through its river. Perhaps King John was the town's first benefactor.

One of Liverpool's most celebrated sons, Lord Picton, said, that Liverpool never had a 'Grandfather'. Presumably his point was that it had so many founding fathers, benefactors and promoters who shaped it and guided its course that it is difficult to single out any one individual. Many have been the supporters and critics from among its own residents who have taken it forward as a city by constructive contributions. This is one of the strengths of the place. The Liverpool-born author, Linda Grant, in the novel 'Still Here', writes of her native town as a derelict place, with buildings like "dead entities" conveying the impression of a place that was somehow "hanging around long after anyone had any further use for it." Yet, to be fair she recognises the survival of Liverpool is in the quality of its people and that it would be wrong to look for its assets only in buildings. Rather they are to be found in the people who live and work in those buildings.

Buildings played a vital part in Father Nugent's work. Turning them into a home for children, a shelter for destitute mothers and their babies, a refuge for fallen women, a house of correction and acceptance for delinquent youths and places of hope for ex-offenders. People, whether in great need or not, were always to be seen as the primary concern for Nugent in his work .They were his 'balance sheet'. Today the visitor to Liverpool would seem to agree that whatever the defects may be it is the optimism, friendliness and sheer resilience of the people that catches the attention.

The travel writer, Bill Bryson, famously remarked that on arriving in Liverpool he thought he had stumbled upon a litter convention, and many would perhaps agree with him, despite recent improvements. He considered it at first sight as a place with "more of a past than a future" but was proved wrong. Whatever criticisms he had, he still gave Liverpool the distinction of being his favourite city in England and that was because of the community he met there rather than the external features of the town. Some indefinable spirit of optimism and hope for the future seems to offset the more undesirable sides of urban life and allows Liverpool to achieve, in sport, music, the arts - and the art of life itself - a quality which is the envy of many larger and better-resourced cities in the world.

People today look for an icon, an image they can look up to. It may be a pop idol, a film star, a footballer, even a slogan or a designer label. The world looks for a living legend of the here and now but perhaps it is because it has forgotten its history and failed to see that the heroes of the past are, in a sense, still among the movers and shakers of today. Their impact was not just for their own time. James Nugent epitomises this. As with the dispute over The Beatles' statue, opposing views have been reconciled, usually, if not always, graciously and amicably. Good will has often triumphed over divisiveness and in the most troubled moments of its history Liverpool has shown itself able to rise above its problems. There is a proven ability to survive and adapt to the next stage of the human story. The slogans: "The World In One City" and "Faith In The City," - which James Nugent would have warmly applauded not only because he liked slogans, but also because he loved the idea of unity - represent something that is not achievable over-night. Only after painstaking and lengthy effort can worth while things be attained.

Nobility does not come without the joys and pains, successes and failures of a life-long battle, without the hard work needed to make a person's ordinary qualities into something special. Thomas Burke, in his book 'Catholic History of Liverpool' states that Father Nugent's work "raised for him an imperishable monument in the hearts and minds of his fellow townsmen and incidentally raised the status of the Catholic body in a town traditionally Protestant." Yet at what personal cost did this come? It is important to see that his achievement often meant that Nugent was torn and tortured in himself since no human being could fail to experience the self-sacrifice entailed in such an enterprise. He battled to the end.

Death bed scenes can be defining moments which capture the essence of a life-time. To look at the manner of someone's death can often be a way of looking deeply into their lives. This, it seems to me, is based on the obvious premise that we see the complete person at the end of their life but we see very little by looking at the new-born baby. What then were the observable elements at the moment of Father Nugent's death?

Nine columns of obituary in the local paper and tributes in many national and international publications suggest that a remarkable man had left the world a little richer on his departure that sad yet blessed day of his death - 27th.June, 1905. It is significant to note that the ministry of Father Nugent on behalf of the poor and destitute was one of the longest and most notable of any Churchman during the 19th.Century. His had been a mission on his own doorstep, among his own community, a "hands-on" application of the Gospel in the streets and amongst the ordinary families, the marginalized, victimised and unfortunate ones whose lives were blighted by various social evils and whose lives, he often lamented, were "running to waste in the gutters". Quick to defend as well as to condemn, he frequently gave it as his opinion that there were many in the streets "whose plight was their misfortune not their fault." He saw them in a different light, as people who had slipped, willingly or unwillingly, through the net of provision and for that reason were the very ones needing to be saved. It was a remarkable and determined crusade of rescue that he could look back on at the end of his life.

The love which motivated his mission came from a deep religious sense, a sense of God's love, a father's love for his children. They may have been "Nobody's Children", they may have been "desolate and homeless wanderers of the streets....." "without a heart to love them, or a hand to guide them", they may have been "rowdy duffers, thieves and convicts", but they were also, in his view, precious children of God and it pained him to see them deprived of their God-given rights.

James Nugent would have endorsed the comment by Charles Dickens that in the little world where children have their existence nothing is more finely felt than injustice, and he recognised that the injustice at the heart of British society in his day affected the children more severely than any other group. In the prisons and workhouses of Britain at that time children and young people formed a majority and in 1846 and 1847 it was estimated that there were 12,508 children in England's prisons. No wonder that when the opportunity arose for him later, as prison chaplain, he was anxious to make this experience known among his fellow Catholics and engage them too in the many-sided work of rescue and reform.

Prison was for Nugent not only a house of correction but also a house of Providence. What gave it special appeal was that it should be a place of respect, where salvation was at work. In her book "My apprenticeship" Beatrice Webb attests to this truth, vital for our understanding of Father Nugent: "an unquestioning, all-out effort to serve the poor and give unstintingly without condition, was not only a means to an end but an end in itself and one of the main channels through which the individual entered into communion with the supreme spirit of love at work in the universe". Only at the very end of life can this insight be grasped,

When Monsignor James Nugent finally gave up the long struggle with pneumonia and fatigue and quietly went to his Maker at four o'clock in the morning of Tuesday, 27th.June 1905, his close friend, Father Edmund Walsh, of St. Thomas's, Waterloo, who had witnessed his holy death, recorded for posterity, with the reverence and respect arising from genuine friendship, this memory: "the monsignor's face seemed lit with radiance, with expectation of a bliss beyond the tomb, while he bowed his silvered head in recognition and content before the inevitable decree", he recalled for the mourners on the sorrowful day of the funeral (30th June) "his body lay cold and lifeless, but his life's work was fresh and fair before them and stirred all hearts with sympathetic love." No one would disagree with the sentiments, and as they looked back on a remarkable priestly life, all would concur that "so long as there remained evils to be faced and remedied he contrived to find a solution."

Victorian obituaries may be full of hyperbole but not necessarily devoid of sincerity, and behind the florid style we can discern the true appreciation. As if to emphasise the sense of universal mourning, the flags on public buildings were lowered to half-mast, and the obsequies were arranged with great ceremony, attended by a wide range of people of every class and occupation, representatives of many countries, religions and backgrounds. Memorial cards were sold in the streets (a final signal of his fund-raising prowess!) In almost every home Father Nugent had become a household name, especially in his native Liverpool, and everywhere there was great acclaim for his achievements as a champion of the Poor, as a pioneer of child care. Only in time could he be understood more profoundly as one of the architects of a renewed Catholic community in Britain.

Venerable with age and weary with labours, Monsignor James Nugent died peacefully in his own bed, in his own home at 'Harewood House' at the corner of Duke Street and Freshfield Road in Formby near Liverpool. He had his wish granted that he should die at least within range of his beloved Liverpool, surrounded by friends and relations, supported by faith and by prayer. He would not be "without a mourner to follow his coffin" for ten thousand would follow the route of his funeral cortege to Ford Cemetery in tearful tribute. He would not be "buried in a pauper's grave", as had befallen so many of the young street urchins he had met. The death of 'The Monsignor' was a cause of widespread sadness and a sense of loss fell over the city, shared by the girl flower-sellers and the boy shoe-blacks, by the Mayor in the Town Hall and the Pope in the Vatican, by a wide range of Church and Civic figures and by the ordinary man or woman in the street whose lives he had influenced perhaps without him even knowing it.

He had obtained the house in Formby where he died, by means of his usual combination of determination and guile. He bid for it at an auction and when he thought the was going against him he raised a question to the Auctioneer as to how long it would be before this building fell down, and the interest immediately dropped. When he had set his heart on something he generally got it one way or another. Nearly all his aspirations had been fulfilled, his wonderful life and many accomplishments had won him great renown. Yet, the dying words sealed the attitude of a life-time; though he died amidst a wave of public adulation for his work, there was a word of self-reproach on his lips as he lamented the fact that he had let slip through his hands many opportunities for doing good.

This paradox, at the end of his days, seemed to typify the contradiction which ran like a refrain through his whole life. In public there was success and achievement but in private a sense of dissatisfaction. He seems to have had a life-long anxiety that everything had to be resolved quickly and he could not rest until the next problem was addressed. Here was a rather tortured spirit in some ways, always with one more project up his sleeve, one more mission to undertake. This approach was driven as much by the boundless social needs he saw in the community around him as by the dictates of his own restlessness. In the early years it had led his bishop, George Brown, (first Catholic Bishop of Liverpool from 1850-1856) to make the observation that he had " a soul too big for his body" and Bishop Alexander Goss to remark that "he had about him more of restlessness than of useful activity". It was certainly a view shared by some of Nugent's fellow clergy that he displayed more zeal than pragmatism, and many were left floundering or bruised in the wake of the world-wind of activity.

In a more general way, this also reflected the nature of the Victorian society of which he was part, where a constant tension existed between success and failure, between respectability, progress and wealth on the one hand, poverty, inequality and deprivation on the other. The tension has never been resolved and whilst great progress brings wealth it also brings misery.

During his life-time two worlds existed side by side: the world of the rich and the poor, of which we are now much more acutely aware. Jane Austin in her novel 'Emma' once wrote: "one half of the world does not understand the pleasures of the other." It may equally be said that one half of the world does not understand the miseries of the other. Today even more ostensibly than was seen in Nugent's day, the world is divided into more segments of rich and poor, and when there is a meeting of the two worlds is a bit like a wealthy passenger on a great ship wandering down from his first class cabin to stumble across the squalor and discomfort of the crew in the steerage berths. This was the contradictory world James Nugent knew all too well, he saw it in the Old Country and the New World, in the damp cellar and the glittering banquet hall, and the contrasts shaped and influenced his mission.

The town of Liverpool was in his bones, in his soul, a "busy, smoky, noisy and money-getting place" it may have been, but it was also Britain's second biggest port, the western gateway to the Empire, door to the untold wealth of the New World. The bustling and growing town of Liverpool in James Nugent's younger days had produced millionaires more rapidly than any other place in Britain outside London, but the unwelcome by-product of its success was the wretchedness and misery and poverty of the left-behind generation. The concentration of destitute poor gave rise to the description of Liverpool as the "Black Spot on the Mersey" - a title we could not contemplate using today and one that sits uneasily with the city's proud heritage, but it was once an undeniable fact.

During his life-time of eighty-three years James Nugent witnessed in Liverpool, under the impetus of its meteoric rise as a seaport, a growth that was nothing short of spectacular. Between 1820 and 1850, as Liverpool grew, Nugent also grew up. This parallel growth had a profound part to play in his own self-identity and purpose. With that strong memory that stood him in good stead for his role in public life, he was able to recall the extent of the town he had known as a boy. Speaking many years later in the Adelphi Hotel he regaled and surprised his audience by recalling that the confines of the town he once knew had been from "Blue Bell Inn in London Road to the milestone at Mile End Road (Scotland Road)" and all the shipping activities of Liverpool then could be contained within the area occupied by Princes Dock and Brunswick Dock. No doubt his listeners were amused to hear a confirmed Tee-Totalism Campaigner admit, along with all good Liverpudlians, that the pubs are always the landmarks for those seeking their way around Liverpool!

Our story has not portrayed a life that is a seamless robe. Father Nugent's humanity and obvious vulnerability is what endeared him to people. The personal differences that arose in the relationship between Father Nugent and his bishop, Bernard O'Reilly, probably worried Nugent more than he admitted to others. He could be opinionated and impetuous, as we have seen, and the occasion when he damned with feint praise the new Bishop O'Reilly in a somewhat infamous and perhaps ill-conceived letter in the 'The Catholic Times' in 1873, was an error that was never totally reconciled. "We can foretell a most useful and solid Episcopal career" Nugent had written, adding that in this choice of bishop some people "may have expected a man of more intellectual strength." But O'Reilly had proved himself a pastoral champion of the people of Liverpool as a priest who had cared for the plague victims whilst working at St. Patrick's parish and indeed nearly succumbed to the plague himself. Despite the unsettled relationship with his superiors and the spats with colleagues as well as friends, Nugent came to see that his work could not be done without them.

In fact it was through Bishop Goss that Father Nugent was able to launch and sustain his famous "Save The Boy" campaign, at the Sessions House in Liverpool, in 1864, a turning point in a distinguished life of service. It was through Bishop O'Reilly's initiative in 1877 that the Rosary Sunday tradition, started by his predecessor Bishop Goss, was revived and the Collection on that day for the needs of poor children, a Collection that continues to this day, was initiated. These were an important part of the new culture as much as the new regulations and policies that brought Child welfare into the modern era. Yet Nugent was often wrong-footed by his bishop, especially when the latter made clear his dislike of party political involvement. When he found himself writing to the bishop this disclaimer: " I am not one of the clergy who are anxious to mix in politics" - it was nevertheless evident that more than once he had clearly suggested people vote for a Catholic Candidate in elections regardless of their political stance.

The slogan "Save the Boy" that threw Father Nugent into the glare of publicity above all others was attributed not to Bishop Goss or to James Nugent but to another unlikely ally and friend John Denvir, who played a special and significant role in his life. For three years or more he reported in the 'Northern Press' (Catholic Times) the sermons, speeches and other occasions of significance in Father Nugent's ministry, providing the vital oxygen of publicity for many of his projects. He wrote articles and was responsible for the distribution and promotion of the 'Catholic Times'. The power of the press was as powerful then as it is today. John Denvir also played a part as secretary of the Boys' Refuge in St. Anne's Street, and he boasted the distinction of being the first person to enrol in the 'League of The Cross for Total Abstinence,' taking the pledge publicly three times. In 1873, Denvir was appointed Secretary of the Catholic Club which gave him a position of influence to express his strong pro-Catholic, pro-Irish views that led him into what was later called The IRA. James Nugent found in him a sympathetic and useful helper, perhaps his closest one among the laity.

In his 'Personal Notes,' written for an American audience around 1870, we find this central statement of Father Nugent's whole mission: "To Save The Boy from the fatal influences of ignorance, pauperism and crime and the temptations of the streets has been the chief aim of my life......Save The Boy is my motto - inscribed on the flag which I unfurled years ago in the old country, and altered circumstances only bind me more faithfully to its call. I seek to Save The Boy from what? Not from labour, which is his birthright, for which he may be thankful to heaven yet, before he dies, but from temptation." The pre-occupation of the Victorian middle-classes with morality and the work ethic, with social respectability and strong loyalty to a cause, can all be seen in this statement. The rallying-cry of a moral crusade for children, which motivated Nugent so powerfully, became the banner around which all sorts of activists, politicians and churchmen and women gathered.

It is impossible to appreciate Nugent properly without reference to this slogan, a 'sound-bite' of its time that he used so effectively. It was heard on platforms in speeches at home and abroad. It echoed around the narrow streets, in the homes of the people, in public buildings, in railway station waiting rooms and in the pubs where it was emphasised further by the presence of collecting boxes marked 'A Million Pennies' to Save The Boy. It was heard in conversations at cosy firesides, it crept around the hulks of the Training ships anchored in the mist over the Mersey River, it was on the lips of all sorts of people, high and low, rich and poor, boys and girls, Town Hall officials, Church leaders, Catholics and Protestants.

Father Nugent's more observant admirers recognised that the experiences of his early life as a priest and his own natural sympathies for the needs of children intensified during his career to produce this slogan until - "there was no more familiar term in everyday speech among the Liverpool public life, nor one more closely identified with him, than the cry to "Save The Boy." So, even if he himself did not coin the phrase, it was a God-send in his missionary endeavours.

One thing has become clear, the mission was never the work of a single man. Many people, in collaboration with one another, helped to bring about the changes and benefits among Catholics and in the general community of Liverpool during this time. Activists of the time helped to lobby for less discrimination and greater equality, freedom from oppressive laws, for better housing, food and clothing, sanitation, jobs and education for those left out in the cold by industrial progress. A great tradition had built up in the town that included the contributions of many : William Rathbone, Josephine Butler, William Roscoe, Kitty Wilkinson and William Duncan standing out among them. They formed the context of Father Nugent's mission in Liverpool. This network of contributions fashioned Liverpool's heritage in the pursuit of Scholarship, Faith, Learning, Literature, The Arts, Citizenship, Justice and, very importantly, good humour.

Within Catholic circles too the legacy of Nugent's achievements must be set in the context of figures like Mother Magdalen Taylor, and Julie Billiart, Founders of the Religious Congregations which influenced so deeply the Catholic ethos of Britain and whose charisms and dedication Father Nugent appreciated so much. Only with such support could he have done what he did in taking the Catholic Cause further than almost any other Catholic reformer of his kind in that generation. To have done so at a time when there was in society what Thomas Burke records as "a base spirit of prejudice and intolerance which prevented Catholics from living in perfect harmony with their neighbours," represented a major achievement.

What are the defining elements of Father James Nugent's character, life and work with which to finish this account? What are the elements of his legacy to us that matter most and that we would want to retain? A summary of Nugent's contribution to social history must inevitably be put it the context of his own personality, his motivation, the people he worked with, his strengths and weaknessess and finally the effectiveness of the campaigns he led. The campaigns often led to social change.

Without doubt he was a complex character, a man of many parts, many talents and not a few anomalies. Contemporary accounts of him attest to his physical and mental strength, to his being a man fired by the gospel and zeal for God's poor, a true Christian missionary. His physical strength is evident; when other clergy succumbed to the effects of their contacts with the victims of the cholera and typhus epidemics, which reoccurred during the 19[th.] Century, he survived and kept on going. In the midst of illness he tried to keep on going when lesser men would have given up. Thomas Burke, in his 'Catholic History of Liverpool' describes him simply as 'indefatigable'.

The disastrous Cholera epidemic of 1849 was closely monitored in the columns of the Catholic Weekly 'The Tablet' of that year, and although focussing on London, it has to be said that none suffered more than the clergy of Liverpool who contracted the sickness through their ministrations in the dockside hovels and cellars. Whilst he may have appeared accident-prone and subject to illnesses arising from overwork, as during his student days and in 1856, when he was thirty four and the work to establish the Catholic Institute took its toll, and yet again in the 1870s suffering periodic and lengthy bouts of nervous mental and physical exhaustion, James Nugent was a battler and a survivor. In 1878, at the time of his prison ministry he fell ill with what was described by the local press as "a painful and dangerous illness" and weeks of dark depression dogged his steps. Such was his resilience that he was said to have been spotted, even at this time, canvassing for moral and financial support for his latest project.

What was really going on during these episodes of illness is frustratingly difficult to discern. They appear as gaps in an incomplete jig-saw and they challenge the general reputation he had for tireless work. 'The Tablet' took an interest in his later work and in July 1905, following his death, observed that in his long life two words entirely alien to James Nugent were lethargy and despair.

It became quite usual for him to be the subject of curiosity and interest in the local press, pursued by the equivalent of the paparazzi of the day. As we have seen he featured in 'The Porcupine', a local paper which, as its name suggests was a satirical magazine offering sharp comment on current political and social events. Generally it was favourable in its references to Father Nugent, though it tended at times to probe any mistakes he might have made. Its editor did not like secrecy in any form. One of the 1865 issues of 'The Porcupine' gave a pen-portrait of Father Nugent as "a man of short stature and slight compact figure", whose features are "small but distinct in outline" forming "an intelligent expression." It proceeded to describe an "expansive forehead," which it said "bespeaks a mind capable of a more catholic grasp and temper than Catholicism is thought to require". His grey hair was thought to denote mature years (in fact he was only forty-three when this was written) and "perhaps the military closeness of cut, which reminds one of a Roundhead clergyman, is not the only soldierly peculiarity of his appearance. He is obviously a man to command - a sort of 'Little Corporal' in affairs ecclesiastical." ('The Porcupine' 1865).

Later, in 1893, he was to be described in the 'Liverpool Legion of Honour' as "a venerated ornament of the Roman Catholic Church, a man of much public spirit with broad views and a capacity for organisation and command." Someone has said that praise is fine as long as you don't inhale!   The public acclaim and press attention Nugent received at times, does not seem to have turned his head.

These descriptions of Nugent's military bearing were probably more perceptive than their authors realised, for as we have noted James Nugent's antecedents were fighting men from France during the Norman Conquest and some of his forebears were numbered among the Jacobite Armies. Nugent himself came to espouse the Nationalist cause in Ireland and he was familiar with the work of the Army Chaplain as one of the longest-serving Chaplains to the 4th. Irish Division and a supporter of the Boer War. Yet the warrior instincts he had were channelled into the battle for souls in the streets of Liverpool, and any inherited qualities of determination and toughness manifested themselves in the pursuit of a good cause.

The hard exterior he sometimes portrayed when dealing with authority changed to an attitude of compassion and humility when dealing with the poor scraps of humanity on his doorstep, a woman in rags on the street or young boys and girls in prison. After all, he was noted for recommending that those who wanted to help even hardened criminals should, "speak a kind word to them and lead them gently by the hand." This combination of an iron fist and a velvet glove was in some ways the secret of James Nugent's success in the prison service. In another way it represented a frustrating contradiction in his nature since his quick, Irish temperament was unable or unwilling to suffer fools gladly, whilst it served to help him deal with difficult characters such as hardened criminals. Occasionally he left behind a few bodies in his breathless pursuit of the things he passionately believed in. His actions and his words could be powerful weapons for good, and sometimes they could hurt. He was once asked if he was having trouble with his mouth and he said: "Yes, keeping it shut".

He developed powers of oratory during his long and distinguished career and learnt the art of dramatic presentation with the skills of an accomplished actor. From his student days he had a love of the theatre and a passion for debate. He probably never envisaged, in his student days, how much he would put this to use later. He became much sought-after for talks and after-dinner speeches on a vast variety of matters, ecclesiastical and secular, and was looked to eagerly for advice on all sorts of issues of the day; his advice on music, cooking and even his considered opinion on the comparative merits of the water closet and the privy in the courts and slums of Liverpool was sought and valued!

Newspapers reported how "His Irish tongue could draw laughter and tears" from his audience. He was able to use words as rapiers or bludgeons, depending on his purpose and his old friend 'The Porcupine' gave this picture : "always free in his mode of active expression, compensating for the want of nobility in his countenance by the easy action of his limbs, he now and then in moments of temporary excitement brings his arms and hands into very liberal play indeed." These characteristics, both in his speeches on the stage of Public Halls and in his preaching from the pulpit, made him an effective communicator, capable of changing hearts and minds and even political allegiances.

One of the most successful movements of social reform in Liverpool's recent history, his Temperance work, took him all over the country and to America and in it he proved himself to be the Father Matthew of his generation. He possessed a natural "gift of the gab", adopted a strong didactic style in the mould of a Victorian Moral Crusader, displayed an unusual combination of flamboyant theatrical energy and practical everyday insights into human nature. On the stage or platform he could employ all the advantages of "personal bearing and vocal power" as one newspaper described it and in all of this the most striking part of his preaching was the "practical purpose." "He combines, in a rare degree, the qualities of a layman with those of a priest. Few of his hearers doubt that Father Nugent knows as much about the world as they do and he takes care to apply his knowledge with effect... Father Nugent has seen, and every day he sees, too much of real hard life, of low life, of mean life, and most likely of noble life under circumstances most debasing and destructive, to make his religious teaching ought but practical", wrote the editor of 'The Porcupine'.

The Temperance Movement changed James Nugent. He himself had to undergo the transition from a theoretical belief in Temperance as a virtue to a belief in Tee-Totalism as a necessity in the prevention of crime. The reform of morals and the public acceptance of the pledge as an example of this took root deeply in him, sustaining his belief that 'prevention is better than cure'. His prison ministry gradually convinced him that criminal tendencies had to be tackled in their infancy otherwise an incorrigibility set in with offenders as they got older and more hardened to drink-related crime and punishment. It was a hard-fought stance he adopted in his reformatory work, and it was abetted by something very important - the desire to keep Catholics in the fold; to stem leakage from the faith, to keep his co-religionists on the straight and narrow for the sake of the future.

The latter half of the 19th. Century was marked by a considerable falling off from organised religion and church attendance, (as at the present time,) and it became a prime motive in Father Nugent's campaigns to stop this dangerous tendency. He gave a lot of emphasis to drink as the cause of break-up in the home giving rise to the comment that Nugent "rides the teetotal hobby horse a little too hard." ('The Porcupine') Be that as it may, he witnessed first-hand the demonic effects of habitual drunkenness and the downward spiral of degradation it brought to the lives of men and women, especially among the Irish Catholic families committed to his charge; those in prison for drink-related crime, mothers who suffocated or neglected their babies whilst under the influence of drink.

We have focussed on the Temperance question and noted that the immediate motivation for this, his most successful and widespread crusade, came from his visit to America in 1870 -1871 where he was called on to take the message home to Liverpool in the way that Father Matthew had done earlier in America and Ireland. He was often motivated by the example of those who, as his seniors, had led similar crusades in their day. There was a sort of hero-worship element in him.

He yearned for travel and whilst his home town held a fascination and a power that energised his work, Nugent recognised, crucially, that Liverpool was the springboard for overseas travel. The policy of child Emigration has obviously been criticised and radically reviewed since Nugent's day but in The Catholic Reformatory Association at that time there was a belief that emigration was an appropriate way of resolving the problem of homeless Catholic orphans and other youngsters who had little prospect of a home-life, proper education or a respectable job. Those who were in his words "more or less a burden on the parish rates" were also an encumbrance for the local Authority. Liverpool became synonymous with emigration and famous (or infamous) for the arrival of immigrants too. If there was a prospect of a new and happier life in the New World Nugent and his colleagues felt themselves compelled to offer it.

However, even in those days of crisis management not everyone saw emigration as the best way forward for the children, being doubtful about the suitability of some prospective adopting families. With hindsight, such concerns proved, in many cases, to be well founded. In a book with the modest title of 'Liverpool - The First Thousand Years' just six lines are given to Father Nugent and even they are not entirely complimentary! It expresses the view that his good intentions in taking them to Canada or America "turned into ashes in a different kind of hell for some of Liverpool's poorest children." Perhaps this says more about the defects in parts of Canadian and American culture than it does about Father Nugent.

Someone who sets out with reforming ideals has to be ready for opposition too. People generally do not favour change and the perceived threat of change raises defences in all of us. James Nugent had to be aware also of the wider picture and the trends of history. The nineteenth century brought a gradual easing of the laws which had held Roman Catholics in a grip of prejudice for so long. As the reign of Pope Pius IX progressed there came about a growth in self-confidence among British Catholics, and a reclamation of the ancient Faith which earlier generations had staunchly defended - not only the Catholic Irish but also the long-established recusant English families. With social and political reform, and the advance of education, there came a greater tolerance of religious differences.

The Catholic Relief Act of the previous century had already sown the seeds Catholic Emancipation in 1829. Unfortunately, statutory changes do not necessarily mean a change of attitude or a softening of hard hearts and part of Father Nugent's strategy was to uphold the statutory concessions for Catholics as they came in. Relations between Protestant, Dissenter, Non-Conformist and Catholic remained unsettled and frosty throughout the century, often breaking, out like a running sore, into conflict in the heart of the community. It was vital to keep an equilibrium if the different communities were going to go forward together.

Although he was always proud of his Roman Catholic, Irish and Lancashire credentials, he used these to build up community spirit not to draw attention to differences. His collaborative ministry with Major Lester and other prominent Anglican Church figures who had similar ideals to himself, was an essential factor in his mission to the town. It was the beginning of a fight back, despite the sectarianism that barred the path. The desire to restore unity and equality to a people deprived of a fair chance for too long was a powerful motivation. Municipal authorities and church leaders alike joined, where possible, to restore the image of the town and the opportunities for its people.

This set a trend which has continued to the present day and which allowed two Churchmen of Catholic and Protestant backgrounds in more recent times to co-write a book about their Christian partnership and dedicate it "to the indomitable spirit of the Liverpool People." (David Sheppard and Derek Worlock). James Nugent would have endorsed that sentiment.

The prestigious place that Canon Thomas Lester's work earned for him in the affections of the people is well summarised in a tribute by Margaret Simey. Her warm appreciation of his work recalls that "The genuine affection with which he was regarded by the poor lives on in the hearts of succeeding generations." After his death the schools and Institutions he founded were taken over by the local City Council but his example lived on. The famous image which people still hold dear is that of him striding through the streets late at night, a pile of bedding balanced in his head, a small child in his arms and an anxious and weary mother at his side, as he leads them to a place of shelter. He would promise payment later, like the Good Samaritan at the Inn, but everyone grew indulgent towards the fact that he was unlikely to come back and pay! The practical nature of the help he gave made him a natural friend of Father Nugent and the significance of their collaboration cannot be too strongly emphasised in the story of Nugent's life. The symbolic nature of their joint action in a time of great sectarian unrest was obvious and it helped to inspire a note of optimism for future religious harmony.

Canon Lester had a parish of 9000 souls in St. Mary's, Kirkdale, and for many years sustained an annual collection of £4000 for his various charities. It is said that the title of 'Major' that was associated with his name, came partly from a family tradition and partly from a recognition of his efficient, military-style approach to his work. The 'Major' and the 'Little Corporal' then were a very well matched pair. They inspired and encouraged each other. Was it not more than enlisting "the aid of enlightened Protestantism" in the pursuit of his cause? Was it not a genuine belief in friendship and trust between Catholic and Protestant, stemming from the same gospel mandate, that transcended denominational boundaries in the common cause of humanity?

Looking back on Father Nugent's story it seems to have much in common with the hard-hitting novels of the period, though it is more compelling, more subtle than any fiction; because it is less contrived, more real, more human. The abiding images I would want to retain of 'Monsignor James Nugent' are of the good shepherd (albeit in cloak and top hat) waiting to board the ship for Canada with twenty-four small orphans in his wake; the kind father commending to the poor women of his parish the value of thrift and encouraging the use of Penny Savings Banks which he made popular, and rewarding them with gifts of geese and coal at Christmastime; the playwright enjoying scenes in the street of ragged boys acting out Shakespeare Tragedies and child acrobats doing conjuring tricks for money or travelling minstrels and strolling players presenting sketches, their faces scarcely recognisable through the dirt, and "sparing in the use of their pocket handkerchiefs"; speaking with infinite kindness to a wild girl in the dark cell of Walton Prison.

These are scenes that could be straight from a Dickens' novel, rich in pathos and humour, but they are tempered by the reality that Nugent then had to set about feeding, housing and educating them; they were real people, not characters in a book. Scenes such as the gatherings of bedraggled people outside the pawn shop on the corner of Brick Street on Monday mornings, the 'Fish and Money' women who came offering starving people putrid fish in exchange for a loan, re-payment of which was ruthlessly and violently exacted, these were the backdrop of his daily experience in the parish. Only a place with the unique combination of social religious factors of the kind found in Liverpool could throw up a character like 'The Hombre' - the nickname of Francis O'Rourke who was well-known for his bizarre and violent behaviour, especially after he had taken a drink or two. The story goes that he was standing on the roof of his house, naked and drunk, weilding a knife as he challenged anyone to come and fight him. An Irish priest was called in, his parish priest, who fiercely shouted to the man "come down offerit yer dirty lunatic, or I'll cumupper der and beat de livin daylights outer yer." The Hombre turned as meek as a lamb and called back apologetically "alright farder, I'll be down right enough" as he cowered behind a chimney stack. Of such stories is the legend of Liverpool composed. There is no indication that the parish priest was Father Nugent, but it could well have been!

In the great commercial enterprise of the 19th Century, with its pariahs and outcasts of society, its refugees and those seeking asylum from the harsh reality of their own lands, where there was gold and there was dross, we see a distant reflection of our own distorted world today. Even Father Nugent felt compelled to refer to the 'dregs of society' in speaking of those children of Irish immigrants who were left behind to fend for themselves, who had fallen through the wide net of provision after an earlier generation had cut them adrift.

In spite of this everyone came to acknowledge the truth of the statement that "of his varied characteristics few were more definite than his love of Liverpool" and in particular for its poorest people. Patricia Runighan talks of a "love-hate relationship" between Nugent and the Irish people in Liverpool. It is true that he loved them but felt that he was not always rewarded with the response he hoped for. At times he may have been a disillusioned man. It is perhaps more accurate to say that he felt some bitterness towards those who had abandoned the poor to their fate in the search for a more comfortable life or in the name of political expediency or through sheer snobbery.

It is perhaps an open question as to what extent personal ambition drove Nugent on. Some personal ambition is surely a necessary ingredient in human progress. It was the view of some of his contemporaries, such as his archrival and fellow-Catholic Michael Whitty, Editor of the 'Liverpool Daily Post', that Father Nugent was driven more by a sense of personal ambition than by any call from God. Whitty saw only underhand methods of working, saw what he called 'a showman', someone building his own empire. In Nugent's personal, utter commitment to the cause which he had espoused lay both his strength and his weakness. His achilles heal was, in the early years at least, his independence and the 'go it alone' approach he seemed to adopt which sometimes kept others at arm's length.

Nugent badly needed to be understood, to be accepted. He was a hard man to work with and a hard act to follow, as Father Berry discovered to his cost, so that there were many who admired him from a distance but could not keep close to him in the sheer vitality of his mission. Yet, in later life there was a greater mellowness and tolerance in his manner that smoothed over much of the turmoil of earlier times. He had set very high standards for himself and he expected others to follow; an expectation that he gradually realised had to be tempered with realism.

Subsequent generations of clergy could not have known or recalled the extent of James Nugent's early pioneering work or his activity overseas. In a long ministry the early years are all too easily forgotten by those who come later. There were signs that Nugent felt this and that he did not always suffer gladly what he viewed as the failings of the younger clergy who did not share the same zeal. Times had changed and he perhaps clung to old methods. Nevertheless at the close of his life all his accomplishments could be firmly placed in context and recognised as an enormous contribution to the life of the Church in Britain, as groundbreaking work that paved the way for future developments. James Nugent came on the scene at a time when a work of leadership and consolidation was crucial. He made a difference to people lives. The charitable projects which he initiated, in a sense have set the political agenda of our own day.

A fitting conclusion and summary is contained in the tribute given by Father Nugent's 'alma mater', Ushaw College, following news of his death in 1905: "To God and to God's poor he gave the strong enthusiasm of his youth and early manhood, the steadier strength and experience of his maturity, the wisdom and last energies of old age...... courage and faith in the power of good over evil were the mainspring of his strength".

In one of his many historic visits around the world, Pope John Paul II placed into the Western Wall of the Temple at Jerusalem his prayer for forgiveness for all the suffering that had been caused to God's children. As I write these last few sentences it is Holocaust Memorial Day. Recalling that gesture in which the Holy Father was capturing a life-time of desire to avoid a culture of self-indulgence, selfishness and insularity, to avoid a culture of death and instead promote and recreate a culture of forgiveness, mutual respect and life, a culture that says sorry and rejoices in the reconciliation that brings, it seemed the right note on which to end.

These great ideals are part of our own times as much as they were in Father Nugent's day. In the search for an open and practical expression of Catholic Faith today, Pope John Paul's call at the start of his pontificate for a liberal Church - in the sense of a generous, self-giving and open Church that will "Open wide the doors for Christ", already had a precedent, in Father Nugent, a century ago, when he opened a door that would let all the children come in, be at home in their Father's House, and enjoy a Second Spring.

Right Rev. T. Whiteside, D.D.
Bishop of Liverpool, 1894
and first Archbishop of Liverpool 1911

Bibliography

A.   Source Material

Father James Nugent's 'Personal Notes', Volumes I - III

Father James Nugent's speeches and articles: 'Nobody's Children' and
'Incorrigible Women'.

Letters of James Nugent (miscellaneous, 1870s & 1880s)
*(The above courtesy of The Nugent Care Society and Clarence House School
archives with special thanks to John Kennedy, Kathleen Pitt, Pat McEvoy)*

Mgr. James Nugent on the Proposed Refuge and Shelter for Women (Paul Street)
1891.

'Mother as we knew her'. Reminiscences of Mother Foundress
written by the Sisters of her Order, 1871-1900.

Sisters of The Poor Servants of the Mother of God,

Annual Reports of Catholic Children's Protection Society 1884.

Minutes of Chapter Meetings, 1890-1899,

Archdiocese of Liverpool. *Courtesy of Cathedral Archives.*

Diocesan Directories of the period (Miscellaneous).
Courtesy of Cathedral Archives.

Correspondence and Newspaper Articles of the period (Miscellaneous).
Courtesy of Cathedral Archives.

B.   Biographical

An Introduction to Father Nugent of Liverpool
*by Ray H. Dunbobbin, unpublished, as background to 'Black Spot on the
Mersey' – by Ray H. Dunbobbin, a script for dramatisation shown at The
Liverpool Play House. 1970.*

The Life Story of an Old Rebel, by John Denvir. 1910
Published by Irish University Press.

Father Nugent's Liverpool. 1849-1905, by Patricia Runaghan.
A Countyvise Publication. Birkenhead 2003.

Father Nugent of Liverpool, by Canon John Osmond Bennett
Published by Nugent Care Society (Second edition) 1993

Father Berry's Homes by Canon John Osmond Bennett
notes for intended publication.

Liverpool Shadows, by Richard Whittington-Egan.
Published by The Bluecoat Press. Liverpool 2002.

Catholic History of Liverpool, by Thomas Burke.
Published by C. Tinling and Co. Ltd. 1910.

The Edwardian Story, by Peter Doyle and Leslie McLoughlin.
  Published by Creativa Limited. 2003.
The Autobiography of a Liverpool Slummy, by Pat O'Mara.
  Published by The Bluecoat Press.

C.   Articles and References

Merseypride. Essays in Liverpool Exceptionalism, by John Belchem.
  Published by Liverpool University Press. 2000.
Popular Politics, Riot and Labour, (Essays in Liverpool History
  1790-1940) edited by John Belchem.
  Liverpool University Press 1992.
Catholic Men's Society Magazine,
50th Anniversary Conference Brochure, 1899.
The Parish of St. Vincent de Paul, Liverpool
Centenary Brochure, 1852-1952.
Child Care Pioneers, by Margaret Weddel.
  Published by The Epworth Press. London 1958.
'Caring' Newsletter For Supporters of the Nugent Care Society
  Numbers 56 & 57 2003/04.
The Nugent Care Society Annual Report 2002-2003
  & Strategic Plan 2004-2009
  courtesy of Nugent Care Society, Liverpool.
William Henry Duncan, First Medical Officer of Health.
  Notes from The Duncan Society based on Duncan of Liverpool by W.M. Frazer.
The Ushaw Magazine,1896 & 1905,
  courtesy of Alistair MacGregor and Father Michael Sharratt.
Found Worthy. Biographical Dictionary of Secular Clergy of
Liverpool Since 1850, by Brian Plumb.
The Pool of Life, A public health walk in Liverpool
  by Maggi Morris & John Ashton. 1997
Father Wilfrid Carr – A local example of the Church's Social Teaching, with
  special reference to "Rerum Novarum" written by Pope Leo XIII.,1891.
  (Dissertation submitted for MA in Ecclesiastical History (1997),
  by Father John Seddon
The Gillows and the Growth of Catholicism in the North of England in the
  Nineteenth Century,
  (Dissertation submitted for MA in Ecclesiastical History (1997),
  by Father Peter Morgan

Philanthropy in Preston

The Changing Face of Charity in a 19th Century Provincial Town
   Phd Dissertation. University of Lancaster 1990 by Meg Whittle

The Porcupine (Liverpool Magazine) Volume 7, 1865, &
   Volume 14, 1872.

Liverpool History Society Journal. 2002
   Liverpool Records Office.

The Liverpool Review 1878/1885/1891/1896
   Liverpool Records Office

The Liverpolitan Volume 1 No. 2. July 1932.
   Liverpool Records Office

Liverpool Legion of Honour by B. G. Orchard. 1893
   Liverpool Records Office

Liverpool Leader Alum Part 1, No. 10. 1874.
   Liverpool Records Office

Catholic Ancestor Volume 5 No. 6. November 1995.
   Liverpool Records Office

Catholic Institute Magazine. Spring 1909.
   Liverpool Records Office

Catholic Family Annual. 1906.
   Liverpool Records Office

Catholic Record, Volumes 18-19, 1948-1949.
   Liverpool Records Office

Directory & Guide to the Quarante'Ore. 1940.
   Liverpool Records Office

The Rambler (Miscellaneous)

The Tablet (Miscellaneous)

Recusant History Vol 15. No1. May 1979

D.   Background Histories

History of Liverpool, by Ramsay Muir.
   Published by Liverpool University Press. 1907.

History of Liverpool by George Chandler.
   Published by B.T. Batsford Ltd. London. 1957.

Liverpool, The Place, The People. Official Guide to the City of Liverpool.
   British Publishing Company. 1996.

The People's History of Liverpool, by Peter Aughton.
   Published by Carnegie Press 1990.

Herdman's Liverpool.
   The Gallery Press. 1968.
Liverpool, Our City Our Heritage,
   by Freddy O'Connor. 1990.
A Pub On Every Corner. Volumes 1 and IV,
   by Freddy O'Connor. 2001.
Liverpool, It All Came Tumbling Down,.
   by Freddy O'Connor. 2000.
Liverpool. Images of A Great Seaport.
   Published by Editions Limited, Bluecoat Chambers.
Alex Laing and Deirdre Morley. 1989.
St. Alban's Blackburn 1773-1973.
A Study in two centuries of Blackburn Catholicism,.
by Mary Conlon.
   Published locally, June 1973.
Liverpool. The Irish Connection, by Michael Kelly.
   Published by Print Origination Ince Blundell 2003
Liverpool – The First 1000 Years,
   by Arabella McIntyre – Brown and Gary Woodland
   Published by Garlic Press.University of Liverpool, 2002
Black Spot On The Mersey A Study of Environment and Society
   in 18th and 19th Century
   by I. C. Taylor.
Liverpool. (Unpublished Thesis 1976. University of Liverpool)
Democracy and Sectarianism. A Political and social
History of Liverpool, by Philip J. Waller.
   Published by Liverpool University Press, 1981.
An introduction to Nineteenth Century British History. 1800-1914, by Michael
Lynch. (Access to History series).
   Published by Hodder & Stoughton. 1999.
Industry and Empire, by E. J Hobsbawm and Chris Wrigley.
   Published by Penguin Books (revised edition) 1999.
The Victorians, An Age in Retrospect by John Gardiner.
   Published by Hambledon, London. 1991.
Dicken's England – Life in Victorian Times by R E Pritchard.
   Published by Sutton Publishing Ltd. 2002.

Mid-Victorian Britain (1851-1875), by Geoffrey Best.

Published by Fontana Books 1979.

Victorian Lancashire, edited by S. P Bell.

Published by David & Charles (Holdings) Ltd.

Newton Abbot 1974.

Churches and the Working Classes in Victorian England, by K. S. Inglis.

Published by Routledge and Kegan Paul Ltd. London. 1979.

The Great Hunger (in Ireland) (1845-1849), by Cecil Woodham-Smith.

Published by Penguin Books. 1991.

Trade and Traders in mid-Victorian Liverpool, by Graeme J. Milne.

Published by Liverpool University Press. 2000.

The Training Ships of Liverpool, by Bob Evans.

Published by Countyvise Ltd. 2002.

Charitable Effort in Liverpool in the 19th Century, By Margaret Simey.

Published by Liverpool University Press. 1951.

Politics and Elections in 19th Century Liverpool, by Neil Collins.

Published by Scholar Press 1994.

Her Benny, by Silas Hocking.

Published by Gallery Press. 1968.

The Making of Liverpool, by Mike Fletcher.

Wharncliffe Books. 2004.

Progress and Poverty, by Henry George.

Published by Robert Schalkenbach Foundation

(Second American Edition, 1998)

Liverpool wondrous Place, by Paul Du Noyer

Published by Virgin Books Ltd. London, 2002

The Last Journey of William Huskisson, by Simon Garfield.

Published by Faber & Faber Ltd. 2002.

Still Here by Linda Grant

Published by Abacus 2003

Appendices

An extract from James Nugent's editorial in
'The Catholic Times' February 1873, on the
appointment of Bishop Bernard O'Reilly

...."The important position which the diocese of Liverpool holds in the Catholic world in England, the fact that the town itself is the stronghold of Catholicity; the good will and growing disposition of public bodies to do justice to Catholics than was done in past time; and the immense responsibility resting on the shoulders of the prelate, might induce some of our fellow Catholics to desire the appointment of a man of more striking brilliancy, and of larger experience in dealing with public questions, or of one whose practical knowledge of Church affairs abroad was more personal and more intimate; but on these heads we experience but little fear for Dr. O'Reilly, as we feel that his sterling peity and his innate good sense will supply any such deficiency".

Incorrigible Women

Incorrigible Women – What are we to do with them?
By Rev. J. Nugent, Borough Goal, Liverpool

The question which I have undertaken to discuss is one which is each clay pressing itself' more forcibly upon all those who have a practical knowledge of the female population of our prisons. Whilst of late years there has been at marked diminution in certain classes of criminals, there has been at the same time a large increase in the number of commitments. Throughout England this is observable. If we analyse gaol returns we shall find that there has not been a proportionate increase of individuals but the increase has been made up by the repeated commitment of the same persons. In 1854 the number of adult females committed to the Borough Prison of Liverpool was 4(197: in 1874 the number had increased to 05(14: vet in 1854 there were 1341 females who had never hear it) prison before whilst in 1874 there were only 1136. In 1854 there were 1754 who had been four or more times in prison and in 1874 there were 4107. In the large towns of this country there is each year a gradual increasing criminal population. who are committed again and again to prison and who are not only a burthen upon society, but whose behaviour and vices are its scourge and plague. No better or more forcible illustration of this can be given than what takes place in the Borough Prison of Liverpool. From the 1st of October 1875 to the 30th September 1876. there were committed to the Borough Gaol 13,317 prisoners - 6501 males and 6816 females. Thus there were 315 women more than men. No other prison in the world presents a parallel to this, of the women exceeding the men. If these figures were closely examined, it would be seen that only about one in six of these had been in prison for the first time, so that a very considerable portion of them come under the class incorrigible- having been in the prison 20.

30. 40. 50 and one over 130 times. A few cases selected from the calendar of the year will confirm this:

M.B.   age 40 : 66 times : four times this year : 6 mos. x 14 days
M.M.   age 52 : 61 times : three times this year : 7 mos.
M. D.   age 24 : 49 times : six times this year : 6 mos. x 21 days.
        this woman from Jany. 4th 1873 has been in prison 14
        times and spent there 2 years and eight months.
M.R.   age 3? : 47 times : five times this year : 9 mos. x 14 days.
J.C.   age 37 : 74 times : four times this year : 9 mos. x 7 clays.
J.K.   age 37 : 65 times : six times this year : 4 mos. x 14.days.
A. L.   age 26 : 27 times : nine times this year : 8 mos. x 5 days.
A.W.   age 28 : 27 times : four times this year : 8 mos.
C.W.   age 28 : 68 times : four times this year : 8 mos. *x* 7 days.
M.C.   age 27 : 29 times : seven times this year : 8 mos. x 21 days.
J.W.   age 37 : 75 times : five times this year : 3 mos. x 21 days.
E.W.   age 26 : 40 times : five times this year : 9 mos.

These women from their age and the number of times they have been committed may be fairly looked upon as incorrigible; the prison has no deterrent effect upon them and it has certainly failed to reform them. Drunkenness, prostitution and acts of violence arising out of drink are the charges upon which they have been committed.

Constant and excessive indulgence in drink and the deleterious quality of the drink they consume have weakened their brain and will. Self-control has gone and with it all self respect, so that they abandon themselves to a life of infamy and animal indulgence. When at liberty they stupefy themselves with drink and as long as they can obtain it, care but little what becomes of them. Prison and its penalties exercises no deterrent influence over them for many of them have been within its walls 35, 40, 41 and even 74 times and their last sentence was only seven days; what care they for that, in fact they have been known to seek it so that they might see some of their companions who were doing Iong-time.

The question then what are we to do with these incorrigible women may be considered, first as to how they ought to be punished and secondly by what means reformed.

Women who are determined to set law and order at defiance and to adopt a criminal life, ought to be dealt with by, a cumulative system of punishments in the earlier stages of their career. A girl of 17 coming to the prison for the first time on the 17th of April of this year and having been committed 7 times up to the 28th of September, and each time, with one exception, receiving only seven days, becomes even in her teens an incorrigible. Once or-twice in the prison van, contact with hardened criminals, the easy means of obtaining large sums of money, with such trifling punitive consequences, all conspired to strip the prison of its horrors and to produce a hardened and troublesome class of female prisoner. Crime ought to be checked before it grows into a confirmed habit and the young must be taught by deterrent means, with a longer sentence, hard labour, scanty food and solitary confinement, that it is odious and loathsome in the eyes of the public. If women under twenty years of age, who were known to have adopted a vicious mode of life, were after their third or fourth commitment to receive a recorded sentence of three months and after this if they appeared again were sent to Sessions, as the law permits, such a course would have a deterrent effect both in and out of the prison. Young girls would thus be taught that they could not adopt an infamous life and prey upon society with impunity. Those who have had experience with the criminal class can confirm what I state, that short sentences fail to effect any reformation and that a prison Chaplain may in vain try to persuade this class to abandon vice. It is only under a long sentence they can be brought to reflect upon their condition, to receive instruction and to make the best effort to return to the path of virtue. A long sentence withdraws them from the habits, temptations and companionship by which they were surrounded; besides a large proportion of these are ignorant of their duty to God and man and have had no education or moral training. A long sentence provides the opportunity of receiving both.

Some years ago in my daily round of duty in the prison; I was asked by the matron to visit a girl of 18, under punishment in the dark cell. I was informed that she was the most violent and troublesome girl that frequented the prison; threatening her officers, using foul language and destroying goal property. When the door of the dark cell was opened she bellowed more like an animal than a human being. Watching my opportunity, I asked her to whisper rather than shout. This novel request induced her to desist for a moment, when I spoke kindly to her, showing her the folly of such conduct. She burst into tears saying "Oh Sir, you are the first person who ever spoke a kind word to me in my life, what can you expect from me. I was dragged up on the streets of Liverpool. I never had a father or mother. No one ever cared for me." I answered her that if she behaved herself until the following morning by ceasing to shout and beat tunes with her heels on her cell door, then I would intercede with the Governor to allow her to return to her cell. She did so and the favour was granted. I found this girl did not know the existence of a God, could not say a prayer, did not know a letter in the alphabet. I promised her that if she behaved herself she would at once be placed under instruction, would be taught her prayers and even to read and write. Fortunately for her she was under a long sentence. She learned to read and write, was instructed in her religion and became most exemplary in her conduct. She was placed in the laundry, where she proved herself useful and industrious. I saw that she was a girl of quiet character and firmness if the opportunity was afforded, she would prove herself a good and careful woman. At the expiration of her sentence I provided her with an outfit and found the means for her to leave the country. She is now doing well in Canada. I saw her there in 1876 holding a most responsible situation and her photograph, which I have in my hand, is an evidence of her changed life of respectability. This is, I think, a strong case in favour of long; sentences in the earlier stages and all previous experience shows that reformation is seldom effected except on the first or during a long sentence.

But there is another class of incorrigible women and these a large class, who have been 30, 40 and even more than 50 times in prison. What can be done with them? Some who have given this subject their earnest attention suggest that the law should be amended and that women who had been in prison say 15 times and who are known to be incorrigible should be sent to Quarter Sessions and that such women should be sentenced according to their condition to three or five years to a Certified Prison Industrial Home, where they would be forced to work at such industries as would not only he profitable, but by which they might at the expiration of their sentence gain their living. They would be under a less stringent discipline than in an ordinary prison, for the character of these institutions would be industrial and reformatory. Whilst a sufficient scale of diet would be adopted, industry and an increased amount of labour would be rewarded with a more generous and plentiful supply of food. The idea is first to rid the streets and prison of an incorrigible and violent class of women, who through their intemperate and criminal habits cannot control themselves and are a burden and pest to society by their vicious lives. Secondly to utilize this wasted power and energy by making these women work and to raise them up by gradually forming them to acquire habits of industry, self-respect, self-reliance and self-control. This can only be accomplished by complete isolation from drink, companionship and the circumstance of their former life. Experience proves that circumstances more than choice make criminals.

This idea of a Certified Prison Industrial Home is not fanciful or impracticable. The time of labour of these incorrigible women may be so utilized as to make such an institution almost self-supporting in certain localities. These women, when under a long sentence behave well, work well, and are found the most efficient hands in a prison laundry. In Liverpool, Manchester and London, large laundries are a profitable investment and women working in them gain good ways. I quote the prices as paid in one large establishment in Liverpool. First class 18/- per week; second 15/-; third 12/-; fourth 10/-. The Reformatory Refuges all make a very large income by this source of female industry. Here then is the labour and the market too is at hand. With three or four years training these women may not only regain their character, but be taught to love honest industrious labour and when their time is expired they will have a character, will know how to work and will experience little difficulty in obtaining employment. I repeat that ignorance, neglect and circumstances have made these women what they are.

Instruct them, let them feel that they are cared for, take them by the hand, give them a fair opportunity of gaining their bread and they will prove that such treatment can change incorrigibles into useful and virtuous women. In an institution like the one I have suggested there would be other industries besides laundry work; especially there would be domestic work, cleaning, cooking, baking and such opportunities would afford variety of labour and thus open up the means of sending forth these women with improved ideas and habits. The system of granting a licence as in Reformatories might with advantage be adopted.

The object of this paper has been to bring this important question before the public and to awaken both discussion and action in its behalf. The many duties that are incumbent upon me have prevented my giving that time and attention to it which it deserves, but I have said sufficient to prove that the present system of dealing with incorrigible women demands a different class of sentence and some amendment in the law.